WITHDRAWN
FROM STOCK

Couture
& COMMERCE

UBCPress   ROYAL ONTARIO MUSEUM

Published by UBC Press in association
with the Royal Ontario Museum.

A ROM Publication in Arts and Archæology

Couture & COMMERCE

The Transatlantic Fashion Trade in the 1950s

Alexandra Palmer

Printed in Canada on acid-free paper

National Library of Canada Cataloguing in Publication Data

Palmer, Alexandra, 1957–
Couture and commerce

Published in association with the Royal Ontario Museum.
Includes bibliographical references and index.
ISBN 0-7748-0826-8 (bound); ISBN 0-7748-0827-6 (pbk)

1. Clothing trade – History – 20th century. 2. Fashion – Social aspects.
3. Clothing and dress – Social aspects. I. Royal Ontario Museum. II. Title.

GT525.P34 2001   391.2'09'045   C2001-910754-4

This book has been published with the help of a grant from the Humanities and Social Sciences Federation of Canada, using funds provided by the Social Sciences and Humanities Research Council of Canada. We also gratefully acknowledge the generous support of the Royal Ontario Museum, Toronto, Canada.

UBC Press acknowledges the financial support of the Government of Canada through the Book Publishing Industry Development Program (BPIDP) for our publishing activities.

Canadä

We also gratefully acknowledge the support of the Canada Council for the Arts for our publishing program, as well as the support of the British Columbia Arts Council.

Published by UBC Press in association with the Royal Ontario Museum.

The Royal Ontario Museum gratefully acknowledges the Louise Hawley Stone Charitable Trust for its generous support of this publication.

Printed and bound in Canada by Friesens
Set in Cochin and Futura
Editor: Camilla Jenkins
Designer: Mark Timmings, Timmings & Debay
Proofreader: Sarah M. Wight
Indexer: Annette Lorek

UBC Press
The University of British Columbia
2029 West Mall, Vancouver BC V6T 1Z2
(604) 822-5959
Fax: (604) 822-6083
E-mail: info@ubcpress.ubc.ca
www.ubcpress.ca

CONTENTS

Appendices

ACKNOWLEDGMENTS

This book has had the involvement of many in diverse ways. I would like to thank all of those who took the time to talk with me about their experiences buying, shopping, selling, making, and wearing haute couture. In particular, I am indebted to Patricia Harris, who gave me time, several lunches, referrals, understanding of Toronto society, and interest at all points along the way. Without all this co-operation, the text would be much drier and I could not have begun to unpack the layers of meanings in the designs.

I am indebted to Lou Taylor, Penny Sparke, and Gail Cuthbert Brandt, my dissertation advisors, who guided me and encouraged me to delve into unexpected inquiries. I also owe a great debt to Hazel Clark for introducing me to Lou. Funding at this stage was provided by the Costume Society of America's Stella Blum Grant and the Veronika Gervers Research Fellowship, Royal Ontario Museum, as well as flexible and non-academic employment at the Queen Mother Café.

The private design house archives offer fantastic records and I can only hope that they continue to be preserved and made available to researchers. In particular, I would like to thank the staff at Christian Dior, especially Soizic Pfaff and Philippe Le Moult, Marie-Andrée Jouve at Balenciaga, Marie-Christine Brarda at Pierre Balmain, Marika Genty at Chanel, and Odile Fraigneau at Lanvin. I would also like to acknowledge the assistance of those who took to time to answer my inquires at all the couture houses that I visited. Food, lodging, and company in Europe and New York was always a pleasure due to support from many friends, particularly Catherine Tait, Martine Trebilloid, Christophe Loizillon, Athlyn Fitz-James, Tom Hamilton, Francesca and Oliver Morgan, Geoffrey Robinson, Gary Soroka, and Nancy Allerston.

Sincere thanks and gratitude must also be made to all my museum colleagues, who furnished recommendations, references, guidance, and help in storerooms, notably Amy de la Haye, Joanna Marschner, Avril Hart, Ann Coleman, Jean Druesdow, Katell le Bourhis, Valérie Guillaume, John Vollmer, and Caroline Rennolds Milbank, who originally piqued my interest in couture when I was an intern at Sotheby's New York.

At the Royal Ontario Museum, my colleagues in Textiles, Anu Liivandi, Shannon Elliott, and Adrienne Hood, all provided invaluable assistance. The photography for this book was a project unto itself, and I am most grateful to Esther Méthé, Irving Solero, Brian Boyle, Suzanne McLean, and Carmen Markert. Further, the support of the Louise Hawley Stone Charitable Trust, its committee, and particularly Mark Engstrom and Dan Rahimi, made the photography of the ROM collection possible. The astonishing patience and endurance of Dawn Stremler in the thankless but necessary area of copyright has been unrelenting and thorough — and I am more than grateful.

UBC Press was most patient and supportive throughout this process, and I am more than pleased to acknowledge the work of Emily Andrew, the precision of Camilla Jenkins, and the design of Mark Timmings.

Ultimately the interest and support of my parents and siblings, Susan, Patti and Chris, and the daily compromises and trade-offs by Paul, Wyndham, Hugo, and Askari, made this entire project possible and as complete as it is now. Thank you.

Couture
& COMMERCE

INTRODUCTION

Clothing is loaded with memory and feelings, whether the garments are humble and commonplace or elaborately designed and expensive couture.[1] Because of the intangible power of clothing, we respond to fashion and remain interested in the latest styles, even though we probably have enough to wear, or may not even want those styles for ourselves. This book investigates why and how 1950s couture fashion was important in its own day. It looks at the designs from a commercial and cultural perspective in order to understand the significance of imported couture in North America. Examining the layers of meaning embedded in clothing may also help to explain why so many of these garments exist fifty years later, and why we are still fascinated by such seemingly obsolete designs.

The 1950s are associated with the golden years of haute couture, captured by iconic images of glamorous models wearing dramatic clothes in sophisticated poses and luxurious settings (fig. 0.1). There are many books and articles on the lives and lifestyles of couturiers, on the artistic design process, on celebrity clients, and on couture fashion photographers such as Irving Penn and Richard Avedon who have achieved fame and notoriety in their own right.[2] Yet the study of fashion history, and in particular of haute couture, has only just begun to move beyond uncritical discussions of "fashion as art" or "designer as artist." Very little attention has been given to haute couture from socio-economic and cultural perspectives. This book explores what actual worn garments meant in the context of the international fashion system after the Second World War. It explores the subject from the viewpoint of the Paris haute couture houses and other European couture houses, of North

0.1 Fall 1956 Pierre Balmain model 22313, "Agéna," from the Jolie Madame collection. Haute couture in the 1950s has been captured in iconic images of glamorous models wearing lavish dresses and striking sophisticated poses.

3

American buyers and retailers, and also of the North American consumer, who had specific social requirements for her couture wardrobe.

The strictest definition of "haute couture" refers only to designs produced by accredited Paris haute couture houses that meet standards set out by the Chambre syndicale de la couture parisienne. In this book, the more informal word "couture" is used to embrace all very high-end European dressmaking that occurs or occurred in establishments patterned on the model set by the Paris couture salons. Definitions of couture became confused during the 1950s, and the word "couture" is still used erroneously today to describe any expensive design, usually manufactured by machine and not made to measure at any point in its construction.

My interest in this subject began while I was working with couture clothes themselves in the textile and costume collection of the Royal Ontario Museum (ROM). As I looked at garments that repeatedly revealed evidence of wear — worn hemlines in ball gowns, shortened hemlines, and numerous alterations and careful mends to many delicate and elaborate evening dresses as well as to day wear — I found myself with many unanswered questions.[3] These traces of wear and modification do not support the commonly held assumption that haute couture clothing

0.2 Detail of a handwoven Irish wool skirt from a fall 1952 Sybil Connolly suit. The skirt front has been damaged, perhaps by a cigarette burn or a tear, but patched and mended so that from the outside it is imperceptible. See fig. 4.3, pp. 102–3.

 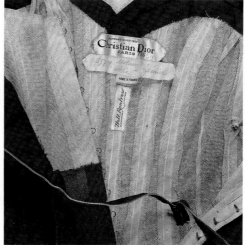

was treated as a disposable commodity, to be quickly replaced by another example in the latest style. The evidence left in the designs clearly demonstrates that the idea of conspicuous consumption in this context is flawed and limiting.[4] The clothes I examined also do not corroborate public opinion that museum collections hold only pristine, "museum quality" couture dresses (figs. 0.2 and 0.3). The dresses themselves clearly indicate that many of the designs had a complex use. In questioning these archetypes, I began to wonder what difference in meaning and value was contained in two Christian Dior designs, one with a Paris label and one with a New York label (fig. 0.4). What was the significance of bond tags buried deep under numerous layers of petticoats in opulent ball gowns?

The relationship between the European couture houses and the North American market was also not clear to me, nor were the postwar rules, regulations, and trade systems for these luxury goods. Couture models were purchased by retailers for public fashion shows and for private consumers, yet during the 1950s the couture

0.3 (left) Detail of a fall 1951 Christian Dior evening gown showing the extended use of the garment in the shortened, worn, and dirty hemline. The hem has been cut with pinking shears, which would not have been used by the Paris haute couture house.   0.4 (right) This Christian Dior red silk faille cocktail dress is constructed over an inner corset that ensures the wearer has an attractive silhouette, determined by Dior. The four labels inside show that the dress was made by the house of Dior in fall 1955 and sold in Toronto by Holt Renfrew. The handwritten tape shows the order number and the name of the design, "Zémire," from the "Y" line. See fig. 7.2, pp. 240–1.

trade was struggling to survive and compete with the numerous couture-inspired designs, copies, and interpretations that finally resulted in *prêt-à-porter* fashions. How did these competing parts of the fashion business intertwine? As well, I was intrigued by the social history of haute couture and the lives of its consumers. I wanted to know where the clothes were bought and worn and what role they played in the wardrobes and lifestyles of the women who wore them. Once I understood this, I could begin to assess the subtle and ephemeral issues of need, value, and longevity that influenced a woman's individual couture purchases.

By investigating not only how the couture designs were marketed but also how the individual clothes were interpreted, accepted, rejected, or modified by the consumer, I began to tackle the complex issue of taste that is often ignored by design historians.[5] Taste is one of the most important and ephemeral fleeting ways in which people classify goods. The association of haute couture with good taste is long-standing and one of its underpinnings. But how was this taste created in the heyday of the trade?[6] Couture consumption in North America was influenced by buyers, manufacturers, retailers, and finally by the private consumer. Tracing the route of a design from its inception at the design house to its trade and retail sale, and finally to the person who wore it and the place where it was worn, I gained new insight into how couture was both designed and consumed. Designs were modified, interpreted, and reinterpreted for local consumption. Consumers then brought their own meanings and values to the couture designs they acquired. My analysis contextualizes haute couture in North America as a commodity within its own economic and sociocultural system, after it left the design house.[7] This has not been done before. It is all these interlocked issues that I attempt to explore through an examination of the Canadian position in a triangle that connected Toronto to Europe and New York in the couture trade.

How did all the clothes end up in Toronto from Europe? What was the distinction between English, French, Italian, Swiss, Spanish, and other couture? Why were the designs I studied at the museum so worn and altered? Who really wore them and for what occasions? What was the story and meaning of the clothes with custom bond tags? I pursued these questions through traditional archival research, newspaper reports, and couture house records and then linked my findings to the actual garments.[8]

Many of the women who wore the clothes were referred to in the records of the time by their husbands' names only, and though I have tried to reconstruct their individual identities, it has not always proved possible. These couture customers were elite women who derived their income primarily from the male heads of households. The husbands were usually executives or professionals such as doctors and lawyers and had high earning power. The wives were responsible not only for child rearing and looking after the home but were also the most important consumers, conferring status on themselves and their families. They upheld their husbands' economic and professional status through social activities, and their couture wardrobes played no small part in this role.

Yet there were several difficulties in analyzing this group of women. Very little information is available about the socio-economic role of Canadian women nationally or regionally for this period. I therefore had to begin with their status as represented by husbands or fathers. Existing studies of Canadian social groups and of the elite examine male society through the lens of financial and political power but do not mention, measure, or assess the social or economic power of women, either alone or in relation to their male counterparts.[9] In 1958, it was a revelation that many Canadian women whose husbands were in a high income bracket actually preferred to work part time. Although a government study concluded that they did so "to get away from the household or to find companionship," in fact, women were engaged in setting up "parallel power structures outside the domestic, commercial and political spheres dominated by men."[10] Women's volunteer organizations were one important facet of this process.

Many of the answers I was seeking were scant in books but still locked in the memories of those who had sold, bought, and worn the dresses. Oral histories were going to prove essential, and were still possible. I first compiled an inventory of donors to the ROM collection, a process that provided the beginnings of a list of Toronto couture customers. This led to interviews with many individuals who had worn the clothes and gave me the opportunity to see more garments still in private wardrobes. In fact, most of the women I interviewed still kept dresses that they could not bear to part with, though they knew that they would never wear them again, underscoring the emotional pull of the clothes and their power to evoke the time in which they were worn. The couture clothes themselves provided a reference point for the interviews. As I asked about where the garments had been worn, I found my research expanding into the unanticipated area of postwar women's volunteer organizations, as Toronto socialites often wore their couture clothes to events that they had organized in the cultural and social service sectors (fig. 0.5).

Tracing social and cultural history through artifacts is a long-accepted practice in the discipline of anthropology but has rarely been done for fashion.[11] Anthropologist Igor Kopytoff suggests that just as people have many biographies, so too do objects. He identifies four categories: the physical biography; the technical biography, including the object's repair record; the economic biography, including its initial worth, its sale, and resale; and the social biography or biographies, or what happens to the object in the social world. He suggests that if one focuses on the object as a key to investigation and identifies its various biographies, the artifact itself can redirect research into areas that might otherwise be left unexplored.[12] This occurred to me several times and was especially important in bringing my attention to second-hand couture use, a wholly unforeseen aspect of the garments' sociocultural value. Material culture can thus illustrate and clarify research, but it can also complicate theoretical concepts and steer enquiry into new areas.

Linking documentary data to material culture is an underused and rich academic tool. As Jules Prown notes, material culture relies on the premise that objects made or modified by humans "reflect, consciously or unconsciously, directly or indirectly, the beliefs of individuals who made, commissioned, purchased, or used them and by extension the beliefs of the large society to which they belonged."[13] Scholars such as Prown have argued for the use of material culture in conjunction with other research methods. Few academics actually succeed in doing this, however, remaining bound in theoretical rhetoric or else using material culture solely as decorative illustrative material.

My research has been greatly informed by incorporating object analysis with standard research tools. Analyzing the objects prompted me to inquire about their history, and theory developed in collaboration with evidence yielded by the dresses. I wedded case studies of specific items of clothing to oral and documentary research to produce a large picture that follows couture from the European design source, through its Canadian distribution system, and into the Toronto social world, where it served an important cultural role. This approach places the couture consumption of

**NEWS OF WOMEN'S CLUBS
AND ORGANIZATIONS**

will be a top feature in

the *Woman's*
Globe and Mail

EVERY THURSDAY

commencing September 1st

elite English-Canadian women in the context of Toronto's postwar culture and society. The result challenges entrenched mythologies of couture and its wearers as stereotyped symbols of conspicuous consumption, and the dresses represent and reveal "the actual brilliance often displayed in the art of living in a modern society."[14]

The period chosen, from 1945 to 1960, circumscribes a rapid cultural, social, and economic expansion in Canada as it gained a place in global politics. Toronto encapsulated this era of change for English Canada, completely altering its physical, social, and cultural profile over these years, largely due to the influx of European immigrants.[15] The same period also witnessed the high point and subsequent international demise of haute couture (figs. 0.6 and 0.7). It was a time when the North American fashion industry depended commercially and culturally on European couture designs and when European couturiers depended economically on the North American market.[16]

When I began my research, I realized that some of the key individuals I wanted to speak with were no longer living. Dora Matthews, Eaton's fashion coordinator, was one of those whom I would have loved to meet. Some of the women I did interview have since died, while others are still vibrant. I feel very fortunate to have had the opportunity to meet them all, often over tea, and to interview them about their wardrobes and their social lives. Yet I did not think that so many of the bastions of Toronto's high-end retail trade — Creeds, Ira-Berg, Simpson's, and finally

0.5 Advertisement for a new women's section of the *Globe and Mail* newspaper, 25 August 1955, dedicated to Toronto socialites and their volunteer events and fundraising parties. These were the venues where they wore couture.

0.6 Spring 1955 Givenchy cocktail dress worn by Toronto socialite Signy Eaton, who was married to the president of Eaton's department store. It is made of silk organdy embroidered with black and white polka dots.

Eaton's — would also not survive into the twenty-first century.[17] In fact, Holt Renfrew is the only major couture retailer from the 1950s that has continued to flourish.

The retail and consumer histories told here are undoubtedly similar to others throughout North America; each city had its own taste and style, which were reflected in the couture worn there. I hope that by documenting the mid-century couture trade in Toronto, this book inspires others to contribute their own investigations of this fascinating era of haute couture and the lifestyles of those who wore the clothes.

0.7 A model wearing the same Givenchy dress as fig. 0.6 stands in front of a painting by Fernand Léger, *Harper's Bazaar*, April 1955, thereby reinforcing the connection between haute couture and high art. Photograph by Louise Dahl-Wolfe.

1 THE PARIS COUTURE
STRUCTURE

"Chic" has nothing to do with money. I who dress some of the richest women in the world can vouch for that. Ginette Spanier, 1959

La Chambre Syndicale de la Couture Parisienne

Today, Paris is touted as the most important design source for women's fashion. This notion is actively perpetuated by the French haute couture as well as by international fashion buyers, the press, and the North American ready-to-wear market, yet the roots of French luxury fashion dominance go back to the late seventeenth century.

Under Jean Baptiste Colbert, controller general of finance from 1665, the French silk industry was restructured and positioned as the leader of international textile design and manufacture. At this time, the fashionability of dress was demonstrated in textile design rather than by a change in silhouette. French silks were the most prestigious and stylish, and were worn by members of the European royal courts and the aristocracy.[1] In the late nineteenth century, Paris fashion designers, or haute couturiers, began to be internationally celebrated names. Their symbiotic relationship with the French silk industry made haute couture design a natural extension of a nationalistic tradition. The so-called "father of haute couture," Charles Frederick Worth, who is often credited as being the first to place his name on a label, was one of many fashion designers who set themselves up as arbiters of taste and style (fig. 1.1)

Worth was one of the most internationally famous couturiers, and one of the most successful in terms of marketing and production.[2] His designs were recognizable by their use of luxurious French textiles and high-quality workmanship. In 1868, Worth was instrumental in founding a governing body to organize and regulate Paris couturiers' production and merchandising, the Chambre syndicale de la

couture parisienne. This agency acted as an umbrella organization to support and promote individual couture houses and Paris couturiers as a collective.[3]

To a large degree, the creation and maintenance of French supremacy in haute couture was due to the structure and energy of the Chambre syndicale. Jeanette Jarnow and Beatrice Judelle account for French fashion leadership by pointing to the technically skilled seamstresses, auxiliary industries that produced handmade trims and materials on a small scale, laws protecting unauthorized copying, and the support of the French government.[4] The role and jurisdiction of the Chambre syndicale are crucial to understanding not only the French haute couture system but also how it managed to regain and keep international dominance after the Second World War.

Marjorie Dunton described the Chambre syndicale as "half union and half guild . . . a judicial and legislative body intended to represent, advise and defend its members . . . It copes with style piracy . . . foreign relations . . . buyers and press."[5] Regulations for the sale of designs and reproductions were laid out in law on 9 April

1.1 Tea gown from around 1895 designed by the house of Worth. This dress is made up in one textile pattern used in two colours and trimmed with handmade lace. The inside shows the petersham waist tape woven with the Worth label. The seams are carefully finished with hand overcast stitches, and the bodice is, typically, boned even though the wearer would have worn a corset underneath. Such fine sewing was characteristic of French haute couture clothes.

1910, and issues of piracy were dealt with under article 425 of the penal code.[6] Couturiers' designs were registered with the Chambre syndicale by "photographies des collections sur film de petit format, avec un appareil à prise de vues rapides," and a qualified individual was to be present to verify that the models were indeed those in the photographs (fig. 1.2).[7]

In 1945, haute couture was divided into two classes, Couture and Couture-Création.[8] The distinction between the two was carefully defined and regulated. Houses in the less prestigious class of Couture could promote their designers and designs as "Artisan Maître Couturier," "Couturière," and "Couture," while those in the Couture-Création class earned the terms "Couturier," "Haute-Couture," and "Couture-Création." The term "couturier" had no feminized equivalent, since "couturière" connoted a lower status. A couture house had to apply for membership in a class, and status was reviewed annually by a jury made up of members of the textile industry and the administrative side of the Chambre syndicale.[9] An application for Couture-Création classification had to meet several requirements: at least twenty-five models had to be created in-house every spring and fall and a sample garment for each made to measure on a live mannequin.

1.2 An example of the type of documentary photography taken by an haute couture house to establish authorship and copyright of a design. The design was then registered with the Chambre syndicale. This cocktail ensemble was designed by Balenciaga for his spring 1950 collection, model 172. See fig. 7.1, pp. 238–9.

(The term "model" in this context refers to the garment produced as a template for production of the particular design.) The collection was then to be presented on live mannequins in an "appropriate" setting in the haute couture house, which had to be situated in Paris. The rules also covered the technical execution of the original models, the repetitions that were to be made in-house to clients' measurements, the number of fittings required and at what stage in the making, and the sale of the designs. The application was followed by a visit to the haute couture salon by the jury, and there was no guarantee that Couture-Création status would be renewed at the annual review.[10] Angry letters appealing rejection of Couture-Création classification demonstrate the importance of this appellation for the houses.[11]

Thus, an haute couture model, or more technically, a Couture-Création model, was not a one-of-a-kind design. It was part of a line that was then repeated and sold, and had complex rules governing sales to private clients, department stores, and commercial buyers. Table 1 shows the total number of haute couture garments ordered from or reproduced by various houses over five seasons from spring 1954 to spring 1955, including the *demi-saison*, or mid-season, which was undertaken by only a few of the larger ones. The table indicates overall quantities but does not reveal the number of repetitions of a particular design. It does, however, illustrate the hierarchy within the Paris haute couture system, as the houses of Dior, Fath, and Balmain were clearly producing considerable volume. Many smaller houses — such as Chanel, which had just reopened and had not yet gained the status and orders it was to attain — sustained themselves at a much more modest production level. Table 1 does make it easy to understand how Dior by the mid-1950s accounted for more than half the total haute couture exports and 5 percent of all French export.[12]

Postwar Problems for Haute Couture, 1945–7

The Second World War and the German occupation of Paris left the French haute couture in a fragile, weakened state. The Nazis had wanted to move the industry to Berlin or Vienna, but the president of the Chambre syndicale, couturier Lucien Lelong, had successfully negotiated to keep it operating and in Paris.[13]

After the liberation of Paris, the haute couture industry had to recapture the North American market in order to reinstate the historical position of France as the production centre for unique, prestigious fashions. This goal would bring with it the

TABLE 1   **Paris couture production, spring 1954 to spring 1955**

Design house	Number of models designed for each collection						Total garments made and sold over the period
	Spring 1954	*Demi-saison*	Fall 1954	*Demi-saison*	Spring 1955	Total models designed	
Dior	237	0	235	0	240	712	5,154
Dior Boutique	65	0	46	0	0	111	1,320
Fath	192	24	177	13	150	556	4,140
Balmain	162	0	133	0	183	478	3,112
Ricci	203	27	182	30	260	702	2,800
Balenciaga	212	0	209	0	186	607	2,325
Heim	193	61	169	28	250	701	2,250
Lanvin/ Castillo	201	0	132	0	134	467	1,729
Griffe	124	24	106	4	130	388	1,650
Griffe Annex	0	0	0	0	0	0	68
Dessès	170	32	110	12	124	448	1,494
Dessès Annex	0	0	0	0	0	0	649
de Rauch	145	25	140	24	140	474	1,200
de Rauch Annex	0	0	0	0	0	0	200
Cardin	75	0	100	0	90	265	900
Givenchy	133	44	124	0	140	441	628
Grès	131	0	102	0	128	361	618
Carpentier	91	15	71	16	70	263	360
Chanel	82	0	0	40	100	222	300

Source: Classification Couture-Création applications, F12/10505, Archives Nationales, Paris.

foreign buyers who were needed to keep the salons in production. It was achieved —
the postwar years are commonly understood as one of the high points of couture
production — but the period was fraught with social, cultural, and industrial change.
Haute couture houses had the seemingly incompatible tasks of catering to private
clients, merchants, and manufacturers. American author Bernard Roshco put it well
when he wrote that "the couturier is . . . serving two distinctly different groups of
clients."[14] The diminishing economic importance of the private client postwar, particularly in relation to the commercial buyer, was clearly reflected in the schedule
of showings of the collections set by the Chambre syndicale. Private clients were
shown the collection only after the North American commercial buyers and then
the Europeans had seen it and placed their orders.[15]

One of the key issues faced by the Chambre syndicale was how to regulate
exclusivity over production and dissemination of haute couture designs when the
houses were introducing boutique lines and negotiating licensing agreements to
expand marketing, as well as selling the rights to make couture copies to foreign
buyers. The Chambre syndicale had to navigate a difficult course to ensure profits
for the haute couture houses while maintaining the haute couture image of exclusive
design, stature, and technical superiority. By the early 1950s, the ongoing closure of
old, established houses and the resulting loss of thousands of hands of skilled labour
was causing concern about the future of Paris couture. The French government
intervened, offering subsidies to the haute couture houses and the textile industry.[16]

The Chambre syndicale was such a successful formula for attracting press,
prestige, and sales for couturiers that it was widely emulated: in Britain in 1942 with
the Incorporated Society of London Fashion Designers; in Spain during the war,
when the Cooperativa de Alta Costura was formed in Barcelona; in Italy in 1951
with the institution of a collective showing in Florence; and in Canada in 1954 with
the Association of Canadian Couturiers.[17] But none of these organizations had an
infrastructure of luxury textile manufacturers comparable to that in France, nor the
ancillary industries of beading and embroidery, "shoemakers, milliners, furriers,
leather merchants, makers of buttons, belts, buckles, handbags, umbrellas; pur-
veyors of ribbons and laces and sophisticated faces; hairdressers, embroiderers,
jewellers," nor, most important, the national backing to achieve anything like the
success of the Chambre syndicale.[18]

During the war, the European and North American fashion worlds were cut off from Paris. In the United States, this gave impetus to local designers and helped to secure the fame and fortune of Americans such as Adrian, Clare Potter, Pauline Trigère, and Norman Norell working in good, high-end ready-to-wear. Canadians not only purchased American designs during the war to replace Parisian and other European imports but also continued to manufacture Canadian designs from such companies as Rae Hildebrand and Alfandri.[19] Because of the hiatus in European imports and the establishment of recognizable North American designers, it became questionable whether North American buyers and members of the fashion press would return to Europe in order to bring themselves up to date with the latest fashion trends, especially when profit was clearly to be found in mass-produced clothes rather than in haute couture. Nevertheless, the uncertain status of the Paris haute couture during the war and what would happen to it afterward were issues of prime importance to the international fashion world, including Toronto retailers and customers.

The Paris haute couture was a paradox: its existence hinged on its craft-based production, but it was increasingly forced to cater to large volumes during the 1950s. Postwar, the Chambre syndicale acted swiftly to reinstate Paris' historical position as the leader of fashion. The luxury clothing and accessory trade had been worth approximately 2,000 million francs before the war, so it is unsurprising that it was considered vital to resuscitate the industry.[20] One of the first successful marketing strategies was the *Théâtre de la mode*, an exhibition of miniature dolls dressed by Paris couturiers and placed within lavish sets, which went on an international tour and gave a high public profile to all the Paris designers.[21] Paris was liberated in August 1944, but it was not until 1947 that Parisian haute couture arrived in North America in quantity and at regular intervals.

After the liberation, news that the haute couture industry had not only continued during the war but that designs had been lavish, along with rumours of collaboration with the Germans, caused shockwaves in the international fashion world. Canadians had supported the French by food rationing and restrictions on clothing and textiles, only to discover that the luxury and opulence of haute couture had continued.[22] In 1947, *Fashion Fundamentals*, a book geared toward those interested in pursuing a fashion career, required an appendix that explained to the reader, in a romanticized style, how and why the Paris haute couture had continued during the war. Fashion expert Dora Miller wrote that despite the war, the luxury trade continued because it was "as important to the economy of the nation as . . . the automobile industry [was] to the United States." She went on to explain, in great detail, the difficulties encountered: "Dressmaking houses were kept open in spite of a lack of material and transportation . . . What this meant in actual suffering, no one in this country can probably ever realize. The workmen continued to sew very fine seams, in heatless rooms, having walked from their homes often in the suburbs, forced to keep themselves alive to work in coats, scarfs and mittens, we can hardly understand. Many of their hands still show chilblain scars."[23] This tone is typical of postwar reporting on the Paris haute couture, which very consciously tried to support the industry and quash public outrage.

The difficulty that the North American fashion world had in coming to terms with this news is illustrated in Canada by Eaton's, the largest national department store at the time. Eaton's had established its own buying office in Paris in 1893 and had been one of the leading Canadian importers of haute couture prior to the war. In order to assess the status and future importance of Paris design, and postwar fashion in general, Eaton's sent one of its buyers to New York during the week of 16 April 1945 to see the stores, attend a New York Fashion Group meeting, and talk to magazine editors. The buyer's report was very significant for Eaton's understanding of fashion retailing and merchandising trends. Of particular interest was the Fashion Group lecture by *Harper's Bazaar* editor Carmel Snow, who presented an "eyewitness account of Paris Fashions . . . answering criticisms that the Paris Couture had profited by commerce with the Germans."[24] The buyer reported, "Mrs Snow pointed out that less than one per cent of the reduced turnover during the occupation was sold to the Nazis. She gave all the credit to M. Lucien Lelong for holding together the remnants of the couture which he leads. In spite of cold, unheated rooms, fashion had come to life again in Paris." Carmel Snow's talk has probably been the basis for most of the subsequent writing on this subject until recently. The talk also outlined specific French couturiers' designs, including features such as rounded, padded, dropped shoulders, small, pulled-in waistlines, and padding placed under pockets at the hips to make the garments stand out at the sides and over the stomach. All the elements she mentioned were synthesized by Christian Dior two years later into his spring 1947 line, which Mrs Snow dubbed the "New Look."

The Eaton's representative attending the lecture also commented that the prices were very high, noting that Carmel Snow had seen such crowds at the Hermès salon that she "thought there was an auction in progress, but these people were *buying*. These customers are the 'Black Market' women who buy to get rid of the extra ill-gotten money that would otherwise have to be explained to officials, and that is one of the reasons for the high prices. At the present time it is impossible for America to buy at French prices. What America obtained for 3000 or 4000 francs ordinarily, now costs 12,000 francs, and is of poorer quality in materials. There is very little wool or silk and mostly wood [sic] and ersatz is used. Materials are very heavy and crease badly, but prints and colours are lovely. Shops keep their best merchandise in the window to attract customers, but they do not sell them." Mrs Snow made no effort to rationalize the connection between the chilblained and blameless dressmakers and the "black market women" who supported them.

Canadians and Americans clearly considered French goods high in cost and low in quality, but still worthy of promotional appeal. At the same time as Mrs Snow's lecture, Canada's *Mayfair* magazine published an article that also commented on the high prices, approximately $500 a garment, and the difficulty of transporting the goods.[25] Any news of French collections still made good copy, however, and the *Mayfair* article boasted of providing "the first authentic description of the Paris Spring Collections, first to indicate the trend of Paris fashions since the Liberation." War correspondent Gwenda Thompson had managed to get exclusive photos and sent her report by "Bomber Mail," via Washington, to Canada in a mere ten days in 1945 (figs. 1.3 and 1.4).

1.3 News of "the first authentic Paris fashions" was sent by "Bomber Mail" to Canada's *Mayfair* magazine, April 1945.

Yet Canadians were still hesitant to promote French design or to appear too eager to market fashion in the immediate aftermath of the war. In order to justify an interest in Paris clothes that were unavailable and outrageously expensive, another article in the same issue of *Mayfair* defended the Paris designers for showing evening dresses. By way of explanation, the couturiers were said to be "keeping their hand in" and the magazine asserted that the designs were not to be sold as there was no opportunity to wear them, a statement that recent scholarship has clearly demonstrated to be false.[26] The same article did go on to acknowledge that there was little real economic or prestige value of this collection, and concluded that the "present limited collections resemble a wedding without the bride; the bride being the foreign buyer — American, Canadian, English."[27] Thus, even though French haute couture was being produced, it was not deemed significant without the crucial role of North American buyers and the international fashion press in attendance and passing judgment. The Paris haute couture needed its myth makers.

Even if buyers had been present for the 1945 Paris collection, they would not have been legally permitted to export any clothing. Had exports been allowed, the clothes were limited in quantity, extremely expensive, and not easily transported

1.4 One of the first photographs of postwar Paris haute couture, a design by couturier Madeleine Vramant from spring 1945 that "conjures up postwar pleasures with this evening gown called 'Cendrillon.'" The name of the dress, Cinderella, connotes the romantic and transformative power of haute couture that was especially important just after the war.

overseas, so it is unlikely that much would have been available. Instead, the designs were sold in Paris to private customers such as Torontonian Mrs Berschinger, who purchased a Jean Dessès knee-length lace dress that she wore to dinner at the elite Parisian restaurant Maxim's.[28] In the early postwar period, the only haute couture client was thus the private one, a situation unknown since the origins of haute couture in the mid-nineteenth century.[29]

Though North Americans thus considered Paris an unstable market immediately after the peace, Eaton's did buy English couture in 1945.[30] Canadian buyers were very aware of the economic difficulties in Britain and made a conscious effort to buy British. British clothes were further considered a safe buy, as the less extreme designs and lower price tag suited English Canadians' taste as well as their pro-British colonialist sentiments. British imports were so sought after that when Eaton's wanted to promote them in a small fashion show at the Ensemble Shop couture salon in its flagship College Street store, its buyer, Miss Weaver, reported that the clothes were already sold.[31] By 1947, however, fashion co-ordinator Dora Matthews noted, "The clothes in the [London] collections that year looked similar to the fashions we had at home, not new and very expensive." She went on to comment that she and her Eaton's colleagues had difficulty gaining admittance to dinner at London hotels and restaurants in their "smart new New York or Paris dresses. We were wearing what was called cocktail or dinner dresses in North America." The cocktail dresses were in the new length above the ankle, whereas those already admitted were wearing floor-length "tatty old velvets and brocades in mid-summer."[32] Obviously there were still marked cultural and fashionable differences between Europe and North America, largely due to wartime shortages, and the new lengths and more modern designs the Canadians were wearing were too avant garde to be recognized as such by hotel and restaurant staff.

Swift Canadian patronage of British couture after the war was recognized by English couturier Hardy Amies (fig. 1.5). Eaton's purchased from him even before the presentation of his first collection, and when he discussed the opening of his house at 14 Savile Row, he wrote, "In the early days I remember being visited by Jack Frost, the London representative of the T. Eaton Co. of Canada, who said, 'The first six models you can make can go to Eaton's.'"[33] Another likely reason for Canadian interest in the British market was status. Canadian buyers had nearly as

1.5 An early postwar design by Hardy Amies in the "New Look" style. The black silk taffeta dress with portrait collar was worn by Dora Matthews, Eaton's fashion co-ordinator. The waist has been shortened, the bodice taken in, and the hem taken up, probably to extend its wear when hemlines rose as the 1950s progressed.

high a status as American ones in England, whereas in France it was lower. Amies commented, "From the beginning we had done as good business with the great stores of Canada as we had with those of America, and it had been hinted that they were a little piqued that I had already been twice to the United States, without bothering to visit them."[34]

In Paris and elsewhere, it was impossible for Canadian buyers to compete with American buyers as their considerably smaller market prevented them from purchasing in the same quantity.[35] Yet Canadian buyers benefited from being massed with the Americans for shows and press openings, enabling them to be among the first to see the collections.[36] Reporter Barbara Stevenson noted that "the top houses rate you according to your importance and you are issued with cards entitling you to view first, second or, in some houses, third or fourth showings. In the *Haute Couture* being known as a *Canadienne* is a passport in itself."[37] Thus, the availability and cost of haute couture, international cultural links, and the social position of fashion and department store buyers all had an impact on what was available in Canada.

The demand for haute couture clothing by individual customers of Canadian retailers was only one aspect of buying. For the department stores, an equally important use of couture was for large-scale fashion shows that were key marketing tools. Fashion shows had ceased during the war, and reinstating them was a delicate question of correct timing. It would not do to appear too eager, mercenary, or unpatriotic. Fashion shows were linked to the revitalization of the local social season, and the big issue was to discover what women would want to wear postwar, and when.

In Toronto, this was a politically charged issue for retailers as early as 1944. A letter from Eaton's Winnipeg branch to the Toronto store recommended that the store "GO EASY" and advised staying away from fashion shows as there were "indications there may be heavy fighting in Europe and with corresponding heavy casualty lists before Summer is over, and with a background such as this the holding of elaborate Fashion Shows would be open to criticism."[38] Another memo referred to the "apparent loss of prestige in Fashion merchandise . . . [We] should consider stressing the 'Importance of Quality' in advertising."[39]

Yet as the war drew to an end in spring 1945, news of the Paris haute couture coincided with the reinstatement of large fashion shows in Toronto. In September 1945, Simpson's department store held its first since 1941, and two large fundraising fashion shows were organized that year by the Women's Volunteer Services of Canada under the chair of Toronto social leader Ruth Frankel, wife of Egmont Frankel. Both shows were held at the Royal York Hotel concert hall. The first, in March, was entitled "Spring Song" and was a collaboration of Toronto's large fashion retailers: Simpson's, Eaton's, Fairweather, Northway's, and Holt Renfrew.[40] The clothes were not identified by designers' names except for an Adele Simpson wool dress worn with "a Paris-inspired but created in London, England . . . hat by the house of M'Arriot" and a Molyneux dinner dress. The second show, "Legend of Loveliness," was supported solely by Eaton's, with an admission price of four War Saving Stamps.[41] The program described eight English couture imports: a day ensemble from each of designers Peter Russell, Hardy Amies, Creed, and Digby Morton; a hostess gown by Bianca Mosca; a tea dress from Worth of London; a dinner dress from Angèle Delanghe; and an evening dress by Norman Hartnell. This marks the first postwar imported couture that can be identified.[42]

In November 1946, Eaton's presented "The British Ambassadors of Fashion." This show had been developed and organized by Miss Clayton of the Lucie Clayton School of Modelling in London. The international tour was backed by British manufacturers and fashion houses despite shortages of goods to show. The event featured seven British mannequins, who arrived on the maiden voyage of the Queen Elizabeth and modelled a collection of British sportswear, dinner, and evening fashions. It was "not too successful — English models [mannequins] have not the same appeal for audiences here, was one opinion."[43] Even in 1948, Eaton's continued to make a conscious effort to promote English fashion houses on a company-wide basis as "a gesture towards these British firms who are endeavouring to build up their export trade."[44] Britain was quite aware of this support, as was noted in *The Ambassador*, an export magazine, with the observation that the gross national revenue from all Canadian industry was at a peak in 1946 and had increased by 125 percent from 1938 to 1943.[45]

The First Postwar Paris Haute Couture Imports

The first French haute couture imports arrived in Canada in spring 1946. Eaton's advertised that it had purchased forty-two Paris originals, which it would place on exhibit in the "Aisle of Ideas" in its Queen Street store. A few days later, the *Globe and Mail* newspaper reported that "while isolated samples from Paris have already

arrived in Canada, this is the largest collection of Paris models ever assembled in one group in Canadian history. It is also the first postwar collection to be seen here, and these pictures [in the newspaper] are among the first the designers have allowed to be shown from their new collections — fearing imitation."[46] Among the models at Eaton's was a wedding dress from Pierre Balmain's second collection that was purchased and worn by Torontonian Suzanne Stohn (figs. 1.6 and 1.7). The significance of this early postwar design is reflected in the memories of many of the couture wearers I interviewed, who remembered the dress because it was considered very new and special at the time.[47] *Mayfair* also featured photographs of some of the French clothes available at Eaton's, as well as a Molyneux and an Amies for sale at Morgan's in Montreal. Simpson's had not bought French designs that season and showed Canadian and American models in its "Spring Festival of Fashion."[48]

Yet in its fall 1946 fashion presentation, Simpson's was showing Paris imports. The September fashion show featured "world-famous designers" though in fact it had European designs from only the Paris houses of Lucien Lelong and Jacques Fath and the London house of Hardy Amies. Its other designs were American, such as Donn of California, Louis Schrier, and Clare Potter.[49] Yet Eaton's had clearly

1.6 Fall 1946 Pierre Balmain wedding dress, as photographed at the Paris salon. This was one of the first Paris haute couture imports into Toronto after the war. *Mayfair* magazine described it as "a treasure to hand down to your daughter and even your daughter's daughter for her wedding day."

scooped its competitor, holding another exhibition in the Aisle of Ideas for the fall season, this time with forty Paris originals. Georges Couture, a small Toronto boutique, also advertised original Paris and London models in the fall of 1946, and other exclusive Toronto boutiques may well have carried haute couture by this time.[50]

By spring 1947, Eaton's had purchased another forty Paris originals, from "fourteen of the most important Collections . . . by new and familiar stars in the dressmaking sky."[51] The small print in an advertisement ran "not yet offered for sale," however, as these clothes were promotional models used for fashion shows in Toronto, Montreal, and Winnipeg (figs. 1.8 to 1.10).[52] Eaton's also had a private fashion show in the Ensemble Shop and invited "some of the comeliest and best-known girls in the blue book" to model garments, most of which were British.[53] That fall, Eaton's fashion show included couture garments from Paris, London, New York, California, and Canada, but the Paris originals were the most notable.[54] The designs included examples of Christian Dior's New Look, Lucien Lelong, Schiaparelli, Balenciaga, Jean Dessès, Hardy Amies, Digby Morton, and Norman Hartnell (figs. 1.11 to 1.15). Thus, it was with the fall 1947 collection that couture clothing began to be imported steadily into postwar Canada (fig. 1.16).

1.7 Suzanne D. Stohn, née Haas, in her Pierre Balmain wedding dress (fig. 1.6), purchased from Eaton's and worn in October 1946, Toronto. **1.8** (opposite) Eaton's advertisement, April 1947, notifying Canadians that the store had flown the latest Paris haute couture models to Toronto, where they would be shown in promotional fashion shows. Later they would be seen in the Montreal and Winnipeg branches.

Maggy Rouff

Lucien Lelong

Schiaparelli

Jeanne Lanvin

Mad Carpentier

Director of Jean Patou

Jacques Fath

PARIS ORIGINALS

by Air to

EATON'S

Flown here again this Spring from the latest openings of the French Haute Couture. Continuing a tradition begun more than seventy years ago EATON buyers travelled abroad — selected clothes from fourteen of the most important Collections for Spring '47. Distinguished fashions including dresses, coats, ensembles, formal gowns ...* shown first in EATON'S, Toronto, later in the Winnipeg and Montreal stores of EATON'S.

* Not yet offered for sale

Designers Represented

Balenciaga	Marcel Rochas
Robert Piguet	Maggy Rouff
Schiaparelli	Carven
Lucien Lelong	Jean Patou
Jacques Fath	Christian Dior
Jeanne Lanvin	Mad Carpentier
Pierre Balmain	Dessel

1.9 Eaton's spring 1947 showing of the "Paris Originals" set this Schiaparelli design in front of a sketch of Notre Dame cathedral. The dress still reflects a wartime look. Though it is longer than earlier fashions, it does not have the cinched-in waist and full skirt of Dior's New Look.

1.10 The same showing of the "Paris Originals" included this Lucien Lelong design against a sketch of Sacré-Cœur basilica.

1.11 Fall 1947 Christian Dior "Chandermagor" design. This design was sold and worn in Toronto and shows the New Look silhouette, with long, full skirt, small waist, and narrow shoulders.

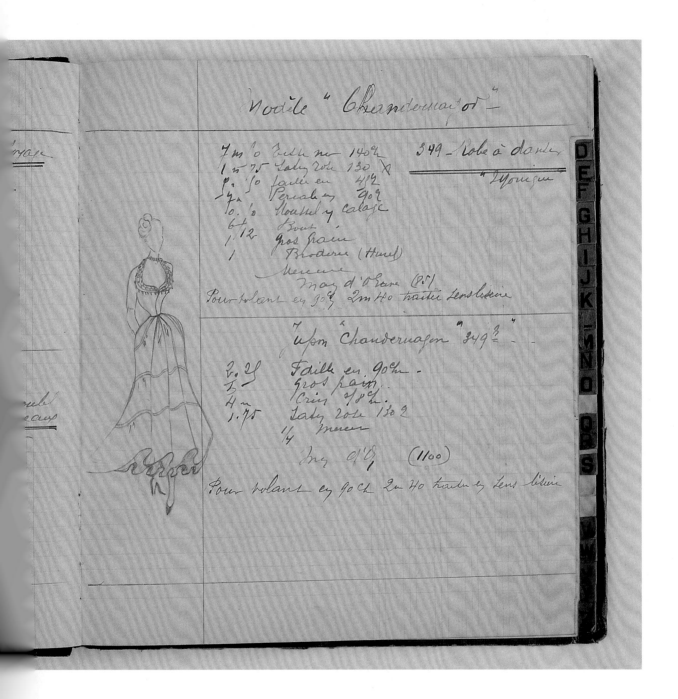

1.12 Sketch and notes for Christian Dior "Chandermagor" design recording the amounts of textile and trim used to make up this haute couture dress.

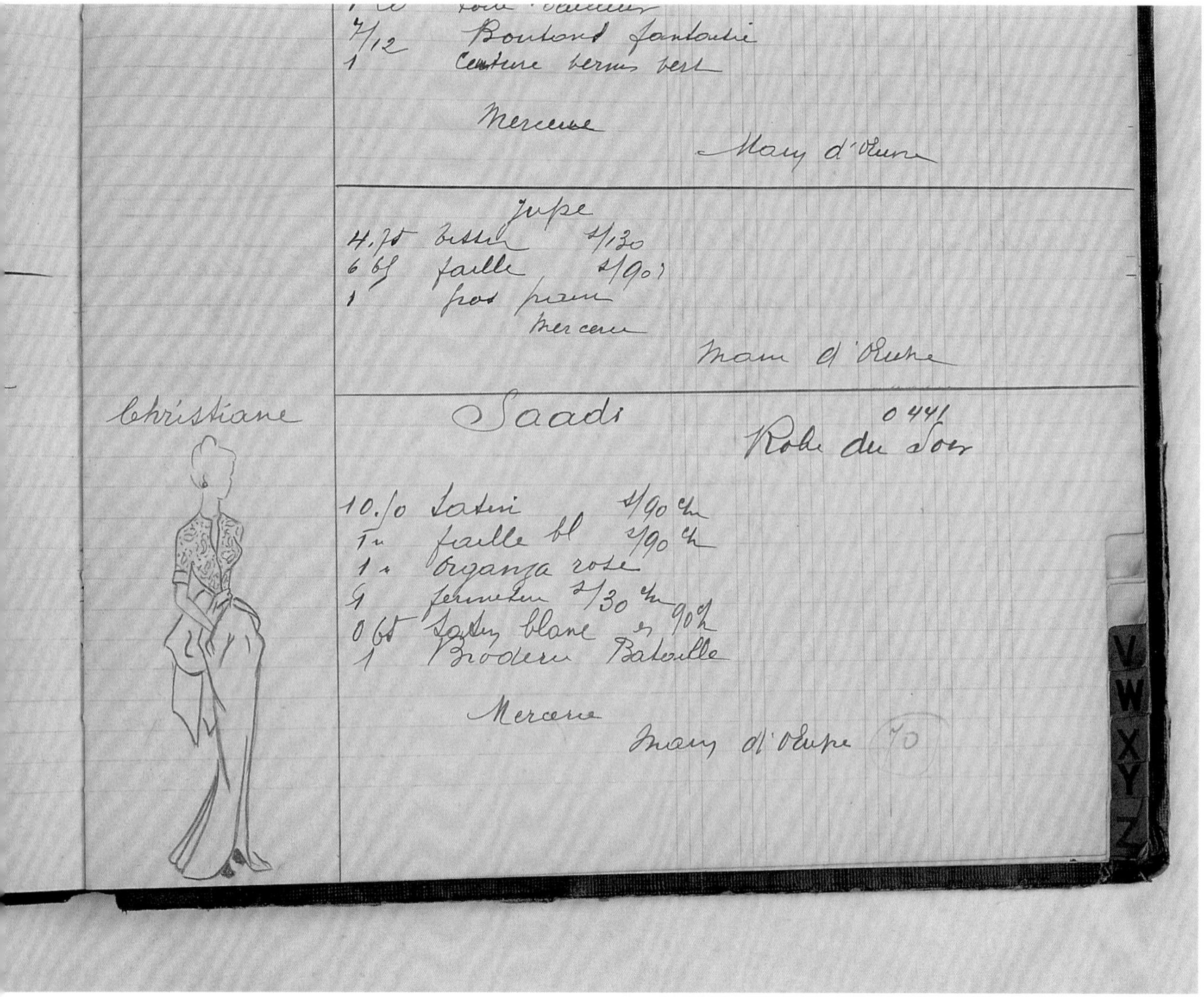

... sous ...
7/12   Bouton fantaisie
1   Ceinture vernis vert

        Mercerie
                    Mary d'Orure

            Jupe
4.75 tissu   1/130
6 ½   faille   1/90?
1   pos presse
        Mercerie
                    Mam d'Orure

Christiane   Saadi   0441
                        Robe du Soir

10.10 Satin   1/90 ch
1 ?   faille bl   1/90 ch
1 ?   organza rose
9   fermeture 1/30 ch ? 90 ch
0 ½   Satin blanc
1   Broderie Bataille

        Mercerie
                Mary d'Orure (70)

V
W
X Y
Z

1.13 Sketch and notes for Christian Dior "Saadi" design from fall 1947, the second New Look collection. This design was influenced by South Asian draped costumes and textiles.

1.14 Couture house photographs of "Saadi" design shown in fig. 1.13.

1.15 Details of the tailoring and luxurious sequin and bead embroidery in a paisley motif from the "Saadi" evening ensemble.

In Toronto, this trade marked a "return to normal" with the re-establishment of the social season. The first postwar debutantes came out, and the pinnacle of the social season, the Royal Winter Fair, started up again.[55] At this time, too, private, retail, and commercial buyers went back to Paris, marking a return to and escalation of international competition for the purchase and exclusivity of European couture. By spring 1948, *Saturday Night* magazine reported that "model after model fashioned from fabrics rare and costly, are being prepared for shipment across the cold Atlantic. Top American and Canadian buyers are flocking to this city . . . Many who hesitated at the high cost and advisability of purchasing Paris models have been lured by the devaluation of the franc, that cuts the actual cost of an original design in half."[56]

The demand for new fashions after the war is reflected in the statistics of Canadian department store sales. The growth in sales of women's dresses, coats, and suits alone was 300 percent in the early postwar period, from $6,469,000 in 1946–7

1.16 The crush at Eaton's department store in Toronto to see the new imported fashions in 1947.

1.17 A coat design in the New Look style by London couturier Peter Russell, spring c.1948–50, purchased and worn by Dora Matthews.

to $19,647,000 in 1947–8, when the New Look took hold at all socio-economic levels. Department store sales rose nationally 19.2 percent from April 1947 to April 1948. The figure was even more impressive over the period from October 1947 to October 1948, during which time sales rose 23.1 percent.[57] These records reflect the strong postwar economy and confirm the seasonal importance of replenishing fashions.

Women's clothing purchases were also influenced by the postwar fashions themselves, especially the New Look of spring 1947, which was designed with a longer and fuller style that made wartime fashions outdated. But the longer length of garments dictated by the New Look was contentious. Just as in the United States a group of husbands founded "The Little below the Knee Club," in Canada, reactions to the New Look were not all positive. An "anti-long skirt parade" was proposed in Toronto in September 1947. The suggestion put forth on a CBC radio program called *What's Your Beef* — that a "Society for the Prevention of Longer Skirts for Women" be formed — elicited 1,500 letters from women across Canada who "just [weren't] going to take the new fashions."[58] Even in the spring of 1948, the popular women's magazine *New Liberty* asked, "Has the New Look caught on?" and replied, "In style-conscious Paris, only [fashion] models and wealthy society women could afford to wear it. The average woman preferred to buy food."[59] Eaton's had to explain the new length in its fall 1947 staff newsletter, exclaiming, "Down with the Hemline! It's a Revolution" and expounding that "skirt lengths are much longer, 14 to 15 inches from the floor for daytime, 12 to 13 inches for afternoon and 6 to 8 inches (and all the way to full length, uneven hemlines, slight trains) for evening wear . . . Yards of material are being used in the lovely new fashions. Voluminous coats with fuller backs, wider skirt sweeps, longer lines; some with hoods, some without" (fig. 1.17).[60] Dora Matthews commented on her own Dior model, saying, "Naturally I had an original. It was smashing but uncomfortable. The full skirt was held out with buckram and the waist was very tight. It was black wool."[61]

The prestige garnered by showing or selling European couture was clearly promoted in Eaton's fall fashion show in 1947, "Overture to Fashion," at which the commentator announced, "To own a model frock means to own a portion of someone's creative mind. It gives a woman a thrill to know she can walk abroad and never 'meet herself' . . . She will be recognized as a woman of taste and discrimination wherever she goes."[62]

2 THE PURCHASE OF HAUTE COUTURE BY PRIVATE CLIENTS

Women would come and want help getting an outfit, usually for a special occasion. Often they would drop in after to tell me what a success it had been. Knowing that you are well and suitably dressed gives one a wonderful feeling of confidence. Dora Matthews, 1984

Buying haute couture was a quintessentially feminine experience. Whether the client shopped directly in the couture salon in Paris, London, or Rome, or in a North American couture salon within a prestigious specialty store or a department store, it was a feminine affair. In all these venues, the relationship between consumer and retailer was carefully orchestrated. Haute couture consumption was like a classical musical composition. It began with an overture, the presentation of the designs in a fashion show. This was followed by a series of formalized movements within which the players each contributed to the sale. At the crescendo of the performance, the consumer, wearing the dress, entered society and had a public reception.

Since the raison d'être of the Paris haute couture was the private female customer, a closer examination of the relationship between client and couture house is warranted. Consumption of family goods, and especially clothing, has been clearly sexed as a feminine occupation since at least the nineteenth century. Recent scholarship has pushed the time frame back as far as the second half of the eighteenth century.

In eighteenth-century Paris, "as shops became more inviting and hospitable spaces for women . . . the relationship between client and merchant — the nature of the entertainment provided by shopping — changed." The increasing number of female shoppers upset the traditional courtship roles of male consumer and female merchant. It was feared that the rise of female consumers and the development of seductive new boutiques "would lead to women's moral corruption, as if the lust for hats would provoke more dangerous desires . . . [Some] contemporaries were concerned that these sanctuaries of frivolity would lead to an equally pernicious character flaw, bad taste." As historian Jennifer Jones so well points out, the female merchant was cast in the role of "promoter and seducer" of the new female customer.[1] The twentieth-century Paris *vendeuse* inherited this role. By the late nineteenth century, the female retailer or saleswoman was seen as the temptress of the female consumer, who was viewed as riddled with uncontrollable urges and usually hysterical.[2] This notion still lingers today, and is profoundly associated with luxury goods such as haute couture. The myth is a far cry from the controlled and judicious decisions that actually framed most female consumption.

The Social Introduction to a Couture House

In the 1950s, a small percentage of North American women still went regularly to Europe and purchased clothing at the couture house. Yet a woman who wanted to buy directly at an haute couture salon could not just walk in.[3] The social contacts required and the etiquette code surrounding the couture system were steeped in traditions resembling gaining membership to an elite club. Some Paris couture houses were much harder to get into than others. This hierarchy was largely based on the popularity of the houses and was usually determined by the fashion press. Prestige also determined prices; the more elite the couture house, the higher its prices. Balenciaga, for instance, was known for being "le plus cher, et clientèle le plus riche." Even in the course of my research I discovered that these rules still apply.[4]

The private customers who purchased directly at the haute couture house can be divided into three groups. The first was an established, elite prewar group, the members of which had inherited an introduction or gained it through wealth and who passed on this tradition of consumption to the second group, their daughters. Very few of the daughters continued to buy haute couture regularly in Europe after they were married, however, even though they had inherited the *entrée*. They would usually buy only if it was convenient when they were in Europe, or if they needed something very special. The third group comprised women with new postwar wealth, some of whom became regular customers and some of whom bought infrequently or only once. For this group, the introduction usually came either from a friend who was already a "member" of the haute couture club or through social-professional connections that could be established through a society *vendeuse*. Others in this group obtained recommendations from local department store contacts.

The experiences of several Torontonians illustrate the typical process of introduction for postwar women. Rosemary Boxer was initiated into haute couture buying by her mother, who went regularly to Europe with her husband, an international lawyer. In 1946, Rosemary Boxer was married in a Norman Hartnell gown, even though her mother usually dressed at Molyneux. Molyneux, however, was known for "never doing wedding clothes" so they went to Hartnell, "who was a friend."[5] The referral system made the transition from one house to another easy. Another society leader, Mona Campbell, was introduced to the system of buying directly at the design house by her mother. Her first couture garment was purchased in 1937, a full-length black evening coat with fox collar and muff from Olive Todd, a couturier on Dover Street in London, England. She was living in London at the time, attending a finishing school before she came out in Toronto that same year.[6] Signy Eaton went first to Europe with her mother, who went annually to both Paris and New York.[7] Alternatively, some women went only once or twice to an haute couture showing, often while they were travelling in Europe with their mothers before getting married. The experience was considered part of their European tour, not expected to be assimilated as a regular pattern into their future married life, and the clothes they bought functioned as a form of trousseau. The process reflects the difference between prewar and postwar clients.[8] Once a client was accepted into an haute couture house, the system of looking at the collection and selecting a purchase was also controlled by rules of haute couture etiquette.

The Role of the Paris *Vendeuse* and the Society *Vendeuse*

A *vendeuse* was the saleswoman in an haute couture house who sold the merchandise to clients.[9] The job was complex and required a great degree of social skill, as she was the liaison between the house, workroom, and client.[10] Her duties encompassed the following: "to see that the purchaser is completely pleased. It is she who puts the order through to the *atelier*, checks fabrics, colours, trimmings — everything — to make certain all are in accord with the original garment and any changes requested are recorded. She supervises fittings and checks on the progress of the garment so that the promised delivery date is met . . . Each *vendeuse* has one or more assistants, also known as *secondes*."[11]

The ideal *vendeuse*-client relationship was long term, and the house attached a great deal of importance to it. Ginette Spanier, *directrice* for Balmain, commented on this in her memoirs: "One of my jobs is to give the right *vendeuse* to a client, because the agreement, psychologically, between the two often is very important to the happiness of the customer."[12]

This private relationship is very difficult to research because even today *vendeuses* protect their clients' intimate details. They are privy to informal chat and details of clients' personal lives and social activities. They keep notebooks on clients and sales but are not willing to share the specific information as it is considered personal and would break the established haute couture etiquette. Clients are also reticent and forgetful. Nevertheless, the stock books from the British house of Lachasse record its transactions from before the war until 1989.[13] The records are organized by client name and *vendeuse* and testify to a rapport often lasting decades. Mrs Arthur Milner of Castlefrank Drive in Toronto went to the male *vendeuse* Peter Crown from 1955 to 1966. The records have the name "Effie" crossed out and Peter Crown's name written above. It seems likely that Mrs Milner's original *vendeuse* was Effie, who retired or left the house, and that she was then passed on to Mr Crown, who was with the house for a long time as a tailor and salesperson and would have been known to Mrs Milner.[14]

An haute couture design purchased directly from the couture house was an insurance of exclusivity for a client's wardrobe. Her *vendeuse* acted as a type of insurance agent who would be familiar with the client's lifestyle and social circle, thus providing security against the client encountering someone else in "her" design. By the 1950s, a more serious issue was to safeguard a private client against buying a "Ford," a design that would soon be knocked off in the mass-produced clothing market. This became such a problem that an idea was discussed, though never implemented, that part of the French collections be reserved for sale exclusively to private clients.[15] Thus, a refined and complex record-keeping system was important to maintain the relationship between a client and *vendeuse*. Christian Dior described the system:

Each private client has her file, which tells her name, address, passport number, measurements, credit rating, publicity value, workroom and vendeuse. *In other columns are written the money she spends at every collection through the years, her personality (hard or easy to handle), her place of birth, how she came to us and her favourite department — clothes, furs, hats, the boutique . . .*

We also keep a model file containing the name of each dress, the name of the mannequin who wears it, its number in the show. It also gives the names of the private clients who buy it, their standing, their nationality and date of ordering.

For professional buyers, the file shows whether they purchased the paper pattern, canvas or the original dress. There is also a file by countries which will tell you in half a minute how much America, Greece or Italy spent during any season of the year.[16]

Tantalizing as this is for researchers, I have not been able to get access to any of this type of record and was repeatedly told that they did not exist. Either they have been disposed of or, more likely, are considered either an infringement of the client's privacy or too commercial to support the myth of couture as art.

The *vendeuse* acted as a taste editor on behalf of the haute couture house and directed the client's final appearance and image. It was the responsibility of the *vendeuse* to assure that garments fit correctly and were appropriate for her client's figure, age, and lifestyle, thereby demonstrating the workmanship and taste of the haute couture house. For the client, the *vendeuse* was a key person, saving her time and unnecessary or inappropriate purchases by knowing the collection, her taste, and often how the new acquisition would fit into her existing wardrobe.

In the 1950s, there was another type of *vendeuse*, who had probably existed early on in the haute couture system. Celia Bertin called her a society *vendeuse*, which she defined as one who "dealt only with customers she herself introduced, receiving 10% commission."[17] Mary Picken and Dora Miller called her a *vendeuse mondaine*, meaning a woman who had a "social following and can bring desirable business to the house . . . Many ladies of title serve the great houses . . . She receives what in the United States is called a drawing account (enough salary for actual expenses) and in addition she is paid a commission on all her sales. A vendeuse mondaine's job is to look chic, to evidence perfection in grooming, to be on intimate terms with the international and theatrical set and keep customers coming to the house."[18]

Prewar and postwar, a very influential woman performing such a role for North Americans in Paris was American expatriate Laura Bacon. She lived in the Ritz and would furnish introductions to Paris couture salons to women who were anxious to make the socially correct purchases but did not know where to start. Introduction to her services was through word of mouth. Laura Bacon left New York for Paris in the 1920s and worked for Anne Morgan, daughter of the American banker John Pierpont Morgan. In Paris, she met and married Howard Bacon, who worked for *Barron* newspaper. In 1927, she set up a business helping wealthy North Americans to experience the luxury services of Paris.[19]

She would tell you what to do in Paris . . . When [Americans and Canadians] came to Paris they looked her up and she shopped with them. When I first knew her [before the war] she was in Molyneux's as a vendeuse *but she didn't go in except when she was helping someone to choose clothes . . . She knew a lot of very well-to-do people coming over from the States who were friends of hers . . . She always lived at the Ritz in Paris, never lived anywhere else . . . She finally went into business for herself . . . helping people shop . . . She had an office in the Place Vendôme across from the Ritz. If you went there she could take you wherever you wanted, whatever it was [you wanted] purses, jewellery, or clothes, or whatever . . . She was an amazing person.*[20]

Laura Bacon probably began to work professionally as a type of cultural ambassador because she was constantly being asked for advice about other aspects of society Paris. She is remembered as the first person in Paris to provide a complete shopping service for foreigners, a role she created for herself. She set up arrangements with all the leading luxury trades — couture and accessory houses, hairdressers, florists — and established a system whereby she sent them clients on the understanding that she would receive a commission.[21] As one Paris couturier told me, "She knew a lot of rich Americans with no taste."[22] Her clients came to her by referral.[23] If she did not personally escort the client she would call ahead to the establishment and make an appointment. The client would go with her business card printed with "Laura Bacon suggests . . ." It was then the responsibility of the *vendeuse* who had served the client to call Laura Bacon with details of the sale. This was customarily supplied before evening, or else Mrs Bacon would quickly be on the telephone for the information.[24]

Laura Bacon established her own reputation for exclusivity, as she only patronized the houses with the highest status. Before the war, she sent clients to Molyneux and after to Dior, Fath, Balenciaga, Lanvin, Givenchy, and Venet.[25] Postwar, when Torontonian Mary Carr-Harris went to Paris, she had a luncheon appointment at the Ritz to see Laura Bacon, who took her to Givenchy, Venet, Dior, Schiaparelli, Lanvin, and Fath. She had been to Paris before, going annually with her husband when he was on business, and had bought clothes at other small couture houses but never from the prominent names.[26] It was Laura Bacon who introduced her to these top houses, guided her though the experience, and ensured that she made appropriate selections.

How a Private Client Made a Purchase

In 1957, *Time* magazine quoted a *vendeuse* at Dior, who in reaction to a client's dismay at the price of a dress said, "When they hesitate, I always tell them to buy elsewhere . . . Remorse is better than regret."[27] Such an attitude perpetuated a tradition of couture as privileged consumption and linked haute couture with high art collected by connoisseurs. The investment in an haute couture purchase, however, was not only a question of capital but also a serious commitment of time. Time, invested by both the client and the house, is one of the keys to the origins of couture mythology and helps to explain why a couture garment was believed to be priceless.

Buying haute couture in Paris was a structured process. Having arranged an appointment with a *vendeuse*, the client would attend a viewing of the collection or the parts of the collection that would relate to the intended purchase or purchases (fig. 2.1). These showings were for private clients only. During the 1950s, the collection was shown an average of two to three times a day on live mannequins. The mannequins worked exclusively for individual couture houses, and their quarters were called the *cabine*. At Nina Ricci, the haute couture collection was shown in the morning and afternoon. Later on, with the introduction of the Jeune Femme collection, a show was added at 3:00 p.m., and by the 1950s, the new boutique collection was also shown in the morning.[28]

At Dior, Toronto client Rose Torno would make an appointment, and her name would be checked off a list at the door when she arrived. She would then go upstairs to the salon, where she sat in a chair reserved by her *vendeuse* and watched the daily fashion parade. She would be given a pad and pencil to mark down the dress numbers she was interested in trying and would give these to her *vendeuse* after the show. She then went to "an impossible little dressing room" to try on the clothes, which would not fit because the samples were made to measure for the

2.1 A *petite main*, or assistant, at the haute couture salon of Pierre Balmain in Paris taking the dresses to show to a prospective customer in 1956.

individual house mannequins. Sometimes she would not bother to try on a garment if the price was "astronomical." Having selected her purchases, she usually did not have more than the prescribed three fittings.[29] This system did not suit all customers. Sonja Bata was a client who preferred to look at the clothes on the rack and herself select designs for the house mannequin to model, rather than sit through a show. She discussed the fit with her *vendeuse* and would sometimes disagree. She did not like the tight armhole that was typical of the period, and especially fitted in French clothes, while the *vendeuse* would say it looked beautiful. Even so, she conceded that the *vendeuse* was "frequently right."[30]

It was during the selection of garments that design modifications occurred. This not only guaranteed an "original" design but also permitted personal taste to change the couturier's original conception. Redesigning was a collaborative effort between the *vendeuse* and client. By comparing the original design house sketch to a garment actually purchased, one can see the scope and type of alterations. A Balmain cocktail dress in the Royal Ontario Museum collection, for example, is similar to a model called "Espoirs perdus" from the winter 1956 collection (figs. 2.2 and 2.3). The main design feature of the dress is the diagonal draping that meets at centre-front waist and is clearly seen in both dress and design. The dress differs from the sketch in that it is sleeveless, has no centre-front buttons, and the line of the skirt is much less flared. Another, more subtle example of modification can be seen in a custom-ordered Balenciaga dress on which the waistline has been dropped; the couturier's original concept had a more avant-garde high waist (figs. 2.4 and 2.5). This type of customizing, or redesigning, stemmed from the historical relationship between the tailor or dressmaker and the client before the advent of celebrity couturiers. The ability of a client to redesign is an aspect of haute couture that has been largely overlooked in favour of promoting the designer as artist and quintessential arbiter of taste.

Not only did a client have to schedule time for the initial appointment and the later fittings but her order had to fit into the overall production schedule of the house. The length of time involved in actually acquiring a final garment depended on both the client's schedule and that of the house. The time necessary to obtain a garment thus secured the client's involvement, heightened her desire by developing her anticipation, and increased the significance of the purchase.

2.2 Pierre Balmain cocktail dress that was probably based on the original model "Espoirs perdus." The dress differs from the model in that it is sleeveless, has no buttons, and has a narrower skirt.   **2.3** (opposite) Design sketch for fall 1956 Pierre Balmain dress model 392, called "Espoirs perdus."

392 Espoirs Perdus

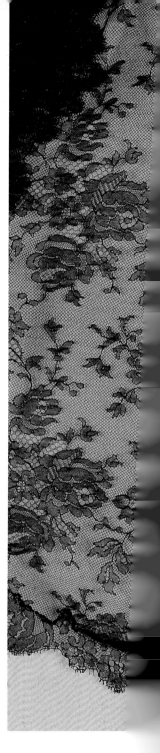

2.4 Fall 1956 Balenciaga black lace cocktail dress ordered by Toronto socialite Rose Torno at the couture house in Paris. Mrs Torno had the waistline dropped from the original design. **2.5** (opposite) The same dress as designed and shown by Balenciaga, model 74. The detail shows how the lace has been seamed by hand to follow the floral pattern.

The *Vendeuse* and the Value of the Garment

A *vendeuse* made her income from her sales commission, so had to be a good sales-woman and encourage customers to buy. Because the business was based on return-ing clients, however, a *vendeuse* had to balance the short-term sale carefully with long-term customer satisfaction. Rose Torno's experiences were typical. She never felt pressured to buy and believed that all aspects of her lifestyle were considered. Having been satisfied with a few houses, primarily Dior, Balmain, Balenciaga, and Chanel, she stayed with them as it was easier for her to go to a house that already knew her, understood her taste, and had knowledge of her existing wardrobe. In one instance, she very much wanted a particular Balenciaga dress but was going to Rome and returning to Paris in five days, then leaving again. She was told it was impossible and that the house could not even make a nightgown in five days.[31] A *vendeuse* thus sometimes had to discourage a sale if scheduling did not permit its creation. Even a regular client could not have all her wishes satisfied and had to "earn" garments, thereby justifying the expense and personal involvement in haute couture production. Denial of some garments also heightened the pleasure of the successfully obtained clothes. It is also possible that in this instance the *vendeuse* did not think that the client would be happy with the design she wanted — it had been requested as an afterthought to the main order — and used this tactic to deter her.

By contrast, another Torontonian's experience at Balmain reflects the effort made by the houses to capitalize on a client's desires. Grace Gooderham was a reg-ular client at Balmain. In 1956, she was buying day clothes but had seen a ball gown that she liked very much but considered expensive (fig. 2.6, and see fig. 7.20, p. 273). The *vendeuse* knew that she admired the design, and when Mrs Gooderham was having fittings for her day clothes, the *vendeuse* would bring in the ball gown to tempt her. Finally, toward the end of her stay she decided to order it even though it could not be completed before she left Paris. She had the inner corset of the strapless dress fitted before her departure, and the garment was then finished and shipped to her in Canada.[32]

That haute couture purchases were contemplated on a number of levels relates to another important aspect of the non-economic value of couture. An haute cou-ture dress had a value that went beyond the monetary because it was considered a rare design object that conferred status on its wearer. This image was publicly advocated by the couture houses and is validated today by museums, couture collectors, and rising auction prices for these designs, as well as by the fact that many women who wore couture still have pieces in their wardrobes years later even though they will probably never wear them again.

Grace Gooderham's Balmain ball gown was embroidered after it was sewn together, making it impossible to alter without ruining the design and impractical to mass produce. The high price of the gown, its technical complexity, and the fact that she ordered it directly from the design house were a form of insurance of its scarcity.[33] At the time, Mrs Gooderham did consider the dress to be expensive, but she also judged its value in terms of design, workmanship, and exclusivity in her Toronto circle. She wore the dress to the Artillery Ball that year when her daughter came out as a debutante.[34]

The purchase of this particular gown is also an example of "impulse buying" within the couture system, as Grace Gooderham had gone to Paris with the express purpose of filling in her day wardrobe, and the ball gown was an "extra."[35] Colin Campbell defines this as "consumption rhetoric," which he explains as the difference between need and want. He suggests that while people typically make lists for the things they need, they do not do so for what they want, "as there is little likelihood of forgetting one's desires. How consumers cope with the 'chore' of simple replacement need-shopping, therefore, is to 'compensate' or 'reward' themselves for performing it by indulging one or more 'wants.'"[36]

These different experiences, the denial of the Balenciaga design to Rose Torno and the fulfilment of Grace Gooderham's desire for the Balmain, illustrate the complexity of the private haute couture sales system, which was geared toward controlling the production of quality garments in order to maintain its elite and exclusive image. The Paris *vendeuse* was pivotal in this process and served as a type of taste broker. Her Toronto equivalent, who was just as influential, was the saleswoman in the couture salon of the local department stores, specialty shops, and boutiques.

Toronto Couture Salon Buyers and Sales Staff As Taste Makers

By the 1950s, most North Americans shopped for couture locally instead of going to couture houses in Europe. Torontonian Rosemary Rathgeb, who did buy in Paris, explained that she preferred to buy from local stores as this gave her time to think

2.6 This fall 1956 Pierre Balmain ball gown of silk faille, "Agéna," was ordered at the Paris haute couture salon by Grace Gooderham, who wore it to the Artillery Ball in Toronto for her daughter's debut in the winter of 1956. The dress was embroidered with roses after it had been sewn to fit the customer, making it impossible to alter. See also fig. 0.1, p. 2.

about her purchases. She found that custom-made clothing did not always come out as she expected, making it difficult for her to be satisfied, so she preferred to have ready-made couture that she could try on before buying.[37]

Nonetheless, the Paris haute couture salons were an internationally recognized model for an environment in which to purchase luxury clothing, and local merchants emulated them. Retailers that traded in couture provided richly decorated salons, elegant seating, and fitting rooms for customers. The lavish decor was intended to reflect the lifestyle of those buying the clothes. The setting and the whole experience of the purchase was integral to the sale and a testament to the retailer's understanding of the cultural and social context of the merchandise and therefore the client.[38] Historians Susan Benson and Cynthia Wright have both noted the importance of the "non-selling areas" in defining department stores as feminine space. Gail Reekie has likened the dressmaking room of late-nineteenth-century department stores to a boudoir and the public spaces and selling areas of stores to the drawing room.[39] Department store lounges, dining rooms, exhibition areas, and theatres were intended for women's events and entertainment, thus promoting the store as a social gathering point with links to art and culture.

In Toronto, Eaton's and Simpson's both placed great value on the interior design of their couture departments, attempting to create an atmosphere in which the customer would feel pampered, as though she were in a rarefied European luxury setting. When Ollie Smythe took over as buyer for Eaton's Ensemble Shop in 1955, she described it as "a dreary place with little stock that was very high priced." She asked for the salon to be refurbished as a condition of her accepting the job, and the three small fitting rooms were decorated with matching paint and carpets in pink, green, and blue. The other large department store, Simpson's, sold couture in the St Regis Room, which its couture buyer, Margery Steele, described as having black and white tile that was "copied from Versailles" and crystal chandeliers (fig. 2.7).[40]

Another aspect of private haute couture sales often neglected by scholars was the husband. He could play a significant role as an arbiter of taste, not just as a source of money. He, too, was directly linked to the value and meaning of couture purchases as capital and cultural investments that were a direct reflection of his socio-economic status. Rose Torno's husband would accompany her shopping most of the time, and she said that he was "most generous." Couture salons, though designed as feminine

spaces, also accommodated trappings associated with male comfort, often by including a club chair, serving beverages, and making newspapers and magazines available.

Toronto retail buyers and sales staff were the local equivalent of the Paris *vendeuse*. Ollie Smythe clearly saw her role as a taste and etiquette advisor.[41] Most couture clients called ahead to make an appointment with their saleswomen, who would preselect styles for them and have the garments ready when they came in. In the salon itself, only a few items of clothing would be displayed, as the bulk of the stock was hidden from view. This practice secured the privacy of both stock and price for any potential customers and upheld the exclusivity of the merchandise.[42]

Specialty stores and boutiques operated the same way. At Toronto's Joan Rigby boutique, the young saleswomen were from the same social group as the customers. They "naturally" understood clients' requirements and could offer very personal, insightful advice. Their own dresses were usually purchased from the shop because they got a discount, and this, too, promoted the store because everyone knew where they worked. Helen Stimpson, Lee Allen, and Ardith Gardiner, all saleswomen at Joan Rigby, were photographed and their dresses described in the local

2.7 The St Regis Room in Simpson's Queen Street branch in the mid-1950s.

newspaper when they appeared at Woodbine racetrack during the King's Plate in May 1947.[43] As the occasion was social, no reference was made in the newspaper to Joan Rigby, but it would have been understood by knowledgeable readers and by the women's friends that their ensembles were from the shop. Thus, they championed the reputation and merchandise of the store within a purely social context.

A well-known Toronto model told me that she would wear clothes from the exclusive store Creeds to the members' enclosure at the racetrack, where her dress would be noticed and understood to have been from that store. This sort of "silent" promotion of haute couture worn by recognizable, fashionable individuals was successfully employed in the late nineteenth century, when actresses wore couture on stage, and by such early-twentieth-century designers as Paul Poiret, who sent his mannequins to the racetrack wearing his designs. It is clearly seen today in the dresses worn by those attending the Academy Awards in Hollywood.

The influence of buyers and sales staff over clients was considerable, in positive and negative ways. Creeds salon, for example, was closely identified with saleswoman Alexandra Dorothea Burton, known as Lexy. She had graduated from Molton College for young ladies at age eighteen and worked for a French milliner, Mrs Nedo, for eight years in midtown premises at Bay and Bloor Streets. In 1930, she went to work at Creeds, where her sister, Eleanor, was the buyer at the time. She was put in charge of sales, and had about thirty-five customers "who bought nothing but the finest French designers." As she said, "I had one customer in particular who . . . if I called her at five o'clock . . . and told her what I had, she'd be down in five minutes and take the whole collection." Lexy said that she would "rather not sell anything than see a woman walk out in something that [didn't] suit her." It was known that "she possessed a keen eye for style, an appreciation of couture fashion and a joy of working with people that made for a success on the floor of the city's most select women's fashion store."[44] She retired in 1988. Lexy noted that her job in sales was "lady-like sort of work because it was the best shop in Toronto, with the best clientele. I had been well brought up, schooled in all the niceties. I had the same savoir faire my customers had."[45]

Ollie Smythe also exerted considerable influence. She recalled having to dress a large-sized client for a special cocktail party. The woman had been referred personally by Signy Eaton, wife of the president of Eaton's, so the situation was infused with importance from the start. Having taken one look at the client, Ollie Smythe knew that she had only a single dress in stock that would fit her and suit the occasion. Nevertheless, the client was taken to a dressing room and shown several dresses before the destined one. The client did choose the only dress possible, but as Ollie Smythe said, "She believed she had a choice and had an enjoyable experience."[46] An opposite tack was taken at Joan Rigby if staff had to deal with customers who did not pay their accounts. They were instructed to show the clients fashions that would not suit them so that they would see nothing to buy.[47]

Consequently, buyers and saleswomen were highly instrumental in understanding and influencing the taste of Toronto's social world. Many of these clients moved in international circles, extending the influence of the buyers and local sales staff well beyond the city.

Department Store Services

Customers had innate expectations of in-store services to accompany retail couture. Deliveries were usually made twice a day, and stores permitted customers to take goods home to be tried on with personal accessories and viewed in the context where they would be worn. Another important service was a reliable in-store fitting and alterations department. Custom fit was synonymous with haute couture, and this attribute carried through to imported, already made-up couture models. In order to retail haute couture successfully outside of the Paris setting, a good alterations service was essential. Clayton Burton, wife of Edgar G. Burton, the president of Simpson's, summed this up when she said, "You're only as good as your alterations department."[48] Selling high-priced clothing, and particularly couture, therefore necessitated having highly trained professional seamstresses available to work on the stock. In Toronto, as elsewhere in North America, many of these were skilled European immigrant women.

The importance of the alterations departments was directly reflected in the staffing. Creeds had an alterations staff of thirty to forty that was run by a forewoman or foreman.[49] Joan Rigby had two fitters, Nellie Cubban and Margaret Curran, who earned $35 a week and were sometimes helped out by another sewer, Bessie Love.[50] Haute couture clothing purchased away from the design house almost always required alteration for a personal fit, a fact that accounts for the high number of alterations in the Royal Ontario Museum collection. The time required for alterations was calculated into the couture shopping process and described in Eaton's staff magazine, *Flash*: "As soon as a customer has decided she wants to buy a certain dress . . . the fitter is called by the salesclerk and there is a deft taking-in here, and a letting-out there . . . indicated by pins, until the garment fits. Next the garment is brought to the workroom where girls expert in their line . . . some for coats and suits, some for dresses . . . do the work indicated by the fitter . . . After the pressers have done their work . . . the garment is hung on a 'finished' rack to be thoroughly inspected before going out."[51]

The scale of alterations varied from small adjustments, such those in a Balmain evening gown that has been taken in at the front darts (figs. 2.8 and 2.9), to major modifications, such as that in a lace Balmain evening dress that has been let out approximately four centimetres at the waist (fig. 2.10). The alteration to the first dress was more difficult than it appears, as the rose embroidery had to be worked around. In the lace dress, a white lace V similar to the original lace has been inserted at the centre back and at the sides of the bust and blends into the rest of the garment. It is further disguised by the addition of copper-coloured sequins similar, but not identical, to the original French sequins on the dress. These dresses and numerous others demonstrate that alterations, either minor or substantial, were not a deterrent to the haute couture consumer but de rigeur to achieve the perfect fit.

For both store buyers and clients, knowing that the clothes would be altered influenced the selection of merchandise. A garment that was designed in a highly complex way, making alterations very awkward or obvious, would be passed over in favour of another style. As the average couture customer was a mature woman, the issue of size was key in determining selections. Buyers tried to order couture garments in large sizes for their clients. A change in scale could change the look of the original design and had to be taken into consideration when placing orders.

The private consumption of haute couture should be viewed as a specialized undertaking. Etiquette, time, money, setting, social connections, and relationships were all integral to a purchase. In-store services including home deliveries, exchanges, and alterations were essential to finalizing sales. But at the same time there existed another set of rules, with its own series of constraints and relationships, governing the mass consumption of couture by merchants and manufacturers.

2.8 Pierre Balmain sketch for the spring 1955 gown "Rose de Paris," altered for Dorothy Boylen (fig. 2.9).

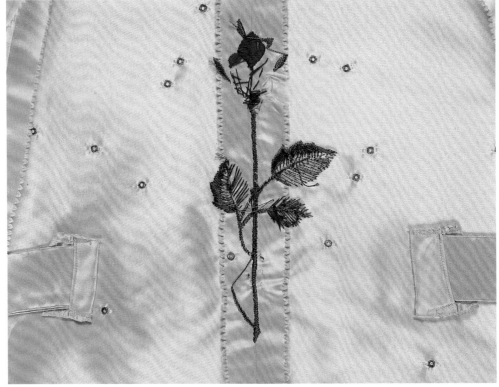

2.9 This Pierre Balmain evening gown, "Rose de Paris," was worn by Toronto socialite Dorothy Boylen and probably purchased at Simpson's. It has had a very small alteration in the front darts, which have been taken in. The roses are carefully embroidered over the centre back seam after the seam has been sewn up.

2.10 This fall 1952 Pierre Balmain ball gown has been has been let out about four centimetres in the centre bodice to accommodate the customer, socialite Ethel Harris. The alteration has been patched with similar lace and sequins to hide the adjustments. See fig. 5.15, p. 162.

3.1 Toronto socialites and members of the Junior League in evening dress at a party at the home of Helen Phelan, president of the Toronto Junior League, prior to the League Christmas Tree Ball, 4 December 1954. From left to right: Mrs Harold Grant, Mrs R.F. Porter, Mrs G.E. Bunnett (Mary Bunnett, wearing Hartnell), Mrs Paul Phelan, Mrs John Bull, Mrs John Weir (Frances M. Weir), and Mrs F.M. Gaby.

3 BUYING AND MERCHANDISING EUROPEAN COUTURE IN TORONTO

In a machine age, dressmaking is one of the last refuges of the human, the personal, the inimitable. In an epoch as sombre as ours, luxury must be defended inch by inch. Christian Dior, 1957

After the Second World War, it is unlikely that many of the European couture houses would have survived without an extensive trade with the numerous North American department stores, specialty stores, and small boutiques that imported and distributed their goods. Examining the operation of couture production and linking the industry directly to its market completely debunks the cliché of the passive female couture consumer and the male couturier as the one dictating styles.

Demand for couture was directly related to the social season. The postwar years in Toronto saw an incredible boom in activities for an increasingly large group of social leaders. In addition to the reinstatement of prewar functions, there was an unprecedented growth in new events instigated by women's voluntary organizations. These quickly became ensconced traditions within the social season (fig. 3.1). The burst of activity was due to Canada's strong economic development and rapid population growth from postwar immigration. Many couture customers were volunteers on the organizing committees that planned these functions. If not directly involved in organizing fundraising occasions, wives and husbands would attend the event itself as a show of support for their friends and for the community as a whole. It was recognized that "a young woman who wants her husband to be successful and, on the way, to achieve her own social ambitions, is well advised to work her way up through a few high-prestige [volunteer] organizations." Thus, the social calendar and season dictated the requirements of a wardrobe, and correct dress was proof of the status of the occasion and of the individual woman's right to be there. The range of social events, both private and public, religious and non-religious, included

committee meetings, afternoon teas, cocktails, evening concerts, dinner parties, balls, and weddings, and all required correct dress determined by time of day and type of occasion.[1]

The significance of the social season was well understood by the leading department stores, which advertised new fashions in the fall. Often incorporated into an advertisement was a list of the upcoming important social events that would require special dress (fig. 3.2). The supply of couture available at stores was closely tied to requirements determined by women's philanthropic "invisible careers" and the entire annual social season.

Interviews with consumers and with the buyers and sales staff who catered to this demand reveal some of the complexity and restraints operating in couture consumption. Selections and taste can then be set within a broader framework of the consumption system, mitigated by intertwined factors of supply, demand, distribution, and economic, social, and cultural influences.

The Couture Retailers

The two most important national department stores in Canada, Simpson's and Eaton's, were long-time business competitors, especially in high-priced fashions, for which

3.2 Simpson's advertisement for evening wear, including one "French Import" and one "European Import," 2 November 1956. The fashions are promoted in the context of nine upcoming social events, held between November 1956 and the end of January 1957, which would require evening gowns.

there was a small market. Couture was seen by stores, and especially by department stores, as cultural capital. The value of featuring couture in fashion shows and having it worn by the leading socialites who patronized the store went beyond dollars and cents. Having these clothes available demonstrated a merchant's links to European design and raised the store's profile and cultural identity within Toronto.[2]

The T. Eaton Company had carried haute couture in its original Queen Street store since the early twentieth century, when it hosted international designers such as Paul Poiret and sold couture by leading Paris houses such as Jeanne Lanvin.[3] With the opening of the modern College Street store in 1930 and its Ensemble Shop in 1932, Eaton's main couture department shifted to this location from the Queen Street store, while the Robert Simpson Company continued to sell couture in the St Regis Room (fig. 3.3).[4]

3.3 Eaton's Ensemble Shop, spring 1932. The shop in the College Street store showed imported fashions from its opening in 1930 until the 1960s. It was designed in the high French Art Deco style.

Other large specialty clothing stores consistently carried couture after the war. Holt Renfrew and Company was a Montreal-based ladies' specialty store founded in 1837. By 1960, it had nine stores between Quebec City and Calgary, all selling high- to medium-priced fashion. Creeds was founded in 1915 as a family-run specialty clothing store and maintained a reputation as one of the most exclusive shops in Toronto.[5]

In 1950, a new store was added to this established prewar order. Montreal's most prestigious shop, Henry Morgan and Company, opened a Toronto branch. The opening of the store was described in the newspapers, and its haute couture collection was highlighted: "The stature of Toronto as a fashion centre will be increased today with the opening of a Henry Morgan & Co store . . . This is the first time it is opening an out of town branch . . . In future one collection [of European couture] will be bought for Montreal and one for Toronto. The large Paris houses from which the store buys include Christian Dior, Captain Molyneux, Balenciaga, Fath, Pierre Balmain and Jean Dessès. In England Morgan's have been buying for some years from Hardy Amies, Norman Hartnell and Peter Russell" (fig. 3.4).[6]

In 1955, Morgan's opened a branch at Lawrence Plaza. This branch was more commercially successful as it catered to a new wealthy suburban clientele rather than competing directly against established downtown Toronto stores with an existing clientele. It was in this postwar period that the department stores pursued new clients into the expanding suburbs.[7]

Numerous small boutiques also carried imports. The largest and one of the most successful in Toronto during the 1950s was Joan Rigby. It was described as a house with big windows and painted grey and white, and was run by Joan Rigby and her husband. The stock was mainly Canadian and American high-priced ready-to-wear, with some European couture imports and a line of suits, dresses, and jackets designed by Joan Rigby herself under the label "Jori." An in-house designer fulfilled the custom orders. Joan Rigby was also a Toronto agent for the British woollen house Jaeger.[8] The shop was on the ground floor and included a bride's room, two large fitting rooms, and two smaller ones that were each equipped with a chair, a mirror, and a stage for marking hems. An accessory department sold gloves and hosiery under the supervision of Yvonne Morrow, one of the top saleswomen. Joan Rigby purchased her imported garments from European buyers who came to Toronto; she never went overseas to buy.[9] She had a strong position within the couture retail

from Morgan's collection of imports
from England, France, Sweden,
Italy and Switzerland . . .

Morgan's
MONTREAL
TORONTO
OTTAWA

community in the city and placed an emphasis on hiring young staff to attract a younger generation and newly married women.

Another similar boutique was called The Billye Vincent Shop. It opened in 1948, on Bay Street just south of Bloor Street, in the heart of midtown. Jeanie Hersenhoren, wife of the first violinist in the Toronto Symphony Orchestra, recalled her mother buying clothes there and giving them to her with the assurance that they would be appropriate because "Mrs Vincent said." Mrs Vincent imported British suits, woollen dresses, junior styles, and cocktail and evening wear (fig. 3.5).[10]

In the late 1950s, Jean Pierce also opened her important boutique, named eponymously. Her success reflects the expansion of the specialty shopping district from the traditional downtown core. Prewar downtown boutiques clustered around Bloor Street, the epicentre of the midtown district. The mid-1950s expansion saw good specialty shops moving north up Yonge Street to St Clair and Eglinton Avenues — the uptown district — and into the new suburban shopping malls.[11] The geographic extension of high-end retailers was a response to the newly developing upper-middle-class suburbs. These merchants captured clientele who either did not have the inherited tradition of shopping downtown or who had abandoned their mothers' habits in favour of local and newer shopping locales. The stores

3.4 Advertisement for imported English, French, Swedish, Italian, and Swiss couture fashions from Morgan's in Montreal, Toronto, and Ottawa, September 1953. The advertisement depicts the appropriate setting and etiquette for wearing these high fashions.

3.5 A summer silk dress purchased at the Billye Vincent Shop in 1951, designed by Simonetta Visconti of Rome. The armseye of the design was under stress when the dress was worn and has been carefully mended, indicating the importance of the garment within the wearer's wardrobe.

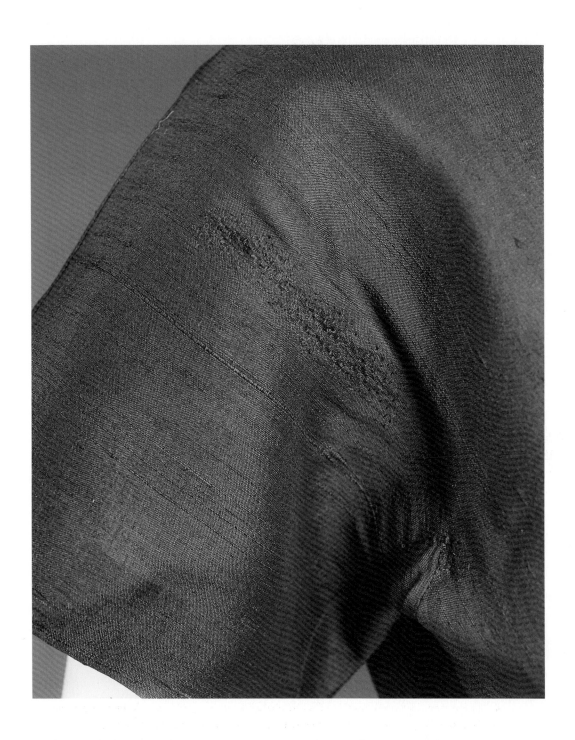

carried some high-end merchandise and were very successful with adaptations and copies of couture models. All the shops that carried imported couture, however, had in common the competition to acquire unique goods. Even if it was only a small fraction of the overall merchandise, carrying imported couture raised their status (Appendix A).

The Purchasing System

The practice of buying and importing couture was similar for all North American stores. Large department stores often established their own buying offices in merchandise centres. Eaton's and Simpson's both had offices in London, and Eaton's also had them in Dublin, Paris, and New York. Here local employees knew the market in their particular area, arranged appointments for the buyers when they came to town, and handled the shipping and customs arrangements. Smaller businesses used brokers and independent buying offices to perform the same functions. These organizations worked for many merchants and profited by taking a percentage of the sales.[12]

Jean Pierce belonged to a New York buying office, McGreely, Werring and Howell, which introduced her to buying overseas. She was assigned to a local woman who knew the market, and the agency took a fee of 5 to 15 percent on the order. Celia Bertin also described the system in Paris, where there were nineteen agencies: "Agents arrange for clients to be accompanied to the couture house, the agent gets in touch with the *vendeuse*, agent pays, takes 10% on amount ordered . . . handles delivery and dispatch."[13]

Yet just as private clients could not walk directly into an haute couture salon, neither could merchants or manufacturers. They were vetted before admittance, and buyers' cards were granted to see the collections. In 1951, American Joseph Barry compared it to "being screened for a sensitive State Department job."[14] Commercial buyers were charged an entrance fee, called a *caution*, to see a Paris collection.[15] The fee was set by the house and approved by the Chambre syndicale, and clearly reflected the status of the house: the more important the house, the higher the *caution*. This cost, was in effect, an unwritten promise to buy and was placed against any purchases. It was an attempt to control unlicensed copying as well as the numbers of individuals who saw the collections.[16] The *caution* was regulated for the different levels of professional buyers and was higher for foreign buyers than for French ones.[17] In 1955, the *caution* for merchants at Balenciaga, one of the most expensive houses, was a minimum of two models; at Dior it was $300 for store buyers and over $1,000 for manufacturers.[18] It was standard practice for manufacturers to pay double the *caution* charged a store buyer, as they would make a higher profit from copies and adaptations.[19]

When a buyer ordered a model, a *toile* (the design made up in muslin), or a *patron à papier* (a paper pattern), included with it was a *référence*. The *référence* gave all the details and costs of the construction, yardage, and sources for textiles, trims, buttons, and belts for the original. With this information, making a copy or knock-off was very easily accomplished as the template was already purchased and the design house had no control over how it was used. The Chambre syndicale recognized that symmetrical *toiles* gave the buyer the possibility of cutting them in half and generating more copies and profit while retaining the information needed in the original. It therefore insisted that the houses sell only *demi-toiles*.[20]

Before the war, private clients had been of key importance to the couture houses. This changed dramatically postwar, when the big buyers were American stores and manufacturers purchasing primarily for copying. The newest and most influential postwar salon, the house of Christian Dior, was keenly aware of the changing role of haute couture and geared the business toward this new market right from its inception in 1947. Dior wrote, "You will remember that I was aiming principally at a clientele of experienced buyers and habitually well-dressed women." He added, "I knew . . . that we could not hope for the lavish orders by the hundred which our predecessors had enjoyed."[21] Dior was perfectly correct, and his astute assessment and the consequent clever marketing tactics of the house are the primary reasons for his huge success, rather than simply the brilliance of his design work.

During the 1950s, adjustments to the haute couture regulations reflected the Chambre syndicale's struggle to maintain the exclusivity of the couture at a time when such a system was becoming obsolete. Commercial buyers constituted the principal market for postwar haute couture. In order to protect the haute couture houses and their good industrial buyers, the Chambre syndicale established a system after the war whereby the press and all those who attended a collection had to "pledge not to make, sell or publish sketches or photos before the release date."[22]

The Chambre syndicale then set the dates annually — usually thirty days after the openings for the new collections — when all Paris haute couture clothes were released to buyers.[23] This was intended to protect the public and private buyers' investments and to control copyright, as all commercial clients received the clothing at the same time. After this, the Chambre syndicale could not regulate who produced the first copies or adaptations from the French designs.

A disparity between the mythology and the reality of haute couture exclusivity was inherent in the system, and it became more exaggerated during the 1950s. Even though haute couture was marketed as unique and special, everyone knew that this was no longer true. The couture houses had to be as careful not to sell designs to private clients or to stores retailing originals if the same designs would end up being copied for mass manufacture. To offset this possibility and to cater to their customers' tastes, stores would also modify designs for their markets, just as the private client could do.

A Balenciaga suit ordered by Holt Renfrew demonstrates the type of design changes that retailers could make (figs. 3.6 and 3.7). The pockets are placed on the jacket, not on the skirt as originally designed, and plain black buttons have been used instead of the larger and more dramatic signature ones on the Balenciaga model. Another simpler design change is seen in a Dior cocktail dress that was ordered by Holt Renfrew in blue silk taffeta, not black, as originally shown (figs. 3.8 and 3.9). Similarly, a Balenciaga day suit was ordered by an American firm, possibly for copying, and the textile was changed from tweed to a plain camel-coloured wool (figs. 3.10 and 3.11).[24] Buyers thus not only selected designs that Canadians would see and wear, but like private clients, they *redesigned* couture to ensure that it would appeal to the taste of their local market. The commercial reality of this process flies in the face of a more romantic couture mythology that positions the garments as iconic designs, far removed from the personal histories of those who traded and wore them.

Overseas Trips for Buyers

Regular buying trips to Europe and New York were part of a retail couture buyer's prestigious role.[25] Ollie Smythe, the couture buyer for Eaton's Ensemble Shop from the early 1950s until she retired in the late 1960s, described her trips. She would go by plane first to London, where she would visit the leading British couturiers, including Norman Hartnell and Hardy Amies. Then she would spend about two days in Dublin, Ireland, where she bought Sybil Connolly and Jack Clark, who had "Country Fashions and lovely Irish tweed suits." From there she went back to London and then on to Zurich, where she would buy primarily Marty of Switzerland models from Harry Marty. After Zurich, she was on to Paris, where she would see small design houses that were cheaper than the big names. Eaton's had an exclusive Canadian arrangement with one on the Rue Royale, which she described as having "everything in the dress, not on it."[26] Though the house did not have Couture-Création status, it did produce couture.

Buyers abroad were representing the store, and as such were treated as business professionals. A chauffeur was available to Ollie Smythe, if none of the store executives were in town. The status of couture was linked to the commercial and social processes of buying it, not just to those who wore it. Ollie Smythe recognized the cachet she gave the store by travelling: "In Paris, [I] could see smart people and what they were doing." Her European experience was very important and gave her unquestioned authority on issues of taste and etiquette, which she would relay to her staff and clientele when she was back in Toronto.[27]

Ollie Smythe's comments are further borne out by her Eaton's colleagues in a letter from the Vancouver branch to the Toronto office: "It is our feeling that the Vancouver and Victoria French Rooms gain prestige in the eyes of their Clientele by having Miss Kaye [the buyer for the region] visit the European Market, and therefore, the additional expense is well warranted."[28] Another letter written two days later on the same subject concluded, "This particular side of our business can not be treated in the same way as other more staple classifications, and much can be said for the prestige value of having a buyer in the market."[29] The executive office concluded that "while the total requisition would not seem to warrant the size of the delegation, it was advisable profit-wise and for prestige, to have the Buyers in the market at regular intervals. Winnipeg and Vancouver consider that such trips should be made annually, while Toronto and Montreal feel that their Buyers should go twice a year," and went on to note that "there is a high gross gain on European goods."[30] Eaton's merchandising of couture was thus linked not only to profits but also, and perhaps more importantly, to cultural status.

3.6 (above left) Original Balenciaga design for model 70, the suit shown in fig. 3.7, with the pockets placed on the skirt.   **3.7** Fall 1959 Balenciaga black-and-white wool suit ordered and sold by Holt Renfrew. The suit has been redesigned from the original model. The pockets have been moved from the skirt to the jacket, perhaps to make the design more conventional, and the buttons have been changed to plain black instead of the more unusual large and textured buttons favoured by Balenciaga.

3.8 Fall 1958 Christian Dior cocktail dress, "Allegro," as sold and worn in Toronto in blue silk.
3.9 (overleaf) Original design and swatch of "Allegro" in black silk, as shown in the Christian Dior Paris fall 1958 collection.

ROBES SOIR COURTES

Strohan Mikado Caracola Favorite Allegro Pianissimo Scherzo

3.10 The Balenciaga photography of fall 1949 suit 117 shows the garment made up in tweed wool, as designed.   **3.11** (opposite) Original sketch of Balenciaga suit 117, showing the tweed wool fabric. This was changed to a camel wool by an American buyer.

Huguette 1951

Paule   117 François

315

futur color
noisette j
gaine

Though buyers visiting Paris brought status to the Canadian stores, the reverse was not so. Eaton's commented in the late 1950s that the small number of models it was able to purchase "disturbed" the couture houses and that "even though Eaton's was one of the first stores to buy from them after the war, while others were waiting to see if they had maintained their fashion prestige, the houses looked down their noses at us because we were buying less [than Americans]."[31] This was to some extent true even in England, where Canadians were generally considered to be good clients. The Canadian buyers' position was directly related to the economic reality that they could never buy in large quantities compared to American buyers, who had a much larger population and clientele for their merchandise.

Buyer Training

Couture departments functioned in a rarefied atmosphere because they were not subject to the same financial pressures as retail departments that dealt in larger volumes and lower priced merchandise. So how did the buyers who were charged with delivering all the associated meanings of couture acquire their training and expertise?

None of the buyers or saleswomen interviewed had received any formal training in merchandising or buying. Their knowledge was gained by first-hand experience on the job, which normally began in more mainstream retail sales. A 1946 Canadian film entitled *Success Story* claimed that "the business of retail selling offers women some of the best opportunities for business careers," though it gave no concrete details on how this was to be achieved. Its message was that one must have dedication and accept responsibility. Though the aim of the film was to encourage women to work, it emphasized that a career in retail was a socially appropriate one for women. This theme was reiterated in a 1950s American film entitled *You Are the Star*, which stated that "success in selling is an opportunity to greater things in life." The clear implication that having more money of one's own could lead to the acquisition of more consumer goods, making a woman more marriageable, reinforces sexist stereotypes of women as both merchants and consumers. This gendered tradition of retail selling was confirmed by a 1951 government report that listed 12 percent of working women in commercial and financial positions as sales clerks.[32]

Formal preparation and training for becoming a couture buyer or saleswoman was non-existent. Ollie Smythe had an eye-opening experience on her first buying trip for the Ensemble Shop in the early 1950s. The trip was to New York, where she received help from Miss Burnett — "a tough cookie, but she knew what she was doing" — who was the dress buyer in the New York Buying Office. Ollie Smythe's previous experience was in sportswear, where she had bought jeans by the dozen to sell at $2.98 each. Her first stop in New York was to the prestigious dress house of Adele Simpson. They were seated to see the line being modelled for them, and Miss Burnett guided her through the sale and wrote all the orders for her. Ollie Smythe was very nervous because the prices were so much higher than in sportswear. A single dress was $119.75, and she had been told that in order to estimate the retail cost, including import taxes and mark-up, she had to triple the wholesale cost. As she said, "I had visions of having to buy dozens," so was much relieved when she realized, with the help of Miss Burnett, that for this high-end merchandise single and small unit quantities were normal.[33]

With quickly learned experience and increased knowledge of her clientele, Ollie Smythe became very comfortable buying couture and high-end fashion. Her selection criteria were based on style, size, and appropriateness for the Toronto season. She explained it as follows: "I had about ten people that I bought for, ten sizes . . . If I could buy for all those different shapes I could fit anybody in Canada."[34] The strength of this statement is borne out by Jeanne Parkin, who was the wife of the Toronto modernist architect John Parkin. She was an Eaton's client and the same size as another client, Mrs E.P. Taylor, whose husband was more financially and socially influential. Mrs Parkin knew that they were often the candidates for the same dress and recalled a certain black Paris cocktail dress "that was so tight you couldn't walk in it." She eventually bought it but not before the dress was shown to Mrs Taylor for first "dibs."[35] Thus, garments were chosen with individuals in mind who were rated in a hierarchy based on their social influence.

Margery Steele, Ollie Smythe's counterpart at Simpson's St Regis Room, had a background in fashion design from Mabel Letchford's school of design. She had worked briefly for a local Toronto designer, Mary Mac, and then had a job selling advertising space for the *Globe and Mail* newspaper. She answered one of the advertisements that she had placed for Simpson's and was hired as a fabric consultant. She eventually became the couture buyer and was placed in charge of the couture sales staff (fig. 3.12).[36] At Creeds, Dorothy Creed, the wife of Jack Creed, was the

buyer during the 1950s.[37] She worked closely with Lexy Burton, who was the top saleswoman.

The department store couture buyer's job was part sales and part promotion, and she was in charge of the couture salon. A leading retailer, possibly Eaton's or Simpson's, placed a newspaper advertisement for a buyer in 1949, and the job description ran: "top fashion buyer . . . she must be . . . thoroughly experienced in selecting and buying women's fashions in the higher priced ranges . . . She should have proven selling abilities in order to direct staff and maintain a high standard of service to a discriminating clientele . . . She will be well paid by a company that enjoys an outstanding reputation. She may be . . . You!"[38] The job of buyer was focused on prestige and etiquette rather than profit. Margery Steele said about the St Regis Room, "For years and years they didn't make money . . . [but] it was good advertising. I would say they were probably in the red more often than not."[39] Similarly, Ollie Smythe said, "Lady Eaton explained it to me as a prestige thing. If I broke even I was a hero." On her first buying trip to Europe she was given no budget and an open requisition to buy.[40]

Typically the owners of small boutiques had a background in retailing, often gained in a large department store. This not only gave them experience in sales but in many cases also prompted customers to follow them to their new premises. Billye Vincent, whose retail fashion career began at a small local store, Miller's, in the 1930s, went on to Simpson's and ended up at the St Regis Room as buyer until she

3.12 Margery Steele, 1998. She was the buyer for Simpson's St Regis Room from the early 1950s until the late 1990s.

opened Billye Vincent in 1948.[41] Other couture boutique owners had similar backgrounds. Jean Pierce had worked for Simpson's in Regina, Saskatchewan, in the receiving department during the Depression. In 1945, she moved to Toronto and set up Pierce-Caldwell, a specialty gift shop selling furnishings and housewares. Soon after, she opened her own clothing business.[42] Joan Rigby had worked at the St Regis Room in 1939 before setting up her own premises on Bloor Street.[43]

Department stores thus provided a training ground in retail for women to pursue careers that could offer advancement. Retail selling also gave women a skill that was transferable locally or to another city. For the few who sold couture, it gave them intimate contact with elite customers, sophisticated associations with Paris and European design, professional and cultural status, and economic independence.

Staff Training

From the end of the nineteenth century, department stores recognized the importance of staff training, and this was particularly true for those working in clothing sales.[44] Eaton's created the Fashion Bureau to promote and co-ordinate the fashion image for the store. In March 1945, Dora Matthews was made fashion co-ordinator (fig. 3.13).[45] She was responsible for all fashion shows and for "keeping the buyers aware of what was going on in all areas of Fashion. Giving talks to the staff, Church Groups, Business Girls and so forth. I went to Montreal, New York and finally to Europe to report." She was in charge of a female staff that was hard to keep: "Top management asked me if I was running a marriage bureau instead of a Fashion bureau. The girls were all pretty."[46] Dora Matthews belonged to the English-Canadian female elite and was a member of the Junior League. She understood etiquette and dress codes. It was she who selected the season's colours, supervised and co-ordinated the fashion shows, wrote the scripts, and was the commentator.[47] She became known as Eaton's "fashion ambassador," so closely was she identified with all of its fashions and events. Her interpretations of each season's styles were highly influential in determining the taste of Eaton's Toronto clients.

One of Mrs Matthews' most significant jobs was laying out the important aspects of the season's fashions for staff training, as sales staff were expected to know all the European trends as well as the store merchandise. Training was accomplished through manuals and demonstrations and, most important, through fashion

shows. Eaton's fall and spring fashion shows were usually preceded by a special showing for all staff, the Eatonians: "There's always an undertone of excitement when the evening rolls around again for the staff showing of the coming season's fashions. Most of those who go to the Monday preview are people who sell clothes, write about clothes or are in some way connected with the fashion departments . . . It's a gala evening . . . First, there's dinner in the Georgian Room or the Round Room, with everybody guests of the Company, and then the show itself."[48] These shows introduced new merchandise, trends, and styles to Eaton employees. Through the shows, staff were educated by the same means as the public on matters of etiquette and taste. Often staff members were given booklets that summed up the fashions, silhouettes, and colours of the season and could be used later for reference.[49]

Eaton's was always considering ideas for teaching its staff the latest fashions and the etiquette of wearing them. In August 1945, the store staged a special staff fashion show to explain postwar changes and the "implications to those who are selling or promoting merchandise." The show was staged as a trial and featured Dora Matthews as counsel for the defence and commentator, while a judge and jury represented "five different types of woman, [who] weighed the evidence and passed judgement on the styles" (fig. 3.14).[50] This "fashion police" format of testing and judging fashions as right or wrong was typical of the period and even persists today.

That same year, the store considered testing employees' taste skills by asking them to select from four models, one of which was dressed correctly in "this season's

3.13 Dora Matthews, 1953. She was the fashion co-ordinator for Eaton's Fashion Bureau.

fashion picture."[51] The idea may have come from a report on a New York trip during which an anonymous Eaton employee saw a group of fashion dolls used by Macy's to demonstrate "right" and "wrong" dressing. The Eaton's reporter commented that this was a successful public education tool, especially pertinent in view of the immediate postwar shortages of merchandise. Interestingly, the use of fashion dolls as a form of transmitting the latest styles goes back to the Renaissance.[52]

For spring 1952, Eaton's experimented. Instead of the usual staff training fashion show it made a training film in its own studio. The film was called *Headlines in Outline* and was directed by Vivien Combe of the Fashion Bureau, supervised by Dora Matthews, and produced by Commercial Photography, a department of Eaton's (fig. 3.15). It was made in three days, using three mannequins, and "the whole story revolves around this season's news in style and colour."[53] The result was shown in Eaton's stores in Toronto, Montreal, Hamilton, Winnipeg, Moncton, and Vancouver. By making the film and distributing it to several branches, Eaton's ensured that a single and unaltered fashion message was promoted across Canada.

3.14 Eaton's fall 1945 "Fashion Goes on Trial" show was held for employees to inform them of the latest postwar fashion trends and what was "right" and "wrong." The show was held in the Georgian Room, a restaurant in Eaton's department store.

Fashion shows were always considered one of the most useful formats for staff training, even into the 1960s. A 1961 spring show for staff training was accompanied by a fashion booklet, *Fashionably Yours*. The booklet reviewed the production as "an educational show designed to illustrate how fashion and selling should be combined for best sales results."[54]

Couture played multiple roles during the 1950s. It was important not only for retailing but also for promoting the stores themselves. It conferred sociocultural status on the wearers and also on the numerous women who bought and sold couture merchandise. The significance of importing couture into North America was clearly tied to several interdependent, status-giving purposes, all of which stemmed from the associated prestige and pre-eminence of couture clothing.

3.15 Still from *Headlines in Outline*, a film produced by Eaton's in its own studio to instruct staff in the Toronto, Montreal, Hamilton, Winnipeg, Moncton, and Vancouver stores on the latest millinery fashions for spring 1952.

4 COUTURE, FASHION SHOWS, AND MARKETING

For the fashion critic, the stürm und drang of the Paris Openings follows on the Openings in Rome, Florence, and London . . . From a matter of some two thousand models . . . [she must] pick out the distinctive dozen of most significance. Alison Adburgham, 1960

Marketing International European Couture

The postwar dominance of European couture as the model for fashion design in North America was fuelled by the fashion press and by retailers. Merchants not only placed advertisements in fashion publications but also gained free advertising when magazines photographed couture models and mentioned where they were available for purchase in North America. American *Vogue*'s Paris correspondent, Bettina Ballard, recognized this mutually beneficial relationship when she wrote, "Social life with the American buyers was an important part of my job. If I could make them feel that *Vogue* took an interest in them away from home, it added to their allegiance to *Vogue* . . . They were always interested to hear the latest Paris gossip and to get tips on any new talent that might be developing."[1] Consequently, the symbiotic relationship between fashion houses, press, and buyers in Europe, and their mutual quest for new designs and new venues, resulted in a consensus of what was fashionable.

As soon as Paris had re-established its prewar position as the leader in style, and was able to command top prices, other European couture centres tried to compete, though it was a struggle to lure press and buyers to cities other than Paris. In 1957, British fashion reporter Alison Settle noted that the Swiss even paid for journalists to come to collections in order to ensure publicity, though others did not.[2] The London couturiers showed their collections before Paris in order to deflect accusations of imitating French designers. But to some extent this tactic backfired, as North American buyers were reluctant to purchase before seeing what Paris presented and on occasion had to return to Britain to place orders once they felt secure about the season's direction as seen in the French collections.[3]

Buyers and press were nonetheless eager to seek out unfamiliar couture sources while on their semi-annual European pilgrimages. For one thing, new markets and cultures made both their trips and their purchases more novel. Bettina Ballard remarked, "I very soon found out, along with the postwar travel-starved buyers and the fashion press, how pleasant it was to travel on an expense account with the legitimate excuse of looking over new fashion markets."[4] Interest in new European fashion centres was also spurred by a decrease in airfares and increase in flights. In 1952, it was estimated that 1,600 Canadians would fly to England for the spring and summer season, and with the introduction of new tourist rates — "flights without frills" — half a million people were expected to fly between North America and Europe. By April, cheap round-trip fares would be available between Paris and other European cities, including Rome and Madrid. In 1954, the invention of the de Havilland Comet turbojet, flown by BOAC, reduced the flying time from London to Rome from four hours and twenty minutes to two hours and forty minutes. All this greatly aided buyers and press in their search for new design and made it possible to cover several countries in Europe within a limited time, increasing the chances of obtaining exclusive models.[5]

Displaying an international diversity of couture demonstrated a retailer's understanding of all European design trends. The importance of presenting an international profile is reflected in an article on Simpson's fall 1951 fashion show entitled "Five Countries Represented in Fashions at Simpson's," and also in a 1958 Creeds fashion show that included designs from seven countries, excluding America and Canada.[6]

Interestingly, though Paris haute couture was the most prestigious, there was an implicit understanding that most French clothes were too extreme for Canadian taste. In 1948, the local Toronto press reported on the new French fashions, recalling how "a couple of seasons ago a new Balenciaga model at a local fashion show brought gales of mirth every time it appeared." By Christmas, however, copies of the same model were best-sellers. The impracticality of French haute couture was headline news in a review of Jacques Fath's fall 1949 collection, which exclaimed, "Fath Skirts Are So Tight, Models Seem on Wheels."[7] Even French models purchased for fashion shows were sometimes modified to appeal to Canadian taste. In 1950,

Dora Matthews reported to Eaton's executives that she had been to the Paris collections at Dior, Griffe, Fath, Balenciaga, Balmain, and Dessès, and wrote, "I hope you will all like the things I have bought, I have set a new pattern, I have cheerfully changed colours and fabrics on almost everything. When a dress turned up in a nice itchy fabric heavy enough for a doormat, we put it in Ottoman [fabric]. It will hang as well and maybe we can sell it."[8]

It was quite a different matter with London couture. British tweeds always sold well and were considered suitable for Canadians due to their conservative design and reputation for quality and durability. This was noted by Miss Weston of Eaton's, who wrote of the Hardy Amies boutique line, "good looking suits — wonderful detail and beautiful material. While these suits are expensive they are requested by our customers."[9] A 1950 article in *Mayfair* clearly identified the position of British couture for Canadians: "From the London designers we do not look for revolutionary silhouettes, fantastic conversation pieces. From them we expect excellent tailoring, fine detail — eminently wearable clothes that are current without being dated."[10]

Canadians also favoured the British notion of fit, which was less restrictive than that of French or Italian designs. The preference was remarked on in 1952 by Alison Settle: "Canada is particularly pleased with London's return to grand but very comfortable evening clothes for wear in the home."[11] Too, British evening wear was widely sold in Canada. Popular were the lavishly embroidered and beaded designs of the Queen's couturier, Norman Hartnell, which were conservative in terms of styling, much less structured than French designs in terms of cut and fit, yet festive in rich use of colour and trimmings (figs. 4.1 and 4.2). Coupled with a good price relative to French designs, these features made them constantly in demand.

Canadian links to Britain, and consequently to British fashion, were perpetuated by the Canadian fashion press. For instance, it focused on the news that a Torontonian, Barbara Stevenson, had married the London couturier Ronald Patterson. In an indirect way, this marriage provided the Canadian fashion press with a lineage within British couture and reinforced Canada's colonial ties, helping to articulate the difference between Canada and the United States. Canadians also embraced Irish design. In 1953, Sybil Connolly was taken up by the international fashion press, as was Irene Gilbert; a year later it was the turn of Irish ready-to-wear designer Elizabeth James. Sybil Connolly visited Eaton's in March 1955, and her clothes

4.1 Black silk velvet ball gown embroidered with diamante pastes and sequins, by British couturier Norman Hartnell, c.1955. The design is loosely based on a formal eighteenth-century court gown, and the restrained but rich trim is classic Hartnell. It was worn by Dorothy Boylen, who shopped at Simpson's St Regis Room and was assisted by Margery Steele.

4.2 An elegant Norman Hartnell taupe crepe evening sheath with pearlescent beading worn by Signy Eaton in the mid-1950s. Mrs Eaton was on the *Toronto Telegram* Hall of Fame list for best-dressed women.

4.3 Sybil Connolly Irish tweed suit, c.1952, worn by Dora Matthews. The skirt has been patched (fig. 0.2, p. 4.). The label promotes the fact that the suit is made from handwoven Donegal tweed.

4.4 Sybil Connolly 1957 navy pleated Irish handkerchief linen princess-line cocktail dress, sold through Eaton's. Her trademark pleated designs required nine yards to produce one yard of the finished pleated cloth, thereby ensuring the production and use of a traditional Irish textile.

were featured in its spring fashion show, which was aired on television. It was Sybil Connolly's ability to capture a quintessentially Irish design, using local fabrics of internationally recognized quality, that made her clothes appeal to Anglo-Canadians, many of whom had Irish ancestral ties. Her sales in Toronto included her trade-mark day suits of handwoven Irish tweed and her cocktail and evening dresses of pleated Irish linen (figs. 4.3 and 4.4).[12]

In contrast to the ongoing relationship between Britain and Canada, Italian fashion burst on the scene after the first collective showing of fashion houses in Florence in February 1951.[13] By that fall, Italian fashions were featured in *Mayfair* magazine and included a photograph of Mrs Reva Nathanson, "one of Canada's best-dressed women," in a Fabiani evening dress.[14] By fall 1952, twenty Italian models were available at Holt Renfrew, which had secured an exclusive Canadian licence to sell Simonetta Visconti and Fabiani designs (fig. 4.5).[15] Canadians valued the detailed workmanship of Italian designs that were available below French prices. Rich detail was considered very European, and was emphasized in the press: "The grand occasion gown with intricate hand-work and surface detail is a specialty of the Roman dressmakers."[16]

In Toronto, Italian designers had a personal advocate in reporter and socialite Rosemary Boxer. She was firmly associated with fashion and beauty, as she was the fashion show commentator for Simpson's, wrote for *Chatelaine* women's maga-zine, hosted a television spot about fashion, and in 1955 opened a beauty school in Toronto. She featured Italian designs several times in her CBC television program and called Rome "now one of the most important fashion centres in the world" (figs. 4.6 and 4.7).[17]

Italian design was promoted as feminine and flattering, and not as faddish as French. In 1955, Rosemary Boxer applauded Italian design that ignored "Dior's shapeless look, [as] the Italian girls demand figure flattering dresses." Such advo-cacy did much to dispel disparaging comments such as those of Pierre Balmain in 1957: "[Italians'] ambition is to design dinner and cocktail clothes, but their ability is to design sports clothes."[18] Rosemary Boxer's championing of Italian designers extended to inviting and arranging for tailor Sergio Mingolini and designer Carlos Guggenheim, of the Roman house Mingolini Guggenheim, to bring a collection to Toronto as a fundraiser. After the show, some of the models were sold privately.[19]

Swiss design also held a strong position in Toronto's roster of imported couture.[20] Switzerland had a reputation for *haute nouveauté*, highly decorative and beaded laces. One Eaton's buyer, in 1953, called Zurich the "city that has become most important, next to London," and at that time purchased coats and suits from Schibili and Solona made of "fine material and beautiful colours."[21] Marty of Switzerland was a dominant Swiss name in Toronto and was associated with top-quality cocktail and evening wear, "an excellent line." Socialite Betty Cassels was photographed in her pink silk chiffon dress for the *Toronto Telegram* as one of the best-dressed women of 1960 (fig. 4.8). She wore another Marty of Switzerland design, a strapless mauve silk peau de soie ball gown, to the National Ballet Guild Ball de Ballet, attended by over a thousand guests and held at the Royal York Hotel with "Duke Ellington's orchestra, champagne, dinner by candlelight, and tickets at $30."[22] In 1958, a local fashion reporter commented in a Creeds fashion show review that "some of the most beautiful evening dresses were from Marty of Switzerland." The popularity of the house stemmed from its conventional designs, good-quality fabric and trim,

4.5 Holt Renfrew advertisement, September 1952, announcing the exclusive right to sell designs by Roman couturiers Simonetta Visconti and Fabiani.

4.6 Apricot silk organza pleated Italian cocktail dress purchased from Creeds, c.1956. The label reads, "Made in Italy Exclusively for Creeds." The intricacy of such Italian designs, which could be purchased more inexpensively than Parisian ones, partially accounted for interest in Italian couture.

4.7 Cocktail ensemble of coffee-coloured silk piped with wine velvet and stencilled in scrolling foliate forms trimmed with beads and sequins, made in Italy by Casa da Silva, 1955. A similar Casa da Silva ensemble was described in Eaton's spring 1955 fashion show program at $195.

4.8 Betty Cassels' pink silk chiffon dress and silk brocade coat Marty of Switzerland ensemble, c. 1960, purchased at Eaton's Ensemble Shop and worn to cocktails, dinners, and the theatre. The high-quality textiles and detailed draping, and couture details such as the coat lining matching the pink chiffon of the dress, made such Swiss designs desirable. See fig. 7.13, p. 264.

Gossip!

TORONTO, ONT.   APRIL 16, 1960

Gossip Limited — Subscription $1
Editor—Mona Clark
Editorial Staff: Mary E. Brown, Ruth Spence, Gwenyth Barrington
341 Church Street, Toronto, EM. 4-8416—Saturdays only, EM. 4-8419
3333 Cavendish Blvd., Montreal
Established 1925 by W. B. Ferguson

Authorized as Second Class Mail, Post Office Dept., Ottawa

Mrs.
Patrick Cassels

President,
Toronto Branch,
National Ballet Guild,
and one of this year's
ten best-dressed
women (Telegram)

Portrait by
Gerald Campbell
Master Photographer
Ashley and Crippen

and the reasonable cost (figs. 4.9 and 4.10). Miss Weston, the Eaton's buyer, purchased other Swiss designs as well, commenting on Lesinger's "very inexpensive, attractive cotton dresses"; and coats, suits, and dresses by Bries, which she noted was "mainly a model house but this year made up a less expensive collection. We are most enthusiastic."[23]

Spanish fashion also held a position in the search for affordable and exclusive European couture. Though less advertised and less popular than Italian fashion, it was available sporadically throughout the 1950s. The Spanish origins of Paris couturier Balenciaga helped to pique interest in the country. Spanish designs were introduced to Torontonians in Eaton's fall 1952 fashion show, which began with "curtains parted on Spain" and showed five designs that had "reached Toronto (by air) only an hour and a half before the first showing."[24] Designers Pertegaz and Rodriguez were the best known (fig. 4.11). Describing the Spanish shows, Canadian fashion journalist Iona Monahan noted that these two leading designers "offer a multitude of new and unusual ideas at prices which are a fraction of those in London, Paris or Rome."[25] Her statement reiterates both the hierarchy and prestige of European couture clothing and consumers' interest in value

4.9 Betty Cassels in "her favourite dress, a draped full-length evening gown of white silk jersey by Marty of Switzerland" on the cover of the local magazine *Gossip!* 16 April 1960.
4.10 (opposite) Eaton's advertisement for a silk satin "theatre costume," by Marty of Switzerland, September 1952, sold in the Vancouver couture salon, the French Room. The ensemble matched a three-quarter-length dress with an evening coat. Similar designs were available at Eaton's couture salons in Toronto, Montreal, Winnipeg, and Victoria.

EATON'S *French Room* VANCOUVER

... devoted to lovely fashions and personalized service.

FROM FRANCE
Madeleine Casalino, Jacqueline Monnim, Georges Boutet, Webe

FROM ENGLAND
Matita, Hardie Amies, Frederic Starke, Stolas, Jacqmar, Marens

FROM ITALY
New-comer Mirsa

FROM SWITZERLAND
Marty, Arthur Schibli and many, many others.

As shown, the glisten and rustle of pure silk satin, deftly designed by Marty of Switzerland. A theatre costume of strapless gown and voluminous cloak in dove grey and seafoam pink. Size 14.

EATON'S FRENCH ROOM
SECOND FLOOR

T. EATON C° LIMITED
BRITISH COLUMBIA
VANCOUVER   CANADA

for haute couture products that were not necessarily French.

Other European couture garments, such as those from Holland, were identified in fashion shows and advertisements solely by country of origin, leaving the individual designers unnamed, and were sold by all the leading couture retailers. The significant aspect of these clothes was that they were European, so had a higher cultural value than most North American designs. That the designers were less well known, or anonymous, was in their favour, for it was assumed that the garments would be well priced and that they would not be duplicated in Toronto.[26]

European couture design was thus promoted by country of origin through the fashion press and by the local retailer. The hierarchy of design was governed by the stature of the country as a cultural centre and by Canadian understanding of that country's taste. Paris designs were dominant in terms of status and price, even if French haute couture was not always the preferred choice for design and function within a Torontonian wardrobe. All this was clearly reflected in prices, which will be discussed later. There was a consensus that all European design was culturally superior to North American and carried with it authority in taste and style.

4.11 Elaborate evening dress based on flamenco costume, designed by Spaniard Pedro Rodriguez, spring 1953, available at Eaton's and bought by Signy Eaton (fig. 7.21, pp. 274–5).

Holt Renfrew and Christian Dior

Competition for exclusive imported merchandise was very stiff among all Toronto merchants, and amplified among the larger stores. Holt Renfrew was the most aggressive Canadian retailer in the 1950s in staking out its authority and control over the European couture system.

In 1951, Holt's secured the exclusive Canadian rights to sell Christian Dior's Paris and New York lines, as well as the right to make reproductions (figs. 4.12 and 4.13).[27] It later negotiated the rights to millinery, hosiery, perfume, furs, jewellery, gloves, handbags, neckties, and the Dior-London collection. Dior had only transacted one other deal like this, the previous year in Mexico.[28] The agreement was

4.12 (left) Holt Renfrew advertisement, May 1952, promoting its exclusive Canadian licensing arrangement to sell Christian Dior clothing and accessories. **4.13** (right) Advertisement for a Christian Dior ensemble available only at Holt Renfrew in Canada, April 1953. The dress was promoted as suitable "from noon on," as the jacket transformed the cocktail dress into a luncheon and tea ensemble.

made by Alvin J. Walker, president of Holt Renfrew, and Jacques Rouët, who was head of the administrative side of Dior. M. Rouët had been with Dior from its beginnings and was described by Dior in his autobiography: "He had no previous experience in the fashion world, but I liked him, and felt complete confidence in him from the start. His role was to provide my castles in the air with solid foundations.[29]

M. Rouët said that Mr Walker had approached Dior and that they had had a discussion over dinner about Holt's obtaining the exclusive rights to Dior for Canada (figs. 4.14 and 4.15). This meant that Dior could no longer conduct business with any other Canadian retailers, such as Eaton's, Simpson's, Morgan's, or small boutiques. The parties signed a contract in December 1951 and Holt's purchased the exclusive Canadian rights. In return, it had to guarantee Dior annual minimum sales.[30]

Mme Ginette Steinman, who was already with the Paris house, went to Montreal to be in charge of the Holt Renfrew workroom. Holt's bought original models and was allowed to make custom-fitted exact copies in its Montreal workrooms, as well as to import from the Paris and New York collections and to make line-for-line copies. The Montreal workroom employed between ten and fifteen seamstresses. Mme Steinman, Alvin Walker, and Leonard Shavick, his son-in-law, chose the clothes. They would usually order approximately fifteen models as designed and would make changes in styling or details to a further twenty. All the *toiles*, *patrons à papier*, and sample models were made in Paris and shipped to Montreal, where they were reproduced. Toronto never had a workroom for reproductions.[31] The advantage of this deal for Canadians was that it was possible to have French-designed

4.14 (opposite) Spring 1955 Christian Dior dinner and cocktail dress with two bodices. The design, "Audacieuse," was ordered and sold by Holt Renfrew in Canada exactly as designed. This ensemble was purchased by Mrs Saul Silverman. The label reads, "Christian Dior Original in Canada Exclusive with Holt Renfrew & Co. Limited." 4.15 Christian Dior/Holt Renfrew label demonstrating the exclusive Canadian licence.

couture made locally, for less than in Paris. If a client had gone to Paris to have the same dress made, it would have cost up to 70 percent more with import duty, not to mention the cost of travel.

Leonard Shavick, who later took over the position of company president from Alvin Walker, commented on why Holt Renfrew had pursued the deal. He explained that Holt's had started to import couture after the war but had quickly realized that it was rapidly becoming very difficult to have anything that was different from its competitors. Having an exclusive agreement singled it out in the local market, allowed the store to have the licence to all the other Dior products, on which there was a profit, and linked the name of Holt Renfrew to the most famous fashion designer in the world at the time. The importance of the deal is clearly reflected in the fact that Alvin Walker received a Légion d'Honneur from the French government in 1963 (fig. 4.16).[32]

Holt Renfrew capitalized on its advantage over its competitors and also signed an exclusive agreement with the Italian houses of Simonetta Visconti and Fabiani in 1952, as we have seen.[33] It gained the exclusive Canadian rights for all the models of these Italian houses and the right to make reproductions and adaptations. Holt's also had exclusives in 1953 on certain Balenciaga models, from which it was entitled to make copies, but this was short lived because the copies were too difficult to make.[34] Nonetheless, these business transactions made Holt's the biggest Canadian buyer at Balenciaga, adding to its standing within the Canadian and international fashion scene.[35]

4.16 Alvin J. Walker, president of Holt Renfrew, receiving the Légion d'Honneur from the French ambassador in Ottawa, 18 December 1963, in recognition of his support of Christian Dior in Canada.

H.R. Jubilantly Acclaims the
New Era of Christian Dior!

On January 30th, practically within minutes after the presentation in Paris of the Dior Spring Collection, the news was flashed around the world that a New Era was ushered in for the House of Dior.

First to be received in Canada was H.R.'s own cable report from which we quote:

"Christian Dior's "Ligne Trapeze" was received with a terrific ovation and enthusiasm by the biggest press attendance on record stop The collection designed by young Yves Saint Laurent, Mr. Dior's favourite disciple. in collaboration with Mesdames Raymonde Zehnacker and Marguerite Carre always closely associated in the creation of Mr. Dior's collections, reflected Mr. Dior's influence in all the categories."

John B. Fairchild of the Fairchild News Service wired to "Women's Wear Daily" . .

"Thanks to 21-year-old Yves Saint Laurent, who in the eyes of the fashion world is a genius, the Maison Dior still wears the Paris fashion crown."

Eugenie Sheppard, Women's Feature Editor, in the Paris and U.S. Editions of The New York Herald Tribune . . "I Never Saw a Better Dior Collection"

Throughout the length and breadth of Canada
All Christian Dior Models are Exclusive with

HOLT RENFREW

Holt Renfrew's aggressive pursuit and successful capture of the leading names in couture at the time suggests very skilful business negotiations. Its liaison with the top fashion houses furthered its position with the international fashion magazines, extending the name of the store well beyond the Canadian magazine *Mayfair*. Purchases of European couture ensured that the Holt Renfrew name appeared regularly in the New York based *Harper's Bazaar* and American *Vogue*, which always identified dresses by local source. Teresa Richey, fashion editor for British *Vogue* during the 1950s, said that shops were more inclined to buy a model if they knew that the magazine had photographed it.[36] Holt's exclusive Dior licence guaranteed magazine coverage, and its stock was listed with that of such respected American fashion taste makers and retailers as I. Magnin and Bergdorf Goodman.

When Christian Dior died unexpectedly in October 1957, the stature of the house of Dior was thrown into question. Holt's took swift action to counteract any doubt in customers' minds about the future stability of the house by placing a special advertisement in the March 1958 issue of *Mayfair* that quoted John B. Fairchild of Fairchild News Service and Eugenia Sheppard of the *New York Herald Tribune* (fig. 4.17). These fashion authorities testified to the success of Yves Saint Laurent's first collection after Dior's death, calling Saint Laurent "a genius." The text

4.17 Holt Renfrew advertisement, March 1958, announcing the success of the first collection designed by Yves Saint Laurent after the death of Christian Dior. The announcement was intended to reassure customers of the continuing strength of the Dior tradition and reputation.

ran: "Mr. Dior's favourite disciple, in collaboration with Mesdames Raymonde Zehnacker and Marguerite Carre always closely associated in the creation of Mr. Dior's collections, reflected Mr. Dior's influence in all the categories." The appointment of a young, unknown designer to take over from Dior was unsettling news, not only for the house and its steady clients but for the fashion world in general. By placing this notice, Holt's aimed to safeguard the value of its licence by reassuring its clientele that the same sort of designs and standards were still to be expected. This assurance was protected by the continued design involvement of two women who had a long history in the house of Dior, and who were similar in age to the clientele and therefore understood their needs. The copy proposed, in hidden terms, that they would understand and carry on the Dior tradition, and, if required, temper the style of the new, youthful male designer. Such strategies were most successful. In 1958, Christian Dior realized over half of the total export figures of the French haute couture industry.[37]

The activity of Holt Renfrew spurred other local retailers to capture a piece of the couture market for their stores. In 1957, Eaton's signed an exclusive with Balmain and carried the largest selection of Paris boutique clothes the store had ever purchased. In 1960, it brought Pierre Balmain to Toronto as part of a store-wide French promotion and to promote his new Florilège collection. This collection, shown every day at 11 a.m., comprised sixty models, including coats, dresses, and suits made up in classic textiles that were less lavish, and less expensive, than those in the haute couture collection.[38] To maintain prestige, Balmain also brought part of his haute couture collection with him, and four mannequins to model it (fig. 4.18).[39] But by this time Eaton's no longer bought original models in any quantity, as its couture buyer Ollie Smythe explained: "We bought three because he brought his haute couture collection, but if anybody wanted them they could order them. But they nearly dropped dead when they found out the white coat, without the beaver trim, was $2,500."[40]

Holt Renfrew and its licensing agreements with European couturiers act as a case study of couture marketing in the 1950s. It exemplifies the problems facing couturiers and couture retailers at the time, as all merchants vied for exclusive couture merchandise that would be seen and sold in a small marketplace. Though the exclusive retailers and large department stores continued to buy couture, its importance

lessened as the decade progressed. By the late 1950s, all the shops were buying and selling more boutique, *prêt-à-porter*, as well as copies and adaptations of couture models.

Fashion Shows

As has already been suggested, a key function of imported couture in North America was for marketing and publicity campaigns, usually involving large, elaborate, public fashion shows. Fashion shows promoted a store's merchandise and clearly demonstrated its style leadership and knowledge of the latest international design trends. Shows were also important within the local community as a vehicle to support local charity groups, usually run by socially influential, couture-wearing volunteers whose patronage the stores valued.

4.18 Pierre Balmain in Toronto with Dora Matthews and his mannequins, 1960. The four mannequins accompanied him to show his Florilège collection at Eaton's "Festival de France" promotion.

American and Canadian retailers were acutely aware of the promotional importance of fashion shows, though historians discussing the origins and traditions of
store merchandising have only begun to investigate this fascinating cultural aspect.[41]
The late-nineteenth-century development of the department store as an exhibition
space and emporium was clearly perpetuated in the postwar period by large, biannual
fashion shows featuring "Paris Originals" and other European imports. Fashion
shows were an essentially gendered construction for women, featuring women, and
usually produced by women, in the feminine space of the shop. The European
format of a couture design, worn by a live mannequin considered an ideal beauty,
placed in a fantasy setting, intended for a female audience, was one of the most
traditional, important, and regular promotional events used by stores. Customers
understood the couture-crafted garments as symbols of new design trends, which
would then be interpreted and redesigned for local consumption. Showing couture
was therefore a non-profit enterprise considered essential to the promotion of the
department store as an up-to-date centre for all products.

The fashion shows put on by Eaton's and Simpson's ran an average of one
and a half hours and were theatrical events with European couture providing the
climax. Eaton's College Street store was spectacularly designed for such occasions.
The seventh floor housed the elegant Round Room, a restaurant-lounge area where
small fashion shows were held, often in conjunction with a women's group committee meeting. Here, too, was Toronto's largest concert and theatrical space, the
Eaton Auditorium, best known now as the auditorium favoured by Glenn Gould
for recording. Cynthia Wright discusses the importance of this "non-selling area"
and its status as one of Eaton's most celebrated attractions.[42]

The significance of Eaton's fashion shows is articulated by the sheer numbers
of them and their large attendance. The semi-annual shows were held twice a day for
five days, one during the day and another at 6 p.m. aimed at attracting "business
girls." The average attendance per show was 800 to 1,000, resulting in an attendance
of approximately 8,000 to 10,000 people during the fashion show week.[43] Imported
couture was the centrepiece, and Eaton's alternated the first showing of the "Originals" — the Paris couture models — between its Toronto and Montreal stores. The
clothes were then shipped across the country to Winnipeg, Hamilton, and Vancouver.[44]
In order to dissipate the expense, the cost of the original models was split among

the stores and each received some of the dresses after the shows. These were either sold at reduced prices to special customers who had asked for them or were put on sale in the couture salon.[45] Thus, the transcontinental fashion shows featuring imported couture as the highlight were seen by thousands of Canadian women, and the influence of couture went far beyond those who actually wore it.

Eaton's and Simpson's vied for publicity and exclusivity of couture designs for their fashion shows, as they did for the mannequins who would wear the clothes. The mannequins themselves were either Eaton's or Simpson's "girls," and followed an unwritten code of not working for the competition. This allegiance was established at the outset of their careers. Norma Wildgoose was from Swansea, Wales, and moved to Winnipeg in 1945, where she worked as a math and science teacher. A friend suggested she might make a good model as she was tall and attractive. She was taken up by Eaton's in Winnipeg and trained at its expense by Pearl Robertson, an ex-Eaton model. Mrs Robertson's husband owned the local movie theatre, and they used the foyer with its tall mirrors for the training classes. Norma Wildgoose was taught how to show the clothes and pose front and back for each garment. When she moved to Toronto she continued to be hired by Eaton's.[46]

The fashion shows were full-blown staged events divided into scenes that were organized by clothing types such as sportswear, day, bridal, and late day into evening, or by themes such as "the new silhouette," "colour," or "millinery."[47] The scenes all reflected the different social uses of the clothes and thus also provided etiquette pointers. The show was accompanied by a live orchestra and included an onstage commentator. The commentator acted as an interpreter for the clothes and scenes, guiding the audience through the nuances of the new fashions. The complexity of the fashion shows directly reflected the significance placed on them by the department stores and the strength of public interest. The fall 1955 fashion show had six scenes, with a finale entitled "The Designers Predict," featuring nineteen British, Irish, and French couture cocktail and evening fashions, in a setting decorated with classical columns, chandeliers, and large floral arrangements emulating a formal ballroom (fig. 4.19).[48] The spring 1953 Eaton's fashion show celebrated coronation year with a set built to emulate the gates of Buckingham Palace, complete with men dressed as palace guards (fig. 4.20). The show also featured an interlude of a colour film showing millinery. The format was so well received that Eaton's made films for

later fashion shows, as the large screen image magnified details that would otherwise be lost for the audience.[49]

Eaton's had its own film studio and used film as a marketing tool to reinforce its underlying fashion show message of up-to-date knowledge of the latest design trends. For the fall 1950 fashion show, a film was made under the guidance of Dora Matthews and featured her as the representative of Eaton's, meeting with British and French designers in Europe. The final version included Mrs Matthews entering and leaving the London design houses of Peter Russell, Norman Hartnell, and Hardy Amies. She was then shown in Paris on Pierre Balmain's houseboat, with a mannequin in a Balmain dress standing in a rowboat, and at Jacques Fath's country château, watching him drape a mannequin beside his pool. The final scene showed her in the Dior haute couture salon with some dresses being modelled for her.[50] The filming of the Paris section alone cost $635.31, but "went over with a bang." It served as a true testament to Eaton's rapport and intimate relations with the leading European couturiers, and was firm evidence of its connoisseurship in fashion.[51] This technique of promotion was continued for the fall 1952 show, when "two designers spoke personally" to the audience on audiotape that had been recorded during Dora Matthews' visits to the Fath and Dessès salons.[52]

4.19 Eaton's fall 1955 fashion presentation set the scene in an abstract, classically inspired European setting, complete with crystal chandeliers, an elegance that was considered appropriate for the formal, imported couture evening dresses. **4.20** (opposite) Eaton's spring fashion presentation for 1953, coronation year. The scene set imported couture evening gowns in front of the gates of Buckingham Palace, and the show came complete with palace guards in busbies.

But fashion shows were not always such highly elaborate events. Eaton's Ensemble Shop held private fashion shows. An example of this was 18 March 1947, when 700 invitations were sent out and 455 invited guests attended over two days. Eaton's tempered its evaluation of the success of this show with concern over the mannequins. It was thought that "as there were many older women in the audience, one mannequin of mature figure might have been presented." This was in sharp contrast to the following show in fall 1947, which featured American Powers models, including two matrons, size 18.[53] The use of matrons was considered an asset and reinforced the reality of the couture customer, who was typically an older woman. This image of the fashionable woman began to give way to a more youthful and thinner model as the 1950s progressed.

Department store fashion shows accomplished more than a high-fashion profile for the store and entertainment for the customer. Women's groups were constantly requesting small and large shows as fundraisers, and this gave stores the opportunity to acknowledge the patronage of their clients indirectly. Many couture customers were on the organizing committees that planned and attended these functions, or if not directly involved, would attend the event as a show of support, as discussed earlier.

At Eaton's, innumerable requests from women's groups are recorded in the minutes of meetings held by the Merchandise Display and Sales Promotion Office. For the fall 1948 show approximately forty requests were received from clubs and organizations for tickets for the evening performances.[54] Eaton's gave away blocks of seats, which the groups then sold. Immediately after the war, Eaton's tried to support as many groups as possible by allotting small numbers of tickets to numerous women's groups. The store administration had discussed that fifty tickets did not appear to be a big enough gesture on the part of the company for many groups, and considered rotating support to accommodate fewer groups but with larger numbers of seats per group. The worry with this was that the larger the blocks of gratis tickets, the less control the store had in ensuring a full house for the shows.[55] Earlier it had been decided to give away fewer seats than requested "so as not to create an illusion of plenty but rather to maintain a high degree of consumer interest, and thus ensure capacity audiences."[56] Thus, the store walked a delicate line between appearing supportive and generous to community groups and the inherent risk that the groups would not sell their allocated tickets, resulting in empty seats and the appearance that the shows were unpopular.

These requests were always politically charged. In 1945, it was decided to co-operate with a request from the Council of Jewish Women for a fashion show, "as the show would be well attended by 400 of the better class of Jewish women . . . Also, as this is a representative Council of all Jewish groups we could gracefully refuse any further requests."[57] By 1948, store management also discussed support for the "larger more important groups requesting an opportunity to sponsor a complete house — such as the Art Gallery Group, Symphony, Fraternities etc."[58] Special consideration would be given in these cases as long as the sponsored shows did not fall in the same season. The Opera and Concert Committee of the Royal College of Music asked to sponsor one of the spring 1948 shows. Eaton's charitably gave away the opening show in aid of the committee's wardrobe fund. The committee proposed to sell 1,200 tickets for a dollar each, whereas Eaton's normally charged fifty cents for afternoon shows and seventy-five cents for evening performances.[59]

Not only were stores solicited for seats for their already scheduled shows, but requests also came in for shows to be put on outside the store. Generally, Eaton's policy was to turn them down.[60] It did put on a few external shows, however, such as one for the Senior Board of Trade at its 15 March 1949 banquet at the King Edward Hotel. Store management accepted the request because "this is one of the more important groups." The rationale for supporting this group and refusing others was that the show was to be held one week after the large show, so some of the fashions could be repeated.[61] The Board of Trade show was followed three days later by a slightly expanded version for B'nai B'rith, also held in the Crystal Ballroom of the King Edward Hotel, and attended by 450 women.[62] These two shows cost Eaton's $1,068.60, approximately the retail cost of two or three Paris haute couture models. If even a handful of women were spurred by the shows to buy a model at Eaton's, the cost would have been recouped and the store's status as a leading arbiter of taste maintained.

One of the social and cultural highlights of the period was a fashion show held in October 1955, when Christian Dior visited Toronto for a special "black tie" Dior fashion show in the new Holt Renfrew store on Bloor Street. Leading socialites organized the event as a fundraiser for the Art Gallery of Toronto. The show attracted a lot

—Metropolitan Photo.

Mrs. J. Thomas Wilson, member of the Women's Committee of the Art Gallery, is one of the commentators for the fashion show being held on Thursday at Holt Renfrew for the benefit of the committee's purchase fund. She looks over the Christian Dior ball gown in petal pink handmade lace which will be in the show at which M. Dior will be present.

Pauline Redsell, sculptor, above, will have examples of her work in the Women's Committee sale, and will also demonstrate some of the technique of her art at the Wednesday open night during Gallery Week.

Paraskeva Clark, artist of many years' standing, and her son Clive, right, both showing their works in the annual Women's Committee sale, use the same room as studio. Clive, a third year architectural student at the University of Toronto, is working on a plastic stabile.

Art Gallery Week
By PEARL McCARTHY

No members of the women's committee at the Art Gallery of Toronto are attempting to pull a long face or put on what Bernard Shaw called an in-church expression as Toronto's Art Gallery Week approaches. The very point of this official Art Gallery Week, opening Friday the 21st, is to indicate the enlightened happiness that all citizens may have by participating in the activities, learnedly grave or gay, of their gallery. And the scheduled events do run a fair range of the more serious and the more light.

On the serious side, there is the welcome fact that the week includes first presentation here of the retrospective exhibition of David Milne's pictures. Here was a Canadian artist who, although never popular in the usual sense, had a rare and imaginative talent of which his countrymen may be proud.

On the gay side, there is the Dior fashion show to be held at Holt Renfrew's next Thursday, and a nice point is scored there. This is the one money-raising activity of the week but, instead of lending their names and asking the public to produce the money, the gallery members are doing the ticket-buying themselves, in the main.

When it comes to real bargains in art, then the public gets an even break with members and committee members. When the women's committee sale goes on its week of preview Friday, the 21st, prior to sales starting on the 28th, anybody may drop in the ballot box his offer to buy the picture at the listed price. This is done because it seems more fair to all, since there are always several who want the same art works. After a preview this week, we can say that it is not only the best collection yet but that, in some cases, the artists are even better represented than in shows of larger pictures. Since the price top is $200, this is the modest collector's one big chance. Paintings, drawings and sculpture are included.

John Steegman, director of the Montreal gallery, comes up on the Monday night for a lecture on Reynolds and his period. The weekend also includes the free Sunday concert by Jack Groob, violinist.

On the Monday and Tuesday there are innovations. The gallery's annual meeting will not have closed doors. If anybody takes it into his head to go and see how things are run, he will get in. On the Tuesday, the women's committee are recognizing by a luncheon the women artists who have work at the sale. On the Wednesday night, Pauline Redsell demonstrates sculpture. You end up the week by the excitement of the opening of the actual sale.

Mrs. George C. Hendrie is chairman of the picture sale. Mrs. Egmont Frankel, assisted by Mrs. Graham Morrow and Mrs. Wm. L. Lovering, chairs the fashion show committee. Mrs. Alan Skaith and Mrs. D. L. McCarthy head the gift shop work.

Painting by William Winter is displayed in showcase at the Royal York. Admiring it are Mr. and Mrs. R. G. Anspach.

Miss Jocelyn Hare of the Art Gallery staff holds an example of locally made pottery found among the Gallery Gifts.

Black Chiffon *de New York*
Mystère de New York
modeled by Vera

of media attention for the store and for its clients. In September and October, newspaper photographs depicted members of the gallery women's committee planning the fashion show, generating free publicity for the store and the women's group (fig. 4.21). Committee members were also photographed entertaining Christian Dior at the Forest Hill home of Mrs T.P. Lownsbrough, the president, along with executive members of the women's committees of the Toronto Symphony, the Toronto branch of the National Ballet Guild, and the Opera Festival. The event was broadcast on national television, 1,400 tickets were sold, and a profit of $3,732 was made for the gallery purchase fund (fig. 4.22).[63]

Requests from women's groups for fashion shows went out to high-end retailers, who all sponsored shows throughout the postwar period. Boutiques were also asked, and Jean Pierce purchased clothes knowing that she probably would not sell them but that they would be used for shows. These forward-looking designs were intended to display her knowledge of current styles.[64]

When a new high-end retailer, Morgan's, opened on Bloor Street in Toronto, women's groups quickly seized on it as a potential new sponsor for their fundraising

4.21 (opposite) Committee members plan for their guest, Christian Dior, and a fashion show of his designs. During Art Gallery Week, 1955, ten years after the formation of the Art Gallery of Toronto Women's Committee, members organized the fundraising fashion show at the new Holt Renfrew store with a guest appearance by M. Dior, "but instead of lending their names and asking the public to produce the money, the gallery members are doing the ticket buying themselves in the main." **4.22** Christian Dior fashion show program cover, 27 October 1955.

work. In September 1951, one of Morgan's first such activities was giving over its premises to the Wimodausis Club, whose members acted as hostesses in the store (fig. 4.23).[65] Morgan's was a Montreal-based specialty shop and sponsoring such an established Toronto women's group was probably done partly in hope of attracting the patronage of this wealthy clientele. Morgan's first fashion presentation in Toronto was sponsored by the Women's Auxiliary of Western Hospital and featured "top designers in London, Paris, Italy with a few from Sweden and from French-designed New York collections."[66] This began a tradition between the store and the Auxiliary that continued throughout the 1950s. One of the highlights of this liaison was Morgan's success in having Norman Hartnell appear in person with his Commonwealth collection for its fall 1958 show at the suburban Lawrence Plaza store (fig. 4.24). The event was publicized in the newspapers and featured on television.[67]

Yet the expense and extravagance of all these fashion shows did generate an ongoing debate about their merit. The spring 1947 Eaton's production costs were $4,160, and the fall 1947 show ran over budget by $1,100. The two-day Ensemble Shop show in 1947 was considered extravagant as it cost $1,470.30.[68] One way to cut expenses was to limit the number of imported models in the show, and there was

4.23 Wimodausis Club members acting as hostesses at Morgan's new store. Their presence indicated how important it was for local retailers to support the charitable organizations of their clientele. Seen from left to right are Mrs Robert E. Grass, chairman of the committee in charge, and Mrs G.B. Heintzman, vice chairman, showing a sheared raccoon coat from Morgan's collection to a customer.

Head-turning highlights
of the
Commonwealth Collection
by
Norman Hartnell...

proving the importance of surface interest in
fabric, touched with the magic of soft,
luxurious fur.

These models, exclusive to Morgan's in Montreal

THE SUIT, in fine wool broadcloth with the
relaxed line, featuring a long open collar of dark
ranch mink. Black or brown,
sizes 10 to 16. 150.

THE COAT, Looped mohair tweed with huge cuffs
of black fox. Royal black, Brown black,
black white. Sizes 8 to 14. 175.

a gradual reduction of originals through the 1950s. Eaton's purchased forty Paris models for its spring 1948 fashion show, and by fall 1952, only twenty. After the show, the Montreal and Toronto stores each received eight models and the Winnipeg store received four to promote and sell.[69] By 1952, Eaton's smaller stores in Moncton, Hamilton, and Vancouver had discontinued the large semi-annual shows.[70] In 1960, Dora Matthews bemoaned the fact that "great, big Eaton's" had only six or eight originals in its shows, while Holt's and Morgan's had entire shows made up of originals. She did not see the situation reverting, however, as "*prêt à porter* is working out so well for us."[71]

Couture was so important for a time that even the disposal of fashion show merchandise was used as a promotional opportunity by the stores. In 1953, an article in *Maclean's* magazine recognized the financial implications of the garments when it noted that "an original gown from the exclusive salons of London, Paris, Rome or New York, is now worn so many times by models at fashion shows in the stores, and before women's clubs and organizations, that when the time comes to dispose of it, Morgan's sells it off for hundreds of dollars less than it cost. Sometimes it is never sold."[72] Eaton's did not advertise its fashion show merchandise but never had

4.24 Morgan's advertisement for Norman Hartnell's Commonwealth collection, September 1958. Hartnell made a personal appearance at the store to promote his collection, and Morgan's gave the event sponsorship to the Women's Auxiliary of Western Hospital, thus supporting a local charity organized by socialites who were potential clients.

a problem disposing of it. Simpson's, by contrast, would price an evening gown at $1,200 and advertise a reduction to $395. Its practice of placing "very high markings" on its fashion show merchandise and then marking it down at "extravagant reductions" did not escape Eaton's notice. Other stores, such as Creeds, advertised dispersal sales of fashion show merchandise as well.[73] These advertisements announced the shows to the community at large and functioned to promote store sponsorship of events even after they were over. Also, by listing the loss that they were taking on merchandise, the stores reinforced their image as community supporters and entertainers, again raising their cultural profile.

A retailer could stake out a national and international position through its association with haute couture. Fashion shows that featured couture were as influential as cultural marketing tools as they were as commercial devices. They promoted the store's image locally and nationally as an arbiter of taste and purveyor of quality goods. The shows were also used as an opportunity to educate staff. For a newcomer such as Morgan's trying to break into the Toronto market, staging a couture fashion show was a desirable and obvious marketing strategy. Fashion shows generated enormous publicity through advertisements in newspapers and magazines, reviews of the shows, and public attendance. They brought into the stores hundreds of Canadian women who wanted to see the glamour and excitement of new European designs. They demonstrated and diffused models of upper-class etiquette and taste for Torontonians, as well as for store employees. They served as public entertainment and supported the community's fundraising projects. Sponsoring fashion shows promoted the image of the store as a generous, community-minded institution and also attracted and retained the elite women who were couture clients.

The lessening numbers of original couture models shown and sold as the 1950s progressed was due to the fast-paced increase in production, availability, and wide price range of couture-related designs. This included North American copies as well as the couturiers' own boutique and licensed designs. Though couture retained its glamour and prestige it was rapidly displaced in women's wardrobes by copies and *prêt-à-porter*.

5 ALTERNATIVE SOURCES OF IMPORTED COUTURE

A lower-priced copy may kill the sales of the more expensive version. This copy will in turn be killed by still cheaper knock-offs. For most manufacturers the basic rule of business is: Try to do what the others in your price bracket are doing — only a little bit sooner and a little bit better and a little bit cheaper. Bernard Roshco, 1963

The struggle to stock exclusive, affordable, and wearable couture resulted in a variety of couture-related designs and labels. In the United States, high postwar duties imposed by the government lessened sales of actual couture garments in preference for a higher number of *toiles*, designs made up in muslin, and *patrons à papier*, paper patterns, on which no tax was charged (figs. 5.1 to 5.4).[1] Few survive because they were used solely as working models by stores and manufacturers for knock-offs and design ideas.[2] In order to compensate for reduced haute couture sales, however, Paris couturiers quickly developed several new forms. These account for the confusion surrounding a clear definition of an haute couture model. Bonded models and new lines, such as boutique collections, finally led to the emergence of couturier-designed *prêt-à-porter* fashions. An active trade in second-hand couture operated as well. All these alternatives resulted in a much wider distribution of couture and couture-related design than has previously been acknowledged. Exploring this dissemination brings to light a broader picture of couture distribution, consumption patterns, and layers of meaning. It also helps to explain the history of the current ready-to-wear fashion system and why the Paris haute couture is still vibrant today.

Bonded Models

Perhaps one of the most interesting and least understood types of couture garment is the bonded model. Bonded models played a unique role for American and

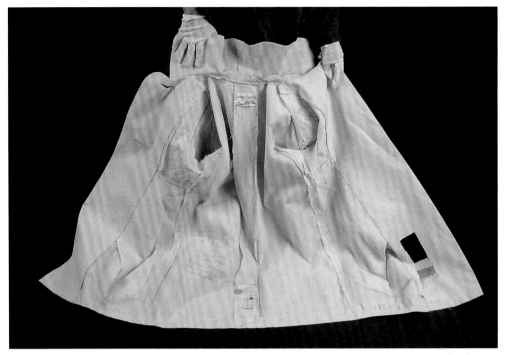

5.1 (top) Bonded Lanvin/Castillo coat *toile* "Borghese," purchased by Original Modes of New York from the 1958 fall collection. The *toile* includes swatches of the linings, interlinings, and the black wool in which the original was made. **5.2** (bottom) Bond seal on Lanvin/Castillo coat *toile* "Borghese." The reverse of the tag shows US Customs entry number 123. **5.3** (opposite) Bonded Lanvin/Castillo coat *toile* "Jessica," purchased by Original Modes of New York from the 1958 fall collection. The inside detail shows swatches of the interlinings, lining, and orange damask from which the original model was made.

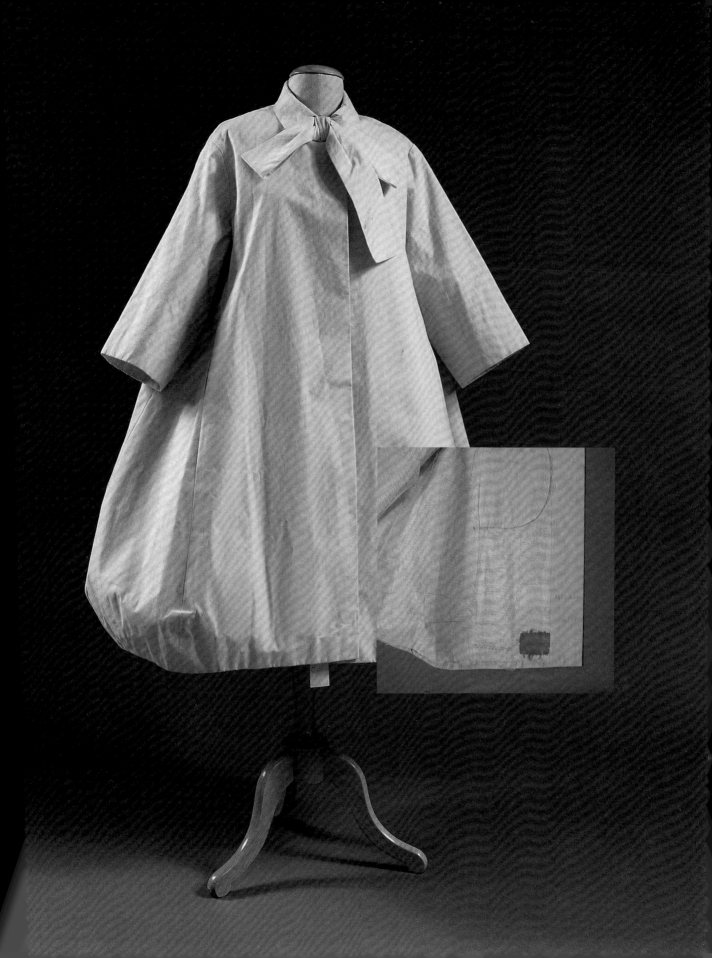

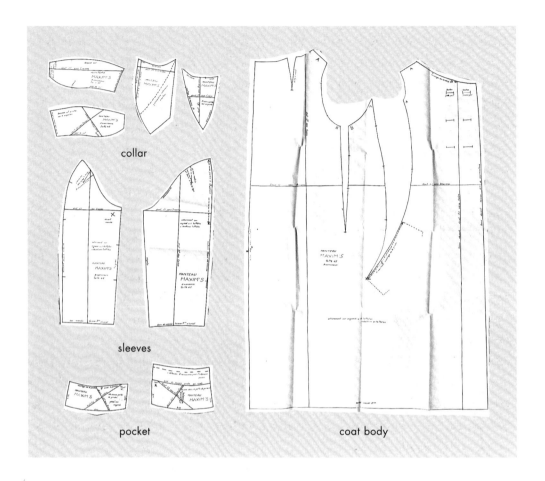

collar

sleeves

pocket

coat body

Canadian retailers and particularly for Canadian couture wearers. The bonded system began in Paris in 1929 in the wake of the Wall Street crash as a legitimate means to sell original European couture garments to manufacturers and retailers that would use them as design sources.[3]

In the United States, bonded models were haute couture designs given temporary admission into the country and held in customs bond in order to get around potentially exorbitant import duties.[4] Celia Bertin noted in the 1950s, "Clothes bought by Americans . . . go up according to weight of material, amount of embroidery, trim . . . as much as 90% of the cost of a model." One of the stipulations of bonding garments into the United States was that the merchandise had to be exported within

5.4 Christian Dior *patron à papier* coat, c.1958–60.

six months or duty and fines would be charged. If American merchants kept the goods for over a year, they had to pay double duty.[5] Even though the models were theoretically rented, selling bonded merchandise north or south of the border fulfilled the terms of the bond and enabled American buyers to recoup some capital on their original investment. Canada and South America were the cheapest and most convenient places for disposal.[6] Other countries also used the bonded system, but the discussion here focuses on its operation between Europe, New York, and Toronto.

There are several reasons why so little has been written about bonded models. Their original function was to create other products: a fashion show, a couture copy, or a cheaper knock-off. The actual bonded model was a disposable commodity from its conception. Its unique role was as an intermediate stage within the larger fashion system. Further, because of the complex pattern of trade and export, bonded garments are not found in the pre-eminent American, French, or other international museum collections. Additionally, very little is now known about bonded models because the French haute couture did not publicize this financial aspect of business, let alone the unglamorous aspect of selling permission to copy designs, which is what the bonded models represent. The Royal Ontario Museum couture collection and probably other Canadian and South American costume collections therefore provide an exceptional resource for understanding and documenting this significant aspect of the couture trade.[7]

Distinguishing bonded models from other imported couture can be done by close examination of the garment. A few still have the bond tags attached, though more commonly they have handwritten cotton tapes sewn into the interior with the customer's name and other order information. Piecing together the history of the artifact through archival research, examination of the dresses, clues such as alterations, and the recollections of Canadian consumers who wore bonded models has revealed many couture garments in the ROM collection to be bonded (fig. 5.5).

The Original Use and Disposal of Bonded Models

American manufacturers and retailers bought bonded models as design sources for copying or adapting and for promotion. All bonded Paris garments ordered by American manufacturers and retailers arrived in New York on the same flight. Bernard Roshco described the arrangement: "Approximately $600,000 worth of

5.5 Norman Hartnell short evening dress, early 1950s, purchased by Bergdorf Goodman in bond and resold by Simpson's to Toronto socialite Dorothy Boylen. The detail shows the lavish sequin embroidery and complex woven textile.

dresses, gowns, coats and suits" arrived together, were checked by the customs inspectors within forty-two hours, and then, at the prearranged date, were released. American buyers had access to the models at the same time, and "the clothes are rushed to 7th Avenue and the semi-annual sprint is on to be the first into the stores with the copies of the latest designs from Paris." The copies would be ready in four to five weeks.[8]

One of the biggest and most celebrated American buyers of couture and bonded models in the late 1950s and 1960s was the New York discount store Ohrbach's. It was famous for its fashion shows, which sent the original Paris model and the Ohrbach's copy down the runway side by side, challenging the audience to identify which was which. Irene Satz, its dress buyer, explained the bonded system: "Ohrbach's did line-for-line copies and we would spend as much on an average as $8,000 per [original] garment . . . We'd bring them in and also try to buy the fabrics that matched and buttons . . . Everything would come in at once, in bond, and it had to go out of the country or else we would have to pay for it." She went on to describe how all the manufacturers competed to make the copies for Ohrbach's: "They made their livelihood out of us. Because out of one garment he had a collar, he had a cuff, he had a hem." In other words, all the latest styling details were used as templates to be replicated in a variety of different designs. But Ohrbach's would give only one model to one manufacturer because it had such a short turnaround time to produce the copies. As well, it wished to protect its investment by curtailing the speed with which knock-offs were produced.[9]

Another large importer was the prestigious New York specialty shop Bergdorf Goodman. Andrew Goodman, the store president, told me that he imported eighty to a hundred couture models from Paris each season. Many were bonded models that were used for in-store fashion shows and for copying in the custom-order salon.[10] One of Bergdorf's bonded models that is now in the Royal Ontario Museum demonstrates how these designs were used (fig. 5.6). The dress is from the Italian couture house of Curiel. Its most distinctive feature is a silk satin and floral velvet draped panel. An advertisement placed in American *Vogue* explained that Bergdorf Goodman had contracted the Italian designer Gigliola Curiel to design fifty pieces "created especially and exclusively for us" as part of Bergdorf's "exclusive ready-to-wear Curiel collection."[11] The collection was aimed at the local American market and used the designer name and the same textiles, in less expensive versions. The dress shown in the advertisement, photographed by Avedon, is a strapless silk satin sheath embellished with the same silk satin and floral panel as the original bonded design at the museum.

The museum dress has an order label sewn into it at the design house that reads "bergdorf's." The evening gown was donated by Simpson's department store, which had purchased it from Bergdorf's, probably as a bonded model not originally intended for retail sale. The dress was probably used as a design resource for the Curiel ready-to-wear collection as well as for fashion shows. When Bergdorf's or any other commercial client ordered a design, it also acquired the *référence* and thus could obtain the same fabric for its own custom salon versions or lower-end copies. The dress at the museum is of a far more complicated construction than the design advertised by Bergdorf's in *Vogue*, but the strong design elements of a luxurious textile and slim sheath line are retained. Interestingly, this dress is illustrated and described in a book on the history of Bergdorf Goodman as "a lovely Bergdorf original."[12]

Another important function of bonded models was for industry fashion shows, in which the dresses served as a "source of advance style information . . . For a fee it is possible for designers to view in two or three hours about a hundred imports . . . The season [to view the dresses] usually lasts three or four weeks . . . The imports are usually 'bought in bond.'"[13] An example of this sort of arrangement was a fashion show held from 8 to 11 March 1949 at the Chanin Theater in New York, sponsored by A.M. Tenney Associates, representatives for Tennessee Eastman Corporation, a subsidiary of Eastman Kodak. The show featured thirty-one original French dresses representing eleven of the leading Paris couturiers and made from French textiles using Estron and American fabrics containing Teca Estron yarns (fig. 5.7). It was part of a series of promotional campaigns to upgrade the fashion potential of postwar synthetic textiles.[14] All the designs were imported in bond and used for the promotion: "We showed these gowns to our mill customers, converters, cutters, etc. . . . After this show the gowns were brought back to our showroom where cutters and designers came in to see and sketch them. At various times, they were sent to out-of-town department stores for special private showings."[15] After much discussion, US Customs permitted fifteen designs to go to the Costume Institute of the Metropolitan Museum of Art and sixteen to the Brooklyn Museum for

5.6 An Italian evening gown by Gigliola Curiel. This was ordered at the design house and imported in bond into New York by Bergdorf Goodman. Bergdorf's probably used the dress for fashion shows in a fall 1955 promotion of its "exclusive ready-to-wear Curiel collection" and then sold the dress to Simpson's in Toronto to fulfill the requirements of the custom bond.

"worthwhile educational value," as they represented "the height of fashion designs for the year 1949." This was unusual in that the bond was legally broken and it was acknowledged that the garments "could be exported and sold." Normally, once the clothes had been seen and copied, they were disposed of within a matter of three weeks.[16]

Bonded models were also used for illegal New York fashion shows. Bernard Roshco noted that model renters waited until the imported models had been used for legal promotion and copying, then rented the garments from the original purchaser to put on "bootleg" fashion shows for "manufacturers willing to wait a few weeks." These shows were mounted in hotels located in the garment district and were attended by manufacturers who paid $300 to $500 for admission. The fee, really another form of *caution*, permitted the manufacturer to return with designers or pattern makers and also to make a muslin copy. For an additional fee, the original model could be "borrowed" overnight. Another aspect of this illicit trade was noted by Irene Satz, who said that Ohrbach's made deals with the manufacturers that produced its copies not to give away any details or sell a bonded model design to other stores until a month after Ohrbach's got its delivery. "Then they were allowed to do anything they wanted, which helped them a great deal. If we were close to them, we'd let them take a rub-off of some of the models."[17]

5.7 This 1949 haute couture afternoon dress by Jean Patou is made from a "luxury textured crepe in a pale aqua shade," a textile woven of Estron yarn and rayon.

Before the bonded models left the United States, they had therefore been worn and handled numerous times and might have spawned numerous versions of a single couture design.

The Relationship between American and Canadian Stores

The disposal of bonded models was an integral part of the bond arrangement. Americans had several options before the bond expired. The clothes could be destroyed, returned to the source, or exported. Andrew Goodman recalled working in Paris in the 1920s and being responsible for getting rid of the returned dresses. He gave them to friends and girlfriends or mannequins.[18] Christian Dior established regulations for the return of models aimed at encouraging higher sales, offering a reimbursement of 20 percent of the original price if the model was returned within two months, 10 percent if it was returned within three months, and 5 percent within four months. Dior hoped that this would be an advantage to foreign buyers who wanted designs for publicity but had difficulty selling them at a full price.[19] The practice was also intended to minimize the copying and devolution of the Dior design. Some models sent back to Paris were sold by the haute couture house at a reduced price, though this practice was not advertised and was "commonly unknown except among French models, their friends, and certain society women from England, Switzerland and Italy who are more endowed with prominence than opulence."[20] The practice of returning clothes to Europe was not usual, however, because of the shipping cost and because it was so easy to unload them for profit to other manufacturers or to Canadians and South Americans.

The most satisfactory method of disposal was to sell the bonded models to another country. This resulted in quite a brisk trade between the United States and Canada. Mrs Clayton Burton remembered the models coming in to Toronto during the 1930s: "Mr Maitland had his own . . . showroom, storage . . . At one point in the depths of the Depression, my husband [Edgar Burton, president of Simpson's] went down and bought up all his stock that he had at a flat price . . . Some were worth practically nothing — they had been pulled apart. He came home, and said to me, "Look these are going to be sold for twenty-five a piece. We're going to have a big sale. Would you like to come down and choose some?" . . . I went down and bought quite a few, six or eight at $25 each."[21]

Postwar, this practice continued and flourished. Creeds relied on bonded models as the mainstay of its couture business in the late 1940s and 1950s. It obtained bonded models from a US Customs broker who worked for American stores such as Macy's and Alexander's, as well as for 7th Avenue manufacturers such as Ben Reig, and who thus assisted them in sending the models out of the country to meet the terms of the bond.[22]

Canadian stores also bought bonded models from Americans by verbal agreement. The garments would be sold approximately two months after the couture shows, at the end of March and October.[23] Irene Satz, Ohrbach's buyer, said, "We made a deal with Holt Renfrew, and they wanted them. They contacted us . . . and they paid us only $250 per garment." Holt's conducted a regular business in bonded models not only from Ohrbach's but also from Alexander's and Christian Dior–New York.[24] Christian Dior–New York samples were made in the Paris workrooms for the New York showroom. By bringing them into New York in bond, the house of Dior avoided the heavy taxes and thus took advantage of the import system devised for Americans.

The numbers of bonded models available to Canadians were considerable, and for many Torontonian consumers and retailers they were as important as the couture models they imported themselves. The dresses were always in demand because they were Paris originals at a cost considerably less than a direct import of the same dress made to order in Paris. Canadian merchants competed for bonded models and advertised their successful acquisitions. One example reads: "a unique collection of 'Bonded Models.' Original Paris models by Christian Dior . . . made in . . . [his] atelier in Paris . . . but because they are 'Bonded Models' we are able to offer them at fractions of their original value."[25] This Holt Renfrew advertisement not only promoted the bonded models but also served to stake out the legitimate and prestigious role of the store in merchandising Dior products.

Toronto retailers had to buy bonded models as a lot and had no control over numbers, size, or designs. This did not worry them, however, as the models could easily be sold at a profit.[26] Bernard Roshco described "one Canadian retailer" who sold the Paris originals for "less than one-fourth of the price the Americans paid. Offering such 'Bargains' as $1,200 Diors for $250, he sells out 15 minutes after the sale starts."[27] In 1948, Christian Dior's rules for resale of models stipulated that the buyer was not permitted to resell the model within two months of buying it for less than he or she had paid. Further, the model could not be sold for below 60 percent of the price paid by the buyer within four months, and the American and Canadian exchange was to be calculated on a rate approved by the French at the time of export.[28] This regulation must surely have been instituted not only in order to control the dissemination of the design but also to curb others from profiting by the trade of Christian Dior designs. The popularity of bonded models is verified by interviews with couture clients, who remember having to rush down to the stores to compete for them as soon as they were telephoned.

Yet in Canada bonded models were wild cards. Couture houses sold limited numbers of a style, since none of the stores wanted what the other had. Store buyers usually purchased with certain individuals in mind for particular dresses and were careful not to sell two of the same model to clients who were in the same social set or city. But such a system collapsed under the arrangement with bonded models, and the meticulous record keeping of the European couture houses, local department stores and shops, and sales staff fell apart. This must have been recognized at the time but was ignored in the competition to offer such desirable merchandise.

A case in point is a design for which at least two models were sold and worn in Toronto. Tracing what Igor Kopytoff has called the "biography of the object" — uniting material culture, oral history, and archival research — a multifaceted history emerges of a Christian Dior ball gown design from the fall 1951 collection. One of the models is in the Royal Ontario Museum and was probably purchased at Holt Renfrew, which had the Dior licence and where the donor, Doris Morrow, was a regular client. An interview with the donor's daughter elicited a sketch of the dress from a contemporary fashion magazine that her mother had saved, suggesting pride in her ownership of the dress.[29] The drawing confirms the design conception as strapless and is verified by additional documentation, which also confirms the date (figs. 5.8 and 5.9). The dress has the remnants of a white tape tag that had the order written on it, but the writing has worn off. The garment has been altered, most noticeably by the addition of grey faille straps. These were probably constructed from the hem, which has been cut and rehemmed, not to Paris couture standards (fig. 5.10). These traces strongly suggest that the modifications were not made at the design house and that the dress was purchased elsewhere.

AUTRICHE

Christian Dior
SOCIÉTÉ A RESPONSABILITÉ LIMITÉE
CAPITAL 35.000.000 DE FRS
30. AVENUE MONTAIGNE
PARIS

HIVER 51~52

Nº

5.8 Sketch of fall 1951 Christian Dior ball gown confirming the original design as strapless.
5.9 (opposite) This realization of the ball gown shown in fig. 5.8 follows the original design.

Ringier

B

Dior
Hiver 51-52

151

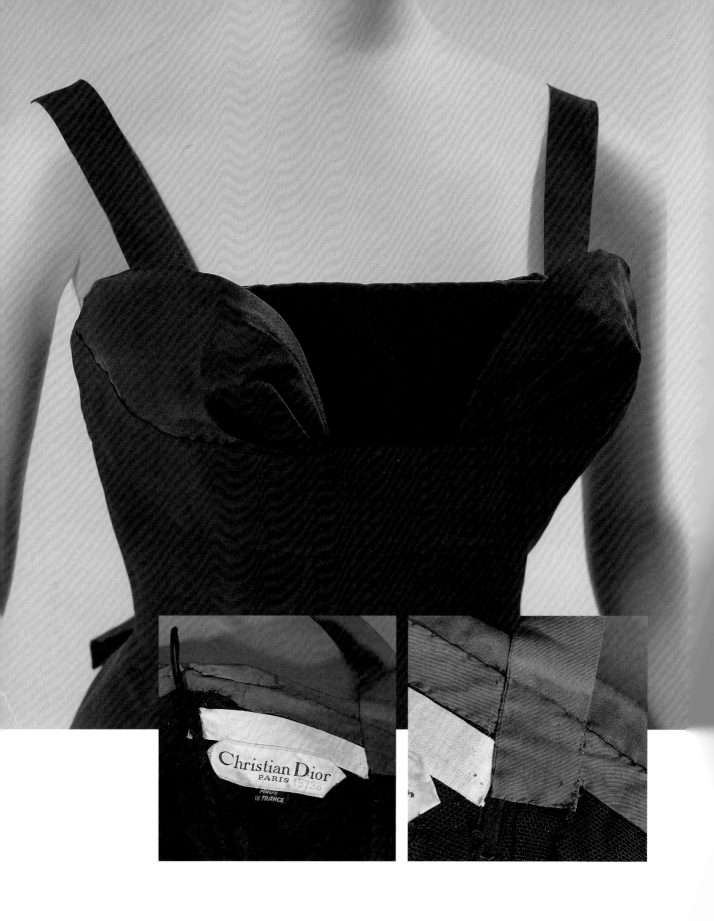

Christian Dior
PARIS 1573a
MADE
IN FRANCE

5.10 Fall 1951 Christian Dior ball gown of grey faille and brown velvet. The design was originally strapless, as figs. 5.8 and 5.9 attest, but straps were added to this garment after it left the design house. The fabric for the straps most likely came from the hem (fig. 0.3, p. 5). The centre back bodice has been let out at the zipper.

Another Toronto owner of the same Dior design, Joan Rosefield Lepofsky, said that it had been worn by her mother and that it was definitely a bonded model.[30] This is confirmed by handwritten labels for the order by a Washington store, partially legible and sewn into the dress. This dress has also had straps added, as it was originally worn to an evening wedding and would not have been considered appropriate strapless. This bonded dress came into Canada within a lot — as all bonded models did — and would therefore not have been selected by either a Canadian client or a buyer.

The two dresses illustrate several important points. First, they demonstrate the breakdown of the exclusive merchandising of haute couture, as both were initially purchased as bonded models by American merchants for promotion, copying, or both. Second, when the design was originally published in the French fashion magazine *L'Officiel de la Haute Couture*, it was described as made from grey faille with a green velvet corselet and back panel in the skirt.[31] Both models in Canada are grey faille and brown velvet, indicating that for North American taste the original colour scheme was probably too dramatic and unconventional. The two dresses also illustrate the uniformity of North American taste as they were ordered in the same colour scheme. Third, the two Toronto consumers of this design were similar ages and, interestingly, made the same alteration, indicating that the new postwar strapless style, called "the naked look," was too avant garde, and inappropriate for mature Canadian women.[32] Unmodified Paris fashion was seen to be improper for North American consumption, and these dresses articulate the role of buyers, merchants, and consumers in ordering the models with specific changes or else altering them to conform to local taste.

Another example of bonded models breaking down the couture system is found in an incident between Eaton's and Holt Renfrew. By the mid-1950s, Eaton's had lost the edge on buying bonded models to Holt Renfrew and Creeds and had by and large ceased to compete for them. In the late 1950s, however, Mr Garnacoult, the merchandising manager for the Ensemble Shop, sent his buyer, Ollie Smythe, to New York specifically to find bonded models. She recalled her trip as follows: "The first place I went to was Ohrbach's and right up on the top floor . . . They had racks of them and I bought them . . . Then sometimes the *toiles* would be included when they arrived. I paid $75 a piece for them . . . for every garment they had.

Garments that they had paid $2,500 for, no matter what condition it was in. If something was pristine new it was $75 or if something was dog-eared . . . Then we went out to Alexander's . . . I kept a cab all day . . . and I had bonded models coming out of my ears."[33] When Ollie Smythe returned, she advertised that Eaton's had bonded models for sale and named the designers, including Christian Dior. Holt's was furious because although it held the Canadian exclusive for Christian Dior, it had been publicly demonstrated that the store was not the only source for the Paris couturier's designs. Yet the shop could do nothing because the models had not been purchased from Christian Dior. The incident clearly represents the havoc that bonded models could cause in Toronto retail circles, while the existence of two identical bonded models owned by consumers of similar age and status demonstrates the social implications of the bonded system.

The original function of bonded models as promotional tools and design sources changed dramatically in their new setting, exemplifying the transformation of meaning and value of designed objects as they move within the social world. In Canada, the status of a garment was not diminished if it had been through the bonded system. Bonded models were treated like any exclusive haute couture models even though they were, in fact, second-hand goods. Toronto stores carefully distributed them to consistent and loyal haute couture clients, who were notified when they were in stock.[34] One client called them "a joy!" and went on to explain their significance for her: "They were three to six months old and it would take you that long to get them made up in Paris. I would have bought the whole lot but they wouldn't sell them to you."[35] Margery Steele, the buyer for Simpson's St Regis Room, recalled that she had a list of clients who would buy only bonded models and said Simpson's could sell them for

whatever we wanted to put on them . . . They were getting a good price no matter how much we made. Some of the names weren't too important, some were . . . It doesn't mean the dress isn't as good . . . We would have a list of customers who were interested in bonded models. As a matter of fact, that's all they'd buy, bonded models. We had list a mile long and we could have had a crowd of people out there praying we'd let them know. Those were the days when the retailer really was in charge . . . We had our loyal customers. They're the ones that got it.[36]

Her counterpart at Creeds, Lexy Burton, had a similar experience. She had the job of "nail[ing] down [bonded] choices for her favoured clients. There was one customer,

155

the fabled late Mrs. N.L. Nathanson, who was known to take 25 or 30 originals at a crack. [Said Lexy,] 'She just loved clothes and she could afford to buy them, so she did.'[37]

Sales staff were careful to control not only the sale of the clothes but also their visibility within the couture salon so that, as with all couture, when a garment was first worn it would not have been seen by the client's social group. The opportunity for a woman's peers to find out what she had purchased at full retail price and what as a bonded model was in this way greatly reduced. Bonded models thus serviced an exclusive couture circle, when in fact a broader clientele could have afforded them. June McLean, whose husband, W.F. McLean, was the president of Canada Packers, described herself as "not in the group" of those who would be called for bonded models. She believed that this was because she was not especially interested in fashion and perhaps did not spend as much money as others.[38] Even among elite customers there was a recognized hierarchy.

Bonded models were considered perks by regular couture clients and formed the backbone of a good wardrobe for many Canadian women. Clients recalled buying them at Creeds, Holt Renfrew, Simpson's, and Eaton's.[39] Margery Steele confirmed that some clients bought couture chiefly when it was on sale or as bonded

5.11 Fall 1965 Balenciaga suit purchased from Holt Renfrew by Barbara McNabb as a bonded model and worn as part of her professional working wardrobe. She wore the navy wool suit with a hat similar to the one shown here and with white wrist-length gloves. If she was feeling "jaunty," she chose her white cotton gloves embroidered with navy polka dots.

models, and sales staff would call to let them know when new dresses were available. Bonded models were also important elements in the wardrobe of professional working women such as Barbara McNabb, who could not afford full-price couture but "wanted to look like [she had] some substance and position."[40] She relied on couture bonded models for her working wardrobe, such as a Balenciaga suit that she purchased from Holt Renfrew for $200, and she also bought high-quality American ready-to-wear to supplement her wardrobe (fig. 5.11).

North American Taste and Bonded Models

The bonded models in the Royal Ontario Museum collection and in private wardrobes raise interesting issues about North American taste in European couture. The various purposes served by bonded models are reflected in the range of designs that American stores and manufacturers purchased from the style leaders of the Paris haute couture such as Chanel, Balmain, and Dior, as well as from smaller names such Henry à la Pensée and non-French sources (fig. 5.12). Garments purchased for promotional fashion shows might differ from those purchased by manufacturers, who were looking for a widely appealing style, the "Ford" that Roshco describes as containing "a blend of novelty and popular acceptability."[41]

For Torontonians, bonded models offered an alternative selection of merchandise from that obtained through the standard couture purchasing system controlled by local buyers. A Canadian buyer would not normally purchase a highly dramatic design for her couture clientele, as it would be considered too expensive and elaborate if imported through the usual channels. The same design might sell easily as a bonded model, however, because it would be seen as a bargain and a prize within the bonded context.

Another interesting aspect of bonded models in Canada is that they were sometimes worn with original design elements missing. Copyists and manufacturers considered trims and furs a non-essential part of the design in terms of basic silhouette and cut, and ordering the garment without them would lower the price.[42] The importance of the trim to the overall design was also a question of taste. A Balenciaga suit, now in the Cincinnati Art Museum, was bought at Eaton's as a bonded model by Torontonian Mary Louise Robertson as part of her trousseau and was purchased and worn without the dramatic detail of velvet cuffs

5.12 Henry à la Pensée bonded silk taffeta ensemble "Ambitieuse," worn by Signy Eaton and probably purchased at Eaton's. The six-month bond tag notes that this was ordered and imported in bond by Current Fashion, New York.

(figs. 5.13 and 5.14).[43] A fall 1952 Balmain ball gown in the Royal Ontario Museum was also very probably bonded, though it contains no bond tags. Both the original design house sketch and a contemporary fashion photograph show that the dress was designed with mink bands at the bodice and in the skirt (fig. 5.15). The actual dress has been let out in the waist, indicating that it was not purchased in a large size or with this client in mind (see fig. 2.10, pp. 66–7). The daughter-in-law of Ethel Harris, who owned the dress, considered it very unlikely that she would have purchased or worn it with the fur as she would have considered it too ostentatious. This is confirmed by a press report describing the dress without the fur.[44] Mrs Harris considered the dress perfectly suitable as it was, however, and several years later chose to wear it for her photograph in the 1955 *Toronto Telegram* best-dressed list (fig. 5.16). Given the extensive alterations and the lack of trim, it is very probable that this model was bonded and ordered without mink to reduce costs as much as possible.

The issue of incomplete bonded models can also be followed through the "biography" of a Chanel model. Some extant Chanel suits retain order labels that list the

5.13 (opposite) Balenciaga suit purchased as a bonded model by Torontonian Mary Louise Robertson as part of her trousseau. The suit lacks the velvet cuffs evident in the design house photograph, though the velvet collar is retained. **5.14** This couture house photograph of the same 1948 Balenciaga design shows the jacket with velvet cuffs.

#405

5.15 Design sketch for fall 1952 Pierre Balmain lace ball gown trimmed with sequins and mink (fig. 2.10, pp. 66–7). The mink bands were not included on a version of the design worn by Toronto socialite Ethel Harris. **5.16** (opposite) Ethel Harris, centre left, wearing her bonded Pierre Balmain ball gown for the 1955 *Telegram* best-dressed list. She has paired the dress with a fur stole, although the dress itself has no mink trim.

Salute to Spring

Mrs. Norman Bell ↑

← Mrs. Donald Carlisle

← Mrs. R. W. Finlayson

← Mrs. W. C. Harris

← Mrs. A. R. Winnett

← Mrs. A. D. McKenzie

Mrs. Arthur Soler →

BEST-DRESSED WOMEN

Marilyn Bell ↑

Mrs. F. J. Crawford →

Mrs. J. W. Connell

All photographs by Gerald Campbell, Ashley & Crippen

163

5.17 Spring 1959 Chanel three-piece Rodier wool jersey suit ordered by the New York firm of Davidow-Schloss as a bonded model and used for making their own copies and adaptations. The handwritten order label contains the Davidow-Schloss name. The buttons and elastic loops keep the blouse down and in place on the skirt. Such dressmaking techniques continued from the late nineteenth century and are found only in haute couture dressmaking by the mid-twentieth century.

5.18 Chanel suit from fig. 5.17 in a Paris setting with classic Chanel accessories. The collarless jacket has been folded back with a brooch to create a lapel effect.

customer as Davidow-Schloss, a large New York coat and suit ready-to-wear manufacturer, founded in 1880, that built its reputation on high-quality sportswear. By the 1960s, the Davidow name was synonymous with the Chanel style (figs. 5.17 and 5.18).[45] The label on one Chanel suit ordered by Davidow-Schloss is actually marked "Exclusive of Ornamentation." Comparison of the suit with a contemporary advertisement does not make it clear what is missing, though the suit lacks the trademark gold chain that was sewn into the inside bottom edge of the jacket for weight, to ensure that it hung correctly. The first buyer would have seen the original design and would also have the *référence*, but the bonded suit was, in essence, worn "unfinished." Joan Rosefield Lepofsky happily wore it with a hat, a slim rolled black umbrella, and no jewellery, resulting in a very minimal treatment (fig. 5.19).[46]

Bonded models met all the social and etiquette requirements of Toronto society. Day suits were available, such as a spring 1961 Dior made of a sandy-coloured loose woven tweed with matching silk blouse, which Mary Bunnett bought for $150 and wore to the annual meeting of the Junior League. Its original import tags show that it was originally purchased by Elizabeth Arden. Mary Bunnett's sister, Frances Weir, also purchased many bonded models, including a Balenciaga day dress of beige wool that she wore with a white or brown wool cashmere sweater for "busy days" when she had meetings and teas. For late afternoon, she sometimes wore a bonded Givenchy silk twill polka dot dress that was originally bought by Bergdorf

5.19 Joan Rosefield Lepofsky in her spring 1960 bonded Chanel sailor-style suit. She wore this with a navy scarf at the neckline. The design was ordered by Davidow-Schloss, a New York manufacturer known for making Chanel-style suits.

Goodman, and for cocktails a black silk design by Jacques Fath. She also bought a bonded strapless Grès 1954 evening gown that probably came via Bergdorf Goodman, the source named for the design in *Harper's Bazaar*.[47] Thus, bonded models ranged from day to evening wear. They included the most famous names in fashion as well as lesser known ones. They gave select Torontonians the opportunity to buy designs that they may not have ordinarily because of the original high cost or because the style was too flamboyant.

The practice of bonding models resulted in a very profitable postwar commercial trade for Paris couturiers and was an enormously important design resource for the North American fashion industry. When bonded models were resold by Canadian retailers, they served as an alternative source of haute couture for clients. From the point of purchase at the Paris design house, through their role in fashion shows and for copying, to their social usage, bonded models have gone largely unrecognized in studies of the couture and ready-to-wear industry. Yet they represented as much as 50 to 75 percent of couture imports into the United States and from there an important percentage of haute couture in Canada.[48] The couture collection at the Royal Ontario Museum is of special importance in this area, as are other Canadian and South American couture collections that can now be studied in a similar manner to provide further insight into cultural and national notions of taste and style.

Couture Copies, Boutiques, and *Prêt-à-Porter*
Exact, Line-for-Line, and Cheaper Couture Copies

Paris in the '50s was not so much imitated as absorbed. Instead of being an all-powerful influence its couturiers were an important source of ideas utilized by other designers who bought, adapted and innovated to meet the desires of their own particular clientele.[49]

The practice of copying, adapting, and essentially redesigning couture clothes was one of the great strengths of the North American fashion industry. An increasingly wide range and number of couture copies were produced and advertised during the 1950s. Toronto retailer Edmund Creed described the selection at Creeds as "Mercedes Benz to bottom-of-the-line Ford." Clear distinctions are difficult to make, and the rhetoric surrounding the copying, geared as it was toward marketing and sales, was imprecise.[50]

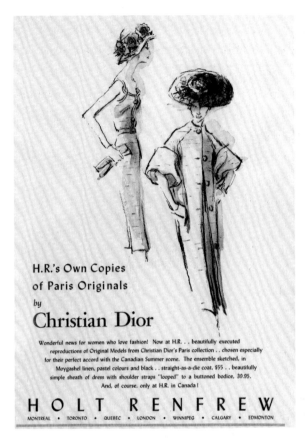

In a high-priced copy, such as the Dior copies made by Holt Renfrew, the design, fabrics, and trims were exactly the same as the original model and were obtained through the *référence*. The product was considered identical to a model ordered from the Paris workroom, complete with three fittings, but the price could be up to 70 percent lower.[51] This could be advertised as an "exact copy." A "line-for-line copy," or "reproduction," implied a close copy of the style, though the fabric could differ. It was based on the couture original but "changes are made; details and workmanship are eliminated. Machine work is substituted for handwork. The result is called a line-for-line copy, though in many cases it should be called an adaptation."[52] Ohrbach's was famous for its line-for-line copies, which were sold to "important, pampered people, with a reputation for knowing French clothes and for spending freely."[53] A copy, reproduction, or adaptation also more generally referred to a garment that loosely reproduced the essential design components of an original model (fig. 5.20). It could differ in terms of the colour, weave, and material, substituting rayon taffeta or satin for silk taffeta, for example; and its production was less labour intensive, substituting machine work for some or all handwork. It could also have minor styling changes.

5.20 A dress and coat ensemble advertised June 1956, from a collection of "H.R.'s Own Copies" of Christian Dior originals by Holt Renfrew "chosen especially for their accord with the Canadian Summer scene." The coat was $55 and the dress $39.95, in Moygashel linen in pastels and black.

The Most Lovely
Lace Dress in Paris

*by Balenciaga
of course!*

H.R. imported the model . .
you will not find it anywhere
else in Canada . . or its
reproductions for immediate
wear . . made in H.R.'s own workroom
in beautiful laces imported from France.

HOLT RENFREW

It is impossible to identify the differences between an original and its copy without direct comparison of the garments. The types of design modifications that simplified a copy and reduced its cost can, however, be seen in a few examples. A fall 1952 Balenciaga design in the Royal Ontario Museum, for instance, is similar to one advertised by Holt Renfrew as a copy (figs. 5.21 and 5.22). The main difference in styling is the omission in the Holt Renfrew version of satin ribbon trim at the neckline and interlaced in the skirt at the hip. It is not possible to determine the differences in quality of textiles and workmanship.

Nonetheless, all copies were costed below the original model. In the United States, for example, a Dior model for fall 1959 was imported for US$1,095, a custom-made copy was priced down to US$775, while a line-for-line copy of the same model was sold for US$159.95 on 5th Avenue and another on 34th Street for US$37.50. Rapidly, even cheaper versions taken from the copies were made available.[54]

The influence of the Paris couture on fashion, and the subsequent relationship between couture originals and all types of copies, became increasingly complex through the 1950s. It could be argued that all couture was, in fact, a copy of a model, or sample, from the original line. But when did a good couture "copy" become a ready-to-wear mass-produced garment that was no longer close to the original model? At what point in production or marketing did this separation take place? I suggest

5.21 A Holt Renfrew reproduction of a Balenciaga cocktail or dinner dress, advertised May 1953, omits the satin ribbon trim of the original design (fig. 5.22). The fan included in the sketch indirectly promotes the Spanish roots of Balenciaga.

that the initial demarcation was made by those who produced and marketed the clothes but that the final distinction was made by the consumer, who placed her own sociocultural values on the copy. Only by taking both perspectives into account can one begin to unravel the significance of copies sold during this period.

The complicated relationship between the original and the mass-produced object is a modern problem and has been addressed extensively in the context of art and design history.[55] French theoretician Jean Baudrillard has argued that the "status of the modern object is dominated by the opposition of the unique object to the mass-produced object — of the 'model' to the 'series.'" His theory can refer to the opposition of the couture model to the copy, but his argument fails to make explicit a comparison he draws between "a dress from Fath" — one of the first and most aggressive French couturiers to enter into a licensing agreement with 7th Avenue — and an undefined clothing "item."[56] One assumes he meant to compare a Fath haute couture dress with a manufactured dress of the same type, but he never clearly identifies the function or the type of "dress" and "item" he is contrasting. The reader is left to assume that the non-couture "item" is a match or copy of the dress from Fath.

In contrast, design historian Peter Dormer, in *The Meanings of Modern Design*, does identify specific designed objects and argues that their status is based on craftsmanship, the display of money, and their role as signifiers of class. He proposes two categories of high-design goods: "heavenly goods," meaning objects designed for the internationally rich to buy; and "tokens," defined as "objects bought by the 'wish-they-were-rich.'"[57] These categories are too simplistic when applied to couture, though, since the North American couture customer often bought both the original "heavenly" garment and the "token" copy. Irene Satz proudly related that her couture copy customers at Ohrbach's were, "You name it. Every name in the papers . . . Everyone, including Jackie Onassis — she didn't come to our shows though — she liked special attention, but she wore our clothes . . . They used to wait in line to get into the store and see our shows and be the first. These glamorous women actually fought to get service and didn't care if they got the same thing."[58]

An essay by Umberto Eco sheds more light on the issue. "Travels in Hyperreality" contrasts European and American cultural values by comparing a fifth-century Greek bronze (the Paris original) with a Roman copy, or "multiple" (the

5.22 Red lace Balenciaga dress that was ordered from model 147, originally designed in black lace for the fall 1952 collection. The dress has satin ribbon trim at the neckline and interlaced in the skirt below the waist, details omitted in the Holt Renfrew reproduction (fig. 5.21).

North American reproduction), and then with a "fake" (the mass-produced copy). He argues that the European tourist's pilgrimage to the *Pietà* at St Peter's (or a Paris couture house) and the American tourist's pilgrimage to a local fake version of the *Pietà* (or Ohrbach's) are both fetishistic because "once the fetishistic desire for the original is forgotten, these copies are perfect." He compares these "almost real" objects — the high-end "multiple" and the mass-produced "fake" — to those at Disneyland, where "it is not so much because it wouldn't be possible to have the real equivalent but because the public is meant to admire the perfection of the fake . . . Disneyland not only produces illusion, but — in confessing it — *stimulates the desire for it.*"[59] I suggest that a similar desire was generated by the North American production of couture copies, which were produced within weeks of the originals being available and "allow[ed] many American women to *feel* they [were] being dressed by Balenciaga, Givenchy . . . at one-fifth to one-tenth of what it would cost them in Paris."[60] The North American copy was swiftly executed, less expensive, and simulated the original couture design. The concept was sufficient, and the customer did not need to have the complete couture salon experience with elaborate decor and numerous fittings. Access to the democratic department store and lower prices opened up the couture-inspired market to thousands of middle- and upper-middle-class women. For many North American women, the copy, or hyperreal, couture became as good if not better than the original because it had been re-engineered for their taste and was cheaper and more appropriate for their lifestyle. As well, the fit in the copy had been "worked out for the American customer . . . A couture model is not really a fit garment."[61]

By the early 1960s, several French designers capitulated with this notion of "fake" couture when they authorized copies of their designs to be sold, with the caveat that their haute couture names were not to be used on copies that they considered "cheap." Thus, Dior became Monsieur X, Fath was Monsieur Y, and Givenchy was Monsieur Z. The store could hint that the designer was, for instance, Dior, but could not actually mention the couturier's name. The names were quickly associated with the letter, however, and general knowledge of the designer behind the initial gave huge cachet to these copies while paying only lip service to the idea that the couturiers' names were still exclusive.[62]

The culmination of this effort to guard the exclusivity of a name and simultaneously to profit from it in the manufacturing market was the suit between Dior and the New York discount shop Alexander's in 1962. Alexander's was not permitted to buy from Dior in Paris, as the house considered the store to be beneath its stature. But Alexander's advertised Dior copies that it obtained from manufacturers who had purchased in Paris. The management of Alexander's did not feel bound by other stores' agreements to use "Monsieur X" and so called a Dior, a Dior. Dior filed a suit against the store, but the American court upheld Alexander's case. Dior then granted it permission to buy from the house if it would use the pseudonym "Monsieur X," which the store did. As Alexander's administration said, however, "Does it make any sense to call a Dior a Ginsberg?"[63]

The problem of exclusivity was a long-standing one. It began as soon as specific names became associated with couture designs in the middle of the nineteenth century. Elizabeth Ann Coleman has demonstrated how Paris haute couture labels were faked in New York in the 1920s, and Nancy Troy has discussed this in terms of fake reproductions of Paul Poiret clothes manufactured in New York as early as the 1910s.[64] The Paris haute couture relied on strong trade with the large retailers such as Ohrbach's, Macy's, and later even Alexander's: "The French-copy mania seems not to have diminished the desirability of good French models . . . It was reported that an estimated 10,000 women had seen the Ohrbach's and Alexander's French-copy showings in New York in one day."[65]

Dior, too, encountered this problem in a different way on establishing his New York line in 1948. The line was designed in Paris specifically for the North American market. Photographs of the New York designs were sent back to Paris attached with prices, number of sales, and comments on the American reception of the garment in order to help the Paris house gauge its new market. One model, for example, number 286 from the spring 1950 collection, was reported to be hard to make in the New York workroom and unpopular with buyers because "many 7th Avenue houses were showing this silhouette." Only fifteen models were sold. Interestingly, Dior was left in the position of being unable to produce his own design because it had become debased by the proliferation of copies.[66]

Copyists had to decide how many of a particular design to reproduce. Line-for-line copies were usually made in limited editions. In the custom-order department of Bergdorf Goodman, a design that produced twelve copies was considered successful, while orders of eighteen to twenty were considered exceptional and the store refused to fill more than thirty orders of a design, in order to maintain some exclusivity for its clients.[67] Even with this control, problems arose. In one instance, a client ordered an US$850 custom copy of a Paris design and on leaving the store saw the same dress advertised for US$250 as ready-to-wear.[68] By contrast, Irene Satz of Ohrbach's would have twelve to 150 copies of a dress made, depending on how high fashion the garment was, and would take special repeat orders.[69] Meanwhile, a 7th Avenue manufacturer would turn out thousands of a successful copy and consider it a "Ford." Nevertheless, usually the more mass-produced and -marketed the design, the more watered down it became in terms of fabric, construction, and overall complexity of design.

To a large extent, even the limited numbers of high-end reproductions or line-for-line copies were marketing devices, just as were original couture models. The power of European couture was such that all levels of copies were marketed with their lineage and still managed to retain strong notions of exclusivity. For this reason, copies themselves began to displace the significance of an original model, and it was hoped that "some of the Paris glamour [would] rub off" on other lines carried by the store.[70] By the mid-1950s, a good copy and a loose affiliation with the original couture garment began to be a perfectly adequate means for Canadian and American stores to acquire the cultural capital that was previously associated only with "real" couture models.

The euphemisms used to exploit copies and their couture sources were abundant. One Simpson's advertisement for a collection of French-based designs identified the garments as "translations," "line-for-line copies," and "interpretations" (fig. 5.23). The text claimed that the original Paris clothes had arrived "on this continent" just fourteen days before and were now ready, having been "interpreted . . . in Misses sizes in pure silk taffetized shantung to look identical to the originals in every respect but price." Importance was placed on the fact that the originals had been studied, that the speed of production ensured completely up-to-date copies, and that they were a bargain. Holt Renfrew advertised a copy of a Grès dress at $135, and the

5.23 Advertisement for line-for-line Paris and London couture copies available at Simpson's "at a fraction of their original price," 7 October 1955. The Fath suit, sketched centre bottom in frontal pose, of "Blin-and-Blin cashmere type fabric" was probably based on a photograph published in French *Vogue*, September 1955, 132.

here they are . . . line-for-line copies of fabulous originals

Copy of Cavanagh

Copy of Balenciaga

Copy of Ronald Peterson

Copy of Norman Hartnell

Copy of Balenciaga

Copy of Balmain

Copy of Givenchy

Copy of Fath

Copy of Hardy Amies

Simpson's

passage clearly stated that the store had imported both the model and the taffeta fabric from France, thus implying that its reproduction retained the "Frenchness" of the original and was authentic. For a Jean Dessès grey flannel suit that Holt's imported, copied, and retailed for $150, it was noted that the dress had been photographed in the March issue of American *Vogue* and also in *Harper's Bazaar*, where editor Carmel Snow called it "one of the most important suits in Paris," thereby giving a stamp of approval to the taste and selection of the store.[71]

Advertisements validated the couture copy by stressing that the store or manufacturer had indeed purchased the original and had it in hand. Close proximity to the source gave credibility and sociocultural value to the copy, while inadvertently making the original less valuable. Few elite couture wearers would want to purchase a couture dress that could be mistaken for an advertised copy (figs. 5.24 and 5.25). For a store to have purchased the original directly from the design house also served to discriminate between the small-run "good" copy over the "cheap" mass-produced one, since some manufacturers sold off their copies to other manufacturers who did not import, as in the case of Alexander's.[72]

Copies were widely advertised in Toronto. By 1951, Holt Renfrew, Morgan's, and Eaton's all sold them (figs. 5.26 to 5.28). Copies of European clothes were available even immediately after the war, and were shown by Eaton's along with an original

5.24 Holt Renfrew advertisement for "authentic translations in the couture manner," 13 October 1960. The Nina Ricci jacket and skirt in the centre of the drawing is a direct copy of the original design shown in fig. 5.25.

5.25 Original 1960 Nina Ricci suit of grey and brown wool double cloth that was also sold as a copy by Holt Renfrew (fig. 5.24). This may have been a bonded model.

Balenciaga's
New Success Suit

The perfect BLACK suit in this great couturier's Autumn Collection. 'Tis said that this model scored the greatest success of any suit presented by the Haute Couture of Paris for this season. The buttoning of the jacket introduces a unique and practical idea .. it's single-breasted above the waistline, then buttons in a double curve below the waist. H.R.'s reproduction .. superbly tailored in fine BLACK worsted material from France .. $110.

HOLT RENFREW
Yonge at Adelaide

copy
of an **Italian**
import . . .
Morgan's
exclusive
'Two-in-One Dress'.

Elegant sophistication in handwoven
pure silk tussah. Square necked,
short sleeved dress with a bloused
look. Slim skirt with overskirt which
buttons on to a tunic effect.
A leather belt completes the outfit.
Natural coloured in sizes 12 to 16

Price $85

import in its 1948 "Overture to Fashion" show. The main differences between the copies and the Balmain original were described in the commentary. Eaton's justified the brown wool crepe it had substituted for the unavailable "tie" [sic] silk used in the Balmain dress by explaining that "our Canadian versions are lighter in weight . . . and perhaps more suited to our often over-heated houses."[73] Eaton's had thus "improved" the French design for its local market.

Canadian reporter Olive Dickason commented in 1955 on Canadian-made line-for-line copies that were available two to three weeks after the original models.

5.26 (left) Holt Renfrew advertisement for a "reproduction" of a Balenciaga woollen suit, 25 September 1950. The original design was published in American *Vogue*, 1950. **5.27** (right) Morgan's advertisement for a "copy" of an anonymous Italian design, May 1958. Designs that could be worn for several types of occasion or in more than one way were popular as they made the investment more serviceable. **5.28** (opposite) Eaton's advertisement for "adapted" designs of French couture coats, 22 February 1950.

EATON'S adapted French Original coats to bring yo...

PARIS CHIC
at a MODERATE PRICE

Our tailors took coats by *Christian Dior, Jacques Fath, Robert Piguet* . . . top-fashion names in the Paris Haute Couture . . . and adapted them, every line, every flare, every pocket, into coats for Canadian fashion. They made them up in fine, soft, wool baratheas. They lined them with tiny-dotted imported rayon taffetas . . . some matching, some contrasting, some with scarves, too, of the lining material. They added belts in bright leathers and the same, soft baratheas. They even imported a special shoulder pad and copied it, to give the smooth, rounded, natural shoulder of the French originals.

These are the coats . . . Paris-inspired, beautiful, exciting . . . and, because we made them ourselves, they're moderately priced. And, of course, they're only at *Eaton's across Canada!*

FOURTH FLOOR
Items marked * also at Eaton's-College Street

Dior's "bint-wing" silhouette adaptation with deep armholes, bloused back, wide shawl collar. Beige with tan lining, navy with navy or tan with beige. Matching scarf. Misses' sizes 10 to 18 included. 69.95

*Dior's fitted coat adaptation with cape-width shawl collar, loose kimono sleeves, softly gathered skirt. Navy with red lining, tan with beige, tan belt or beige with beige. Matching scarf. Junior sizes 9 to 15 included. 49.95

*Fath's versatile coat adaptation worn loose or belted. High-placed pockets, rounded yoke. Navy with red lining, red belt; tan with beige, tan belt; grey with red and white, grey belt; red with red, navy belt; beige with tan, beige belt. Misses' sizes 10 to 18 included. 49.95

*Dior's fitted coat adaptation with high-placed crescent pockets, dropped shoulders, loose sleeves. Grey with red and white lining, navy with candy plaid, beige with beige, tan with tan or gold colour with gold colour. Misses' sizes 10 to 18 included. 49.95

Piguet's little cape adaptation with pastel collar, big round buttons. Navy with red lining. In Junior sizes 9 to 18. 25.00

STORE HOURS: 9 a.m. until 5 p.m. Saturday: 9 a.m. until 1 p.m.
Telephone Order Service opens at 8.45 a.m. Dial TR. 5111

T. EATON C<u>O</u> Limited

181

Of particular note was the high quality and cost of these Canadian-produced copies: "If originals are not cheap, neither are the copies or the first adaptions . . . that start at $80 for a dress and $125 for suits." Interestingly, she went on to note that the availability of styles was not controlled by the speed of the copyists but by Canadian acceptance of Paris designs. Most Canadian women preferred specially adapted garments to exact copies. When buying couture designs, Canadian manufacturers considered appropriateness more essential to sales than the rapid availability of industrially produced copies.[74]

The difference between European and North American taste was borne out in a poll taken in the late 1950s by the Chambre syndicale, asking American women what they thought of French clothes. The poll interviewed 504 women with an annual family income of $7,000 or over, of whom 204 were listed in the 1958 *Social Register*. The conclusion was that "a majority of both groups felt that Paris designed clothes, unmodified by American manufacturers, were usually too extreme for most women to wear."[75] Even at the most elite level, then, the local construct of taste was more significant than income or class when it came to consumption.

The need to comprehend and cater to local cultural ideas of taste was immediately recognized and acted on by Christian Dior–New York. When Dior established his New York collection, Anny Latour noted that he was "aware . . . that the French taste must not be too loud." "Baromètre," model 244 from his spring 1950 collection, is an example of a design that was too "French." Comments from the New York branch noted that the style was "not accepted here. Sold after publication in *Vogue*. Shown first with a skirt. Sold better without a skirt [i.e., as a dress]" (Table 2). This design sold only nineteen copies at a wholesale cost of $110, as it was considered too extreme and probably too fitted for North Americans. Substituting a one-piece dress for the skirt and top made the design more saleable and perhaps the fit more relaxed. Interestingly, a *Vogue* photograph by Irving Penn of this design is an iconic image of a Paris haute couture design, and as the Dior notations attest, did help to promote the style though it was clearly largely unwearable by North Americans despite being designed specifically for that market.[76]

Thus, having established a legitimate system within the haute couture industry for others to produce their designs, the Paris couturiers themselves began to diversify to capture the large numbers of affluent North American women eager to have Paris-inspired clothing.

Couture Licences, Boutique Lines, and *Prêt-à-Porter*

Newsweek estimated that in 1957, Paris haute couture houses had a profit margin of 2 to 7 percent on sales to private customers. On sales of the same model to a manufacturer the price and therefore the profit was approximately double. The manufacturer then reproduced the garment just as designed, without fittings or styling alterations, lowering the cost and raising the profit margin. In that year, a US$400 couture dress ordered by a private client could thus have realized a profit of about US$30 for the couture house but a much higher profit if ordered by a manufacturer.[77] Paradoxically, the same North American mass-manufacturing system that supported the couture industry also left couturiers struggling to maintain their exclusive tradition and wondering how they could tap into some of the profit that so many others were making on their designs.

Immediately after the war, therefore, Paris couturiers began to experiment with new ways to profit from the prestige of their names and designs. They created individual couturier boutiques, special licensing agreements with American and French manufacturers, and finally, *prêt-à-porter* collections.[78] Today we are very familiar with fashion designers licensing their names and celebrities endorsing products. Yet many European couturiers only began to market themselves beyond their couture collections in the postwar period. Paris haute couture houses began to diversify, and the number of designs produced outside the Couture-Création collection quickly grew, though it differed greatly from house to house. Nina Ricci and Jean Dessès had four labels each outside of Couture-Création, while Jacques Heim had five and Madeleine de Rauch three (figs. 5.29 to 5.31).[79]

One of the first non-haute couture lines to be established was often the boutique line. The couture boutique was well established by the 1920s. It was a shop attached to or inside the couture house that sold accessories designed by the house to complement the couture clothing collection. As early as 1949, Alison Settle reported that "Paris dress houses must increase their sales if they and the French textile trade are not to sink into financial trouble . . . The Paris designers are opening shops inside their grand premises, where simplified versions of their models are sold for half the price [of the couture collections] and made to measure at that" (fig. 5.32).[80] This created problems for the Chambre syndicale, however, and it tried to combat the natural assumption that there was hardly any difference between the Couture-Création

TABLE 2 **Notes on selected models from fall 1949 to spring 1950, Christian Dior-New York**

#525 **Manhattan**, fall 1949
$115.00 wholesale
Sold 203 models

    material $29.66
    making   <u>$36.76</u>
    cost price $66.42

Good dress. Complaints on the weight of the
fabric, clients bought it in a lighter fabric.
Complaints on the gussets. Many Reorders

#537 **Petit Duc**, fall 1949
$135.00 wholesale
Sold 183 models

    material $21.95
    making   <u>$51.12</u>
    cost price $73.07

Well made. Sold well. Many reorders.
Very good style for petite women.

#585 **Sargent**, fall 1949
$250.00 wholesale
Sold 46 models

    material $68.15
    making   <u>$54.21</u>
    cost price $122.36

Making very slow — fabulous dress.
Style sold very well.

Note: Photographs and notes on the making and reception of this new line were sent from the New York office to give the Paris office an understanding of the North American market. Model 711 also shown as fig. 7.30, pp. 290–1.
Source: All photographs courtesy of Christian Dior Archives, Paris. Text originally attached to the photographs.

#244 **Baromètre**, spring 1950
$149.75 wholesale
Sold 19 models

material	$23.74
making	$51.17
cost price	$74.91

Not accepted here. Sold after publication in *Vogue*.
Shown at first with skirt, sold better without skirt.

#290 **Pat**, spring 1950
$159.75 wholesale
Sold 262 models

fabric	$25.62
making	$57.13
cost	$82.75

Excellent suit. Many re-orders.

#762 **Life**, spring 1950
$175.00
Sold 104 models

piece goods	$44.55
trimmings	$26.00
labour	$56.21
	$101.02 [sic]

Making ok. Well liked.
Style is good and well liked.

#711 **Avenue Montaigne**, spring 1950
$110 wholesale
Sold 121

piece goods	$21.15
trims	$4.20
labour	$38.64
cost price	$63.99

OK to make. Style well liked.

griffe
grande collection

griffe
vêtements autre que
la grande collection
(petite collection et
vêtements d'origine éxtérieure)

Jean Dessès
AVENUE MATIGNON - 1, RUE RABELAIS
ARIS - VIII° - TÉL. BAL. 45-63

Bas Jean Dessès

Jean Dessès
"DIFFUSION" PARIS

and boutique lines, even though the couturiers were required to label all their collections clearly and were not permitted to use anything in the Couture-Création collection for any other lines.[81]

Though the concept of the boutique line was to sell designs that did not require the selection time, redesign, and fitting process of the Couture-Création collection, clients tended to expect the same perfection. The issue of fittings therefore became one of the most important points of distinction between a boutique garment and a Couture-Création one. A member of the Chambre syndicale committee for review of Couture-Création applications noted in 1952 that repetitions of boutique models were to be made without fittings and preferably without changes to the design. If fittings were an absolute requirement, they were billed at 10,000 francs each rather than being included in the price of the dress.[82] At Nina Ricci, a boutique garment was made for a client from measurements taken by a *vendeuse* and was made up by a *première*, or "first hand." The garment was then cut and sewn partly in the haute couture atelier and partly in a different part of the house, in an atelier not connected with the haute couture one. Making the dress within a physically different system

5.29 (opposite) Labels for the house of Jean Dessès registered in 1955 with the Chambre syndicale to differentiate not only the garments but also the categories of production, in order to keep Couture-Création designs distinct. They also show the beginnings of boutique and ready-to-wear lines. Document conservé au Centre historique des Archives nationales à Paris   **5.30** (left) This Lanvin/Castillo design for the house of Jeanne Lanvin, c.1958, bears a label for licence to Maria Carine, who manufactured the ready-to-wear designs. The suit was sold at Eaton's Ensemble Shop.   **5.31** (right) Jacques Heim Actualité label in dress and jacket ensemble. This diffusion label was founded in 1950 and aimed at a younger clientele then Couture-Création.

5.32 Lanvin/Castillo (left) and Heim (right and facing page) daytime ensembles, c.1958, made outside of the Couture-Création labels. The labels in figs. 5.30 and 5.31 are from these garments.

of production helped to differentiate it from an haute couture garment, a distinction further demarcated because the boutique premises had a different staff from the couture house. At Dior, all boutique models were made in-house. In spring 1952, eighty-two boutique models were designed. These were produced by a Dior staff of forty-six sewers operating out of three ateliers overseen by two *premières d'ateliers*. Dior permitted a maximum of one fitting for its boutique garments, in contrast to the minimum of three for a Couture-Création garment demanded by the Chambre syndicale regulations. Lanvin permitted neither fittings nor changes to its boutique garments, or else charged 10,000 francs per fitting.[83]

The comments of the 1955 Chambre syndicale jurors record some of the many problems they faced in applying the changing rules and regulations. The boutique collection was to be shown separately and after the couture collection, and to be sold only from the boutique premises. Jean Dessès, for example, was typical in having its boutique situated on the ground floor of the couture house. But by the late 1950s, the couture houses were exporting their boutique lines to North American department stores and specialty shops.[84]

In North America, boutique collections and other new lines were quickly exploited, supplanting sales of the original couture models. As early as 1950, Creeds advertised garments from Jacques Heim's Jeunes Filles collection, while by fall 1957, Eaton's noted that it had bought the largest selection of European boutique clothes in its history. At the fashion show for this season, Dora Matthews explained that boutique clothes were "more suited to Canadian figures [than haute couture garments] . . . and were all more wearable and more reasonably priced at around $200–300," thereby implying that these designs were in fact as good as Couture-Création originals, if not superior, though in effect they were the couturiers' own knock-offs inspired by the couture line.[85] Other European couturiers were quick to follow the Paris lead. In 1951, Morgan's carried Hardy Amies boutique clothes, and in 1954, Holt Renfrew obtained an exclusive licence for the Elizabeth James of Cork boutique line (fig. 5.33).[86] Canadian buyers bought boutique garments because they had the association with and glamour of the couture collection for a lower cost, and customers preferred the less extravagant designs.

The term "haute couture" was further eroded in the late 1950s by the explosion of *prêt-à-porter* manufacture, making notions of couture exclusivity even more

Erin's Fashion Invasion
has come to the fore!

And HOLT RENFREW have captured
the smart boutique fashions by

Elizabeth James of Cork

the young designer who is the latest one to join the Irish
Couture . . her distinctive flair and witty approach to
fashion are shown in the stunning coats, ensembles and
suits of the traditional Irish tweeds and homespuns;
also Irish linen dresses and suits . . that you'll find

<u>In Canada only at</u>

HOLT RENFREW

problematic. Several European couturiers took direct advantage of the mass-manufacturing strength of the American garment industry, as well as the large pool of potential customers within the North American population. Dior was one of the first to do so on a large scale with his New York line, but the arrangement was unusual as the Dior business was totally controlled by the Paris house.

Deals were made outside the North American market as well. When the Christian Dior–London collection was being planned, it was announced that the line would sell for "around one-fifth of what Dior clothes cost in Paris, but there they are individually fitted; here fit must depend on alteration hands to recast the intricate clothes for those of stock size." Yet at the cocktail party held "in the great designer's honour" after the launch of the first collection at Harrods, Alison Settle could not distinguish the Paris-made clothes from the London-made ones, as the "elegant guests were so shapely that the dress fit them or they had found perfect alteration hands to produce correct fit."[87]

New types of arrangement were experimented with, such as the one Jacques Fath made with 7th Avenue manufacturer Joseph Halpert. Fath's first American line in fall 1948 was reproduced in the thousands. In the course of two years his

5.33 Holt Renfrew advertisement for the exclusive sale of the Elizabeth James of Cork boutique line, March 1954. She specialized in day suits, coats, dresses, and jackets made from Irish handwoven wools and linens. Cotton linings, often diamond patterned, were a James trademark, as she believed that comfort came first: "If one dressed to please men one would wear satin . . . Well, one can't do that, can one?"

a
Jacques Fath
design for
Joseph Halpert
only
at
Morgan's

Morgan's
MONTREAL
TORONTO
OTTAWA

overall turnover trebled, and more than half of the total was attributed to the American business.[88] In Canada, Morgan's sold "Jacques Fath for Joseph Halpert" garments in its stores in Montreal, Ottawa, and Toronto (fig. 5.34). Other such arrangements included Jean Dessès' first American collection of at-home lounge wear, for Raymond of New York, which was imported by Simpson's in 1951. Pierre Balmain produced his first American collection, Balmain–New York, in spring 1952, followed by a less restrained fall collection, and both were carried by Simpson's.[89]

Having seen the profits reaped by North American manufacturers and stores from Paris couturier-based designs, the French tried to implement a system that would bring profit locally.[90] French ready-to-wear manufacturers and stores were the last to see the Paris haute couture collections, several weeks after the North Americans and Europeans, and for years had seen others copying and profiting from the Paris designs. In 1944, it was noted that models were reproduced and disseminated abroad and that foreigners knew "la mode de Paris" before the French dressmaking industry. Even before the war, American dress manufacturers had captured not only the North American market but also the South American, and the Austrians had done the same in central Europe. The sous-directeur du vêtement of the Ministère de la Production Industrielle suggested that several French manufacturers — who had been left "looking through the keyhole" — pay a fee to see a special showing of the collections to use as inspiration for their own ready-to-wear, though not to reproduce the models.[91]

5.34 Jacques Fath ready-to-wear design for the American manufacturer Joseph Halpert, sold by Morgan's, March 1952.

In 1950, the couturiers made an attempt to deal with this complicated situation. Jacques Fath, Piguet, Paquin, Jean Dessès, and Carven established a label together, "Couturiers Associés," to reproduce and sell their designs to French stores. Each designer submitted seven *toiles* for any combination of dresses, suits, and coats. Each design carried the association label as well as that of the individual couturier who had designed it.[92] The collection was sold to leading high-end stores in eighty French cities that were prohibited from reproducing Paris originals. In addition, the designs were presented in six towns in North Africa, twelve in England, fifteen in Belgium, and five in Switzerland.[93] The designs were also sold in London by Peter Jones department store, but there the clothes were made in British workrooms to avoid duty. The UK/Paris collection was considered comparable to the best British copies of Paris designs.[94] This initiative lasted only until 1953, however, as France did not yet have adequate distribution and marketing systems to sustain and profit from this type of high-end ready-to-wear. As well, because the models had to be produced as designed, the collection could not meet the tastes of such a wide variety of clients, even though the selection of fabrics was left open.[95]

In the late 1950s, Paris couturiers began to produce their own *prêt-à-porter* lines, adding yet another layer to the already complex couture-inspired market.[96] As Alison Settle explained, "French wholesalers had to get their ideas from somewhere . . . so why, they asked, should couture not take a share in mass-producing its own ideas instead of merely having them freely copied?" Some couturiers formed a joint collection called Prêt-à-Porter Création. Clothes in this collection contained the individual couturiers' labels, but the garments were made up by professional wholesalers who "rigidly control[led] themselves on the amount of fabric used in order to keep production costs to figures that the important [US] dollar market, above all, [was] prepared to pay."[97] High-end French manufacturers Maria Carine and C. Mendès produced the collection.[98]

This new couture-based product required an explanation for Canadian readers of *Mayfair* in November 1957: "Fashion-conscious women . . . are now in the position of being able to buy French couturier designs at ready-to-wear prices. This seemingly contradictory circumstance is the result of a venture into fashionable mass production . . . In addition to their couture showings . . . designers are producing Prêt-à-Porter collections . . . These collections offer variations on the current themes with designs that have been simplified for the more impersonal process of French mass production. Prices are a fraction of the cost of a couture original even though the garments boast couturier labels." Iona Monahan noted that Canadian stores had already purchased "in great quantity" and concluded that "while no threat to Haute Couture — [the garments] are nonetheless putting satisfaction within easy reach of every woman who yearns to wear a Paris label."[99]

The problem for Toronto retailers was a familiar one of trying to have different stock from their competitors, so the race for exclusivity on these designs began. Creeds obtained a Toronto exclusive on Pierre Cardin's Jeunesse collection in 1959 and in the same year signed an exclusive for Cardin's *prêt-à-porter* collection, made by the French manufacturer Vaskene SA. This was labelled "Pierre Cardin–Paris" and marked the first time a Paris couturier had clearly put his own name on a ready-to-wear label.[100] By the late 1950s, *prêt-à-porter* had overtaken the importation of original haute couture models, as it was more affordable and conservatively styled but kept a strong affiliation with haute couture collections.

Geraldine Stutz, the buyer for Henri Bendel in New York, remarked on the increased difficulty in obtaining exclusive couture and in 1958 began to buy European ready-to-wear instead: "Until then we could go to Paris and find some sneaky little numbers that nobody else was buying. Other stores would buy the obvious big number, the Fords . . . There was something left over for us — the style with more subtle appeal . . . Then one day we came back and found that everybody else had ordered the sneaky little numbers too. And that was it. No more couture."[101]

Second-Hand Couture

Just as copies and adaptations expanded the numbers of those who could afford couture-inspired clothing, so too did the second-hand trade. The active market for used couture demonstrates that even after the garments had been well worn and discarded by their original owners, they still retained economic, sartorial, and social value in a second life with new owners.[102]

The Sources

"Gently used" couture and other expensive clothing had an important second market based on consumer values of style, condition, and designer rather than the age or season of the couture piece. In 1956, second-hand shops were estimated to be worth $500,000 annually in Canada.[103]

The second-hand couture clothing market in Toronto during the 1950s comprised three stores run by charities and five run privately. The two most significant were the Opportunity Shop on Mount Pleasant and The Clothes Horse on St Clair Avenue, which became the 139 Shoppe.[104] The Junior League, a North American women's volunteer organization, ran the Opportunity Shop, while the 139 Shoppe was privately run. In addition, annual events such as the Hadassah Bazaar and the Toronto Symphony Orchestra (TSO) Rummage Sale were important occasions for giving away and acquiring couture.

The Opportunity Shop was well known for being a good and steady source of better quality clothing, donated primarily by its elite members. The Toronto shop opened in 1928 as a method of raising money for the Junior League.[105] By the late 1950s, it was the largest League shop on the continent and was staffed by 105 volunteers a week. Each League member was required to put in a half day every year, and the strong Toronto membership put in 12,000 volunteer hours annually. In order to secure a continual supply of merchandise, donations to the shop were incorporated into the rules of membership in the League. An active member in 1957 was obliged to donate $20 worth of goods annually and a provisional member $15 worth. Interestingly, the Toronto branch had one of the lowest quotas in Canada, though the average contribution for 1956–7 was valued between $30 and $100. Presumably a high quota was not needed, as members gave quite freely. By 1960, the average donation was $58.55. Though a wide range of clothing merchandise was donated, it was a recurring problem to get enough clothing in large sizes. Another was to keep supplies of "our less appealing stock" for new immigrants who were shopping for themselves or relatives abroad. Unsaleable merchandise was given to Crippled Civilians and the Salvation Army. By Junior League standards, Toronto's Opportunity Shop was a big success. It made the top profit of all the shops in the League for 1956–7 — $27,000 — followed by Atlanta, Kansas City, and San Francisco. By the end of the 1950s, the shop's annual profit was approximately $30,000.[106]

The selling area for couture in the shop was the Next-to-New department, which opened in 1949. Here, the donor received a percentage of the sale price — 60 percent in 1957.[107] All merchandise in this area had to be dry cleaned before donation, and if the garment had not sold within six weeks it could be picked up or given over to the main shop with its value credited to the member's quota. In order to build up the Next-to-New department, members were encouraged to add friends' names to the mailing list.[108]

The success of this part of the shop is reflected in a 1960 telephone survey that reported 60 percent of its members selling their used high-end clothing through the Next-to-New department.[109] It is very difficult to find out who bought the clothes, as customer names were not recorded. One freely confessed client is the late Toronto clothing collector Alan Suddon. Some of his garments illustrate the type of merchandise to be found, such as a lace evening dress by Maggy Rouff and a yellow corduroy afternoon dress by Toronto's leading couturier, Cornelia, which was made for Mrs Signy Eaton. Another Cornelia design, a silk taffeta cocktail dress, was sold through the shop as well.[110] Mrs Eaton made it clear during an interview that she only donated her clothes, never sold them, so perhaps the corduroy dress was sold in this prestigious area without the usual donor percentage.[111]

The Junior League had the support of Canadian department stores. When the Opportunity Shop moved to Yonge Street in 1948, Eaton's provided the decorations for the new premises without charge while Simpson's supplied price tags and contributed donations during the year (fig. 5.35). This charitable assistance for women's volunteer groups was in keeping with the large Toronto retailers' practice of donating fashion show tickets for fundraising events. Stores' support of their elite customers was of mutual benefit, as these women were their most socially important clients.

In contrast to the volunteer-run Opportunity Shop, whose profits were directed to local charity work, the 139 Shoppe evolved into a sustained and substantial private enterprise, typical of high-quality consignment shops in other large North American cities. It was founded in the fall of 1950 by Vera Morrison, and her granddaughter recounted the story: "Her second husband, Dave Sykes, was a stockbroker and established in the upper echelons of Toronto society. They were members of The Granite Club, etcetera. As Mrs Sykes, she and her friend, Rose Calder, who also . . . lived in Rosedale, opened a consignment shop, The Clothes Horse on St Clair Avenue West. The idea was for the store to keep 10 percent and the client 90 percent . . . They didn't need the money. It was really to obtain pin money and to clear their closets in order to be able to refill them."[112]

Vera Morrison and her friend started their business with clothes from friends, and soon it became very successful. Before long Rose Calder backed out, no longer interested in working in an increasingly demanding business. In 1954–5, Mrs Morrison bought a two-storey late-nineteenth-century townhouse in downtown Toronto and changed the name of the store to 139 Shoppe because it was at 139 Cumberland Avenue. Business continued to prosper.[113]

Today's owner, granddaughter Norma King-Wilson, believes that the success of the shop was because "it was one of the first upscale second-hand shops, and

5.35 The Opportunity Shop in 1948, decorated with the help of Eaton's and Simpson's for the Junior League of Toronto.

before that there was only the Salvation Army." Vera Morrison priced the garments based on the original cost but also took into account the condition and style. Clothes that were out of style or too well worn were not accepted, and Mrs Morrison estimated that she took in only half of what she was offered. Another condition was that the garments had to be clean: "We try to make it clear that this is not a rummage shop and tactfully suggest that clothing that does not meet our standards might go to charity."[114] The 139 Shoppe staff consisted of a manager, a bookkeeper, and an average of five saleswomen, who were paid a salary. Mrs Morrison never wanted to pay her saleswomen on commission as she thought that it would cause problems among them and did not want bickering over clients. The sales staff were usually women in their fifties or sixties who wanted some extra money but did not necessarily need to support themselves. They were therefore in a similar social group to their suppliers, and often to the customers as well.

Bookkeeping procedures at the shop continue today in the way that they were established in the 1950s. The name of the person who has consigned goods is entered on a card and given a number, and the merchandise and transactions are recorded. Early ledgers read as a list of names and addresses of Toronto's elite. Most lived in the prestigious residential areas of Rosedale and Forest Hill.[115]

Assigning a value to garments was a delicate process, as Vera Morrison noted: "One big problem is the tendency for the owner to be 'overgenerous' in remembering the cost of the garment." The sale price of the garment was designed to give the owner approximately one-quarter of the original price after the store had received its 10 percent, though there was a ceiling of $95 return on all garments accepted. The most expensive garments were therefore sold at a greater loss to the original owner and at a higher profit for the store. If a garment did not sell, the owner was informed and a new price suggested. If it was still unsold after ninety days and the owner did not want it back, it was passed on to charity. On average, a regular supplier to the 139 Shoppe made $400 to $500 annually on her wardrobe. This equalled the cost of one or two new couture ensembles, but Mrs Morrison pointed out that the money was generally "turned over to charity."[116] It has not been possible to determine whether this was indeed the case. It is also difficult to obtain prices, as the store ledgers are private, but other documents show that second-hand couture was a real bargain (Appendix B).

One of the keys to the success of the 139 Shoppe was knowing who had owned a garment, in order to avoid embarrassment for a customer attending a function at which the first owner of her dress was present. To ensure that this did not happen, Mrs Morrison would occasionally tell a customer the name of the person who had consigned the garment. This sort of discreet information had also been given in the late 1930s by a gentleman who ran a dress rental business in Toronto. He would tell his clients not only who had worn the dress before but also to what event. As Ms King-Wilson said, "People who sell it don't care where it goes . . . but for the people buying it, it's fairly critical."[117]

An inversion of this problem occurred at the Opportunity Shop in 1958, when a "chic dress" was put in the window priced at $19.95. A woman passing by saw it but had just bought the same dress downtown for $59.95 and "had planned her whole spring wardrobe around it." She did not want her friends to think she had bought it second-hand, but there was nothing the Junior Leaguers could do. They were, in fact, pleased to carry such up-to-date stock.[118]

The Next-to-New department of the Opportunity Shop, with its charity focus, and the 139 Shoppe, a private business, were in direct competition with each other for clothes from the same sources. The annual TSO Rummage Sale and the Hadassah Bazaar were also in the running for this merchandise.

The TSO Rummage Sale began in 1950 as a fair held at Sproat's farm on Bayview Avenue in North Toronto, and the profit, $6,800, was considered encouraging enough to repeat the event the next year. In 1952 and 1953, the sale was held at Varsity Arena, at the University of Toronto. By 1953, the event was so successful that the crowds attending stopped traffic on Bloor Street, and the police asked the volunteers to move to a larger venue. Accordingly, the 1954 sale was held at the enormous Horticultural Building at the Canadian National Exhibition (CNE) grounds, and was even more successful (fig. 5.36). At this sale, "Mrs Kenneth Carter [one of the organizers] made the discovery that the second-hand clothing, hats, books and treasures sold first."[119] The sale was so large that the committee used an empty apartment on Yonge Street for sorting and pricing the merchandise.

By 1957, the committee was concerned about its ability to obtain enough merchandise. One committee member said "It's horrifying to have crowds in great quantities and not to have rummage in equal quantities."[120] But the volume became

so large that a "year to collect, a week to price, and a day to sell" became the arrangement. As the size of the TSO women's committee grew, and with it the various subcommittees, the rummage sale acted as a unifying project for everyone.[121] The financial success of the rummage sale increased annually and was a substantial support for the orchestra (Table 3).

The TSO sale was recognized as part of the spring Toronto season, and it was known for generating a great many second-hand couture sales. Alan Suddon worked for the Metro Toronto Reference Library and was first sent to the rummage sale in 1957 to buy second-hand books for the library collection. It was here that he began what became the Alan and Mary Suddon Collection. He was struck by the quality of clothing for sale and made his first purchases for his wife to wear as costumes. The range of couture designers and styles he bought over the years documents the type of couture worn by Torontonians who donated to the cause. Annually, he lined up to get into the sale and paid $10 to $60 per garment. The collection includes a Canadian couture ball gown of pink silk satin designed by John Artibello, given by best-dressed list socialite Dorothy Boylen; European couture by Balenciaga, including a black wool day dress, a purple wool day coat, and a white brocade evening coat; a black net evening dress and a black silk knit cocktail dress by Pierre Balmain;

5.36 Toronto socialites and volunteers preparing for the Toronto Symphony Orchestra Rummage Sale at the Canadian National Exhibition, 1957.

TABLE 3   **Toronto Symphony Orchestra rummage sale profits 1950–63**

Year	Profit $	Year	Profit $	Year	Profit $
1950	6,800	1955	13,240	1960	23,000
1951	7,257	1956	15,993	1961	20,350
1952	7,144	1957	19,090	1962	25,394
1953	10,500	1958	17,000	1963	26,856
1954	12,000	1959	18,255		

Source: Toronto Symphony Women's Committee, *The Toronto Symphony Women's Committee, 1923–1983* (Toronto: Toronto Symphony Women's Committee, 1984), 48.

a Pierre Cardin cocktail dress; a printed chiffon evening dress by Jean Dessès; a Christian Dior silk organdy evening dress, also given by Mrs Boylen; and a late 1940s Paquin evening dress.[122]

The other large annual second-hand sale, the Hadassah Women's International Zionist Organization (WIZO) Bazaar, was held in the fall (fig. 5.37). Toronto Hadassah was begun by ten women in 1917 and by 1959 had over 3,000 members in sixty-five chapters in the Toronto area. The bazaar was the major fundraising event of the year for the organization, and raised $72,000 in 1955. It was another source for second-hand couture clothing and good ready-to-wear.[123]

An interesting aspect of all these charity sales is that the socially elite women who belonged to the organizations also acted as volunteer saleswomen for their bazaars and shops. As customers themselves, they received the best sales attention in the downtown boutiques and specialty rooms of the city, expecting to find, as one contemporary author noted, sales staff who behaved as if "the customer is your guest."[124] Volunteers then emulated the consumption system they patronized by imitating the kind of events and service they expected and received themselves. The ideal Opportunity Shop volunteer was described as follows: "She has an instinctive fondness for 'playing shop' . . . She dignifies each sale with seriousness and with interest, offers praise that is not so effusive that it is unconvincing . . . She is quick

the Woman's Globe and Mail

TORONTO, THURSDAY, OCTOBER 20, 1960

M. V. Kaufman often does her telephoning sitting on the floor as she allocates space on her big plan of the Automotive Building.

Big Bazaar

The giant Hadassah Bazaar held every year on the last Wednesday in October at the Automotive Building is a multi-ringed circus. From the end of one bazaar till the last few days of tying up loose ends for the new one, committee members are on call and continually busy.

—Photos by John Boyd

The Hobby Shop booth gives a wide margin for imagination and Mrs. A. B Clavir (left) and Mrs. Ralph Winberg discuss display items.

Mrs. A. A. Epstein, the general convener, is the focal point for telephone calls from all sides. Answering two at once is common.

...sh cooking is a bazaar specialty, but that takes organization, too. Mrs. Joseph C. Gold combines the two activities.

Mrs. Mark Gross has son Jeffery on her lap while she takes a message concerning her job as publicity chairman.

M. A. Sadowski (left) and Mrs. L. J. Simpson, conveners for the auction ...le, are combining making telephone calls and classifying their stock

There are no office hours for bazaar conveners. Mrs. J. M. Bergman, in charge of commercial display space, gets calls at all hours.

Past chairmen are never allowed to retire. Here Mrs. W. B. Herman, Mrs William Gold and Mrs. Frank Wilson discuss the fashion show.

to adjust from one customer to another."[125] This description clearly identifies the volunteer as role playing. That she "plays shop" connotes that the duty is a short-term activity that will not lower her social status. Nevertheless, the job is then described as having a seriousness designed to create a neutral, respectful attitude toward the customer who, we can infer, might well not share the same value system and class as that of the volunteer. The Opportunity Shop also adopted competition between shifts as a retailing strategy to increase incentive in its volunteers.[126]

Charity imitation of retail consumption and marketing patterns extended to putting on the ubiquitous fashion show in order to boost sales. The 1950 Hadassah Bazaar, for example, held a fashion show featuring dresses given by a local boutique, Simon Ramm, and modelled by Hadassah members. At the Opportunity Shop, it was noted that the clothes tended to sell better if they were modelled: "It's amazing . . . how quickly we can sell a number that has been gathering dust, as soon as someone puts it on and models it" (fig. 5.38) This success led to semi-regular fashion shows and teas that highlighted the better garments.[127] The business of volunteering and running a shop or special event sale was thus treated as a serious commercial undertaking, complete with competition from other women's groups operating in the same Toronto marketplace.

In fact, the contrast between the volunteer-run and commercially run second-hand shops for high-quality clothing was minimal. The saleswomen for both types of shop were from upper-middle-class or upper-class backgrounds, and in both, diplomacy and tact were key to the delicate business of resale.

The Sociocultural Role of Second-Hand Couture

The clientele for second-hand couture was broad, and differed little between the shops and the charity bazaars. Research indicates that women of all socio-economic backgrounds would buy second-hand couture if they saw something they liked. Mrs Morrison said of the 139 Shoppe, "Our store is for the customer who wants to build her wardrobe intelligently . . . We are in the business to satisfy the woman who wants the world's truly beautiful clothing at a price within her range."[128]

The young working woman was an important customer. In 1951, the Opportunity Shop stayed open late on Monday and Wednesday evenings "to give business

5.37 Members of the Toronto Hadassah committee plan for the 1960 bazaar.

girls a chance to replenish their wardrobe in the Next-to-New department."[129] Business women could buy good-quality garments at a very affordable price. One was Barbara McNabb, who also bought bonded models. She was pleased to shop at the 139 Shoppe, which she described as "one very useful fund-extender . . . the first shop offering couture clothes on consignment from first owners." To augment her purchased clothing further, she also made some of her own wardrobe from French *Vogue* couturier patterns.[130]

Society women were customers as well, and not only sold their own used couture but also bought second-hand for their daughters and sometimes themselves. Harriet "Sis" Bunting Weld has a dress her mother purchased at the Symphony

5.38 Junior League members modelling clothing for sale in the Opportunity Shop, February 1951.

rummage sale. It was originally a formal court presentation dress with a train and is made from a pale silk brocaded with pearls and gold thread. The rich material and fine finishing suggest a very good dressmaker. Mrs Bunting had the train removed, making the dress appropriate for evening.[131] By altering it she also made it into her own garment, and because it was a presentation dress it had probably been worn only once, far less than the many bonded models that had undergone a rigorous first life before they were sold in Toronto.

Giving away good clothing was a tradition among the wealthy based on the status and economic value of cloth and clothing. High-quality clothing has, historically, been bequeathed, passed on to servants, and remade. The ethos of recycling clothing was more pronounced during the war and immediately postwar, even though North American women did not suffer the wartime shortages encountered in Europe. In 1947, the continued need in Europe for clothing was recognized by *Harper's Bazaar*. The magazine ran an article listing US and international organizations that wanted clothing, but added that "old party finery, [and] women's narrow shoes" were not considered useful. Velga Jansons, a Latvian Displaced Person who came to Canada after the war, recalled getting very good clothes from the United States when she was in a German camp. Out of one man's houndstooth coat she made a two-piece suit for herself, with a blouse made from a silk slip she dyed green.[132]

Yet for socialites, a stigma was attached to profiting intentionally from the sale of one's wardrobe. An inherent conflict lay in the fact that volunteer associations solicited goods for their charities, but a volunteer-run store such as the Opportunity Shop would reward the donation with a percentage of the realized price. A socialite might therefore profit from her charitable act, but could not be seen to do so on purpose. Despite this coyness, the commercial 139 Shoppe was also very successful, though those interviewed rarely said they sold or shopped there. It must be remembered, however, that the shop could acquire clothes from a broader constituency than could the old Toronto establishment of the Junior League, whose membership was strictly vetted. As Ms King-Wilson said, "Everybody forgets about coming here but they all know it."[133] Many of those interviewed said that they gave away clothing to charity functions or servants, yet few admitted to selling through, or shopping, at the 139 Shoppe. For socialites, selling pieces rather than donating them was seen as mercenary and ran contrary to the "Lady Bountiful" image.

Mrs Morrison did comment on receiving "mistakes," perhaps a dress bought on a shopping spree in New York that the consumer later "detest[ed] in the clear Toronto dawn." Clothes that had been badly or unsuccessfully altered were another kind of "mistake." One example is a badly altered, unworn wool Dior suit that originally cost $250, sold for $79 in a second-hand shop, and was then realtered for $15 into a successful model for the second owner.[134]

As opposed to selling clothing through commercial outlets, donating clothing to charitable causes served several functions. It was a way of letting your peers know that you were contributing to the community. Those peers handled the goods as volunteer saleswomen and could possibly recognize the garments from having attended the events where they had been worn. Donating couture also signalled socio-economic status that was clearly read by social peers through the dress labels, fabrics, and workmanship. To be able to give was also proof of financial and social security as it implied that replenishment of the wardrobe was ongoing. As well, importantly, giving away couture that was no longer useful or appropriate validated the initial purchase, as the garments went on to retain value in a second life.

For buyers of second-hand couture, the resale price was only a part of its value. Wearing these clothes raised their status. There was no stigma attached to the practice, as couture was understood to be of good design and quality. Notions of appropriateness and value were already certified for the new consumer because the garments came from Toronto's social elite, who were national role models for taste and etiquette. Second-hand couture was therefore equated with taste that was beyond reproach.

6   THE VALUE OF COUTURE

The basic wardrobe has a theme which often carries through from year to year . . . Such long-range planning means that you can buy better quality, for the investment is to be spread over more than one season. Amy Vanderbilt, 1954

The economic significance of haute couture from the perspective of the consumer is not easy to assess. Indeed, it has scarcely been addressed before. Such an omission perpetuates the myth that each couture garment is "priceless" and "a work of art," an attitude fully endorsed by the couture houses. They welcome design research and are willing to provide generalities about the systems of sales, the relationship between *vendeuse* and client, and their fashion shows. Questions about prices and costs, however, are another matter. They are met with the implicit response that discussing the monetary value of couture is to demean the artistic value not only of the individual piece but also of the couture system itself, and that such enquiry demonstrates ignorance of the "true" value of couture — the æsthetic.

The absence of advertised prices has helped to build up a fiction, placing couture fashions in a rarefied realm of goods beyond economic measure and making it difficult to document the sums paid by private clients, store buyers, and manufacturers. Asking clients or *vendeuses* about the price of their clothes is to cross beyond the bounds of couture etiquette. Interviewees claimed loss of memory and implied that the question was insignificant. Even when they did recall prices, these cannot be assumed to be accurate forty years after the original purchase. This elusive attitude is part of a social barrier erected around the couture system as a whole, whereby the relationship between the couture house and client is carefully guarded and a new consumer has to be vetted and then initiated into the exclusive circle of couture connoisseurship.

Secrecy about couture prices is reflected in Eaton's fashion show programs. Eaton's began listing the prices for most garments in its fall 1953 fashion presentation but never showed prices for the most expensive merchandise — imported couture models. If a prospective client was interested in knowing the price of a garment featured in the show, a saleswoman was available afterward to answer questions. As the couture import had been used in the fashion show, however, it would be sold at a reduced cost. In this context, its full retail price never really existed. The design was purchased for the fashion show from the outset with the knowledge that it could not be sold for full price and would be a financial loss to the store.[1]

Given the difficulty of obtaining prices from the design houses, I gleaned most retail prices from local newspaper advertisements, many of them placed during sales periods. These were particularly useful in that the discounted price was often promoted by listing the full retail price. Yet the great variation in advertised prices demonstrates one of the problems of defining couture clothing. In the strictest sense, haute couture includes only garments produced by the members of the Chambre syndicale, who were all based in Paris. One might then broaden the definition to include members of the Incorporated Society of London Fashion Designers, in addition to a few other internationally recognized figures such as Italians Simonetta and Fabiani. Typically, though, Toronto merchants advertised all expensive imported clothing together, including original couture models, thus implying a superior design and quality for all their merchandise. As goods from American manufacturers were sometimes considered imported as well, it is often impossible to know exactly what was being marketed unless the advertisement clearly specified the designers or depicted the garments (Appendices C and D).

European couture models were always the most expensive garments. The acceptable price range for couture and other expensive clothes was set within an international and local context, and Toronto retailers understood and supported this norm. They purchased only small numbers of Paris haute couture models, as designs from other nationalities were less expensive, less extreme in design, and generally more marketable. Further, the rapid postwar growth of international boutique and couture licences made it unnecessary to rely solely on the most exclusive levels of haute couture.

Expense is of course only one aspect of the value of the garments. To understand the context in which the purchase was evaluated, it is also important to appraise couture in terms of the more powerful and ephemeral sociocultural values placed on it by the consumer herself. High-quality material, workmanship, and design were essential for a purchase to be considered a good investment (fig. 6.1). These traits were inherent in an haute couture dress, as the standards were regulated by the Chambre syndicale. Quality also assured longevity, as good fabrics and construction helped the garment to hold its shape with continued wear, while hand and fine workmanship justified the expense by adding value to the piece. Quality materials and workmanship also helped to enhance a mature figure. Women wanted a design that was fashionable, flattering, and suitable for the occasion, and couture carried the assurance of all three.

It is clear from interviews with consumers and saleswomen that a couture purchase was very carefully considered. A garment was assessed in terms of its etiquette coding and its conformity to the rest of the wardrobe. What Torontonians were *willing* to spend, as opposed to what they could afford, on any given couture piece was influenced by several factors: the quality of materials and fabrication; the national origins of the design, French being the most desirable; the type of garment, for day or evening; how it fitted within the existing wardrobe; and the requirements of the social season.

The Price of Couture

Couture, or high-end couture-inspired clothing, was not affordable for the majority of Torontonians. The purchase of an imported couture coat at an average cost of $95 to $195 — or even a low-end couture-inspired import at $40 to $95 — constituted a sizeable portion of the family income. Spending at this level was not possible for most Toronto families, whose average monthly income was $221.08 in 1951 and $360.83 in 1961.[2] The wealthiest Torontonians' incomes were at least two or three times higher, but even a wealthy society woman's wardrobe was rarely composed exclusively of couture purchased at full price.[3] Torontonian taste in couture fell into two categories influenced by price: couture purchased at full price; and bonded, sale, or couture copies. In the first category, consumption was very carefully controlled by the couture system and the consumer. In the second category, consumption was not as constrained by the requirements of the wardrobe, as costs were interpreted within a different value system.

6.1 A lavish Lanvin/Castillo strapless ball gown with short cape of silk satin beaded with sequins, pearls, and metallic threads, c.1954, demonstrates the high quality of materials and workmanship expected in haute couture design.

The purchase of full-price couture was controlled by the *vendeuse*, the Canadian buyers, and by the consumer's sense of value, coloured by both personal and national taste. International consensus about the value of couture merchandise was predicated on the quality of fabric, fit, good workmanship, modern design, suitability for different social occasions, price, and national cultural characteristics. All these factors were tempered by "need," itself mitigated by "taste." It is important to realize that women were willing to spend but would have compared the cost of a specific garment to prices for other available couture merchandise. That the couture market was competitive should come as no surprise, yet it has not been presented in this manner, probably because each couture design is marketed as unique and therefore without rival.

Purchases were typically staggered over several seasons. In one season during 1960, for example, a woman might buy a single ball gown at $300, a suit at $200, and a cocktail dress at $200, spending a total of $700 with no allowance for items such as co-ordinating accessories, or staples such as underwear, or clothing for other family members.[4] These clothes would be bought to fit in with garments she already owned. Given that the highest annual family incomes in Toronto in the period were $10,000 and up, this type of expenditure twice a year, spring and fall, would have equalled as much as 14 percent of the family income, on couture alone. This estimate is validated by Elizabeth Bryce, who believed that she spent about $1,000 a season.[5]

The Lachasse house records are an exceptional reference for couture research and provide a rare window into the consumption habits of clients. Lachasse during the 1950s was considered a good-quality British couture house, producing conventional, well-made clothing and particularly recognized for its tailoring. The records show that a Canadian, Mrs Plow of Halifax, spent approximately $630 in the spring of 1959, on two suits and one dress with a jacket.[6] Compared to her purchases in other seasons, this was a larger expenditure than usual. The patronage by Torontonian Mrs Arthur Milner was similar at the same design house. In 1957, she bought a green checked coat and green tweed suit, probably co-ordinating, that cost her approximately $450. This was most likely her 1957 seasonal addition to her day and afternoon wardrobe. If she did purchase any evening wear, it was from another house or store (Appendix E).

The figure of approximately $1,000 a season is only a very conservative estimate, and it is likely that further outlay would go to boutique models, copies, sale models, bonded models, and dressmakers' clothes. Taking all these into account, it is not inappropriate to estimate that 10 to 20 percent of the family income might go to a woman's wardrobe. Investment in couture and couture-like clothing greatly enhanced or helped to maintain a family's social status, practically guaranteeing social involvement in community activities and sustaining women's key roles as professional volunteers for cultural and social causes.

The expanding social season and larger number of people participating in it increased the demand among Toronto women for quality clothing. The need was met by bonded and sale models as well as couture copies.[7] Sale and bonded garments allowed for "perks." Women could purchase more lavish designs than they might when garments were intended to complete a wardrobe. The timing of sales corresponded to upcoming events in the social season, some of the most important of which took place in October and November. The Artillery Ball, in November, served as a debutante coming-out ball, and was closely followed by the Royal Winter Fair, which was a social highlight with its evening horse show. The fundraising Crèche Ball and the 48th Highlanders Ball were also socially significant.[8]

For some Torontonians, a couture wardrobe could be constituted almost entirely of bonded models or sale merchandise. In October 1953, Creeds advertised a sale of one-third to one-half off "original continental models" originally priced from $195 to $325, and in 1955 Simpson's advertised a dispersal sale of its fall fashion show merchandise. The sale included French and British models originally costing $375 to $1,200, now priced at $195 to $295, by designers such as Givenchy, Dessès, Balenciaga, Nina Ricci, and Michael Sherard of London. In November 1956, Holt's advertised the sale of bonded models in the following manner: "Holt Renfrew announcing the annual exclusive collection of ORIGINAL MODELS . . . by 16 of the leading couturier's of Paris, London and Rome . . . Need we say more . . . women . . . know what a presentation of this kind means so early in the season!" A November 1950 Creeds advertisement suggested that bonded models were available by announcing "a spectacular opportunity" of imported originals at half price or less. Such advertisements implied the sale of bonded models while retaining the exclusive image of the merchandise.[9]

The range of couture prices, from custom-made originals to bonded models and second-hand garments, resulted in a wide distribution of actual couture. Prices for individual couture garments were relatively stable between 1950 and 1960, probably due to the increased availability of copies and boutique items. It was therefore unnecessary to increase expenditures on individual items, and in the mid-1950s it was noted that Canadian women were "inclined to spend less on individual garments than did their sisters twenty years ago," but that they purchased more pieces of clothing.[10]

Designer Status, National Identity, and Value

In September 1955, Creeds advertised a Paris haute couture coat, day suits, afternoon dresses, and cocktail wear priced from $195 to $275 (fig. 6.2). The advertised models were from the houses of Rouff, Heim, and Raphael, none of them as renowned and expensive as Balenciaga, Dior, Fath, and Balmain. The advertisement not only includes several garment types but also illustrates the price range that Torontonians considered acceptable for French haute couture merchandise sold by one of the city's most exclusive shops.

A few days before, another advertisement had identified a selection of coats that were "adaptations of original models" made by a "French tailor" (fig. 6.3).[11] The coats ranged from $175 to $210, equivalent to the originals in the other advertisement. The items were high priced because they were adaptations from two of the most famous French houses, Balenciaga ($210) and Balmain ($175), and were serviceable day coats that would be worn for several years. The value of a good copy or an adaptation from a high-status designer was thus equivalent to that of an original by one less celebrated (Appendix D).

Garments were valued not only by the status of the designer but also by the design reputation of their country of origin. The high regard for European origins is illustrated by a 1955 Creeds fashion show featuring an Italian designer whose name "was kept a secret, and added a note of mystery to the show." Mr Creed said that the mystery man created the styles especially for Creeds, and the local newspaper described his style as "typically Italian in his use of colours."[12] If a story told by Toronto couturier Rodolphe is anything to go by, the mystery designer may in fact have been working in Toronto and only Italian in origin, if at all. Rodolphe

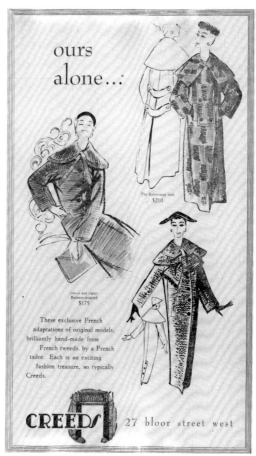

Liska worked for a Viennese menswear shop for fourteen years. In 1953, he came to Toronto and in 1954, started his own business with Alphonse Stehlik. In 1956, he opened his own couture salon. He was also a member of the Association of Canadian Couturiers.[13] In the 1950s, Rodolphe designed a coat that a salesman greatly admired. The salesman had always wanted to sell to Creeds, as it was so prestigious, and thought that the coat was of such good design and quality that the store would want to carry it. He took the coat across the road to Mr Creed,

6.2 (left) Creeds advertisement for Paris haute couture designs priced between $195 and $275, 30 September 1955. **6.3** (right) Creeds advertisement for "exclusive French adaptations of original models brilliantly hand-made from French tweeds by a French tailor," priced from $175 to $210, 21 September 1955.

saying that it was by a French designer who was newly arrived in Toronto. Mr Creed was impressed enough to place an order and also suggested that the newcomer should meet his in-house designer, Sacha, who was French as well. Rodolphe, wearing sunglasses and pretending to be French, went to meet Sacha. In fact, neither Rodolphe nor Sacha were French and each knew the other for an imposter but played along with the fiction. It is more than likely that Mr Creed also knew the truth, yet he placed an order for the coat and it was sold as a high-priced French design.[14]

The significance of this farce lies in its clear demonstration of the way in which European origins gave designs cultural superiority and a higher price. If this value were covertly assigned to Canadian-designed goods, so much the better. The "mystery" Italian designer for Creeds may well have been simply a marketing ploy to play on the cultural capital of European origins. It pleased the newspapers, heightened interest in the clothes, and sold garments, thus satisfying merchants, media, and consumers.

The cost of various types of garments was closely correlated with the status and social importance of the occasion to which they were to be worn, highlighting the importance of these clothes as social constructs. The fact that women's day wear was considered utilitarian reduced its price. A day dress worn when a women undertook private and unacknowledged activities, such as shopping for the family or driving children to school, was consistently the least expensive item in her wardrobe. More was paid for an afternoon dress, in which a woman could attend a tea or more socially important luncheon. The dinner dress had a higher status still. Ginette Spanier, *directrice* for the house of Balmain, commented that "a man will spend more money on a woman's dress if she wears it when she is out with him, more particularly if she wears it when his business associates are around to be impressed. So he will pay more for a dinner dress than an afternoon dress even if the afternoon dress has double the work in it."[15]

The suit, which was, to use Grant McCracken's description of the male working wardrobe, "expressive of ability, discipline and reliability," was a major capital purchase, symbolic of a woman's professional role in the community. In 1956, Mrs Arthur J. Trebilcock was quoted in the *Toronto Telegram* when she appeared on its best-dressed list, saying that she "live[d] in suits."[16] It was the costume in which she and her peers attended volunteer meetings and luncheons. Its cost was justified by the need to acquire the necessary public profile and the importance of the philanthropic work undertaken while wearing this garment. Etiquette books also counselled that a tailored suit "should be of good fabric and well cut" because "it is meant to survive several seasons," thereby validating it as one of the most frequently worn and longest wearing garment types in the wardrobe. The let-out seams in many of the extant garments testify to their serviceability and durability.[17]

The status and value placed on various different garment types was also related to national strengths and characteristics of design. French clothing was considered the highest style and was usually the costliest. Italian designers were recognized for feminine cocktail and evening clothes that were perceived as high-design goods but less expensive than French. British couture was understood to be practical and featured well-tailored suits that were unextravagant in design, affordable, and generally considered good value. British evening wear was less expensive than French yet carried elitist connotations because the leading English couturiers dressed aristocracy and royalty. I could find no Italian suits, either in advertisements or extant in the wardrobes of the women I interviewed, though there were many British and French ones.

Somewhat surprisingly, Swiss cocktail and evening wear held a significant place in the wardrobes of Toronto socialites. Switzerland produced designs that were Paris inspired but not as extreme, as was noted by Eaton's buyer Ollie Smythe. The most expensive dress Nancy Boxer purchased during this period, for example, was a mint-green silk ball dress from Creeds, for which she paid $295. The dress has no designer label, but its good construction, restrained, classic design, and modest use of beading make it reasonable to conclude that it was Swiss. Its high price confirms the quality of the dress, though it was not the most expensive of the designs carried by Creeds. Although Mrs Boxer considered the purchase extravagant, she had received a windfall of a small inheritance and justified her purchase because she was spending her own money. She perceived the dress as an "extra" that needed no discussion with her husband.[18]

The price of a garment was thus established by its position within the wardrobe, the reputation of the individual designer, the national design identity of its country of origin, and the reputation of that country for the specific garment type.

Quality, Longevity, and Value

It is possible for almost everyone to be well dressed. There are two ways of achieving this. Either a good deal of money must be spent on clothes, or else much time and thought given to planning them.[19]

Those interviewed who did spend "a great deal of money" on buying couture pointed out that these two methods of dressing well were not, in fact, mutually exclusive. Often, the more money spent on a piece of clothing, the more planning was given to its purchase. The worth of a garment was evaluated in terms of its cost, appropriateness, exclusivity of design, and place within a wardrobe for the entire season. Such thoughtfulness was also inherent in the couture system, and couture houses developed an elaborate system for clients in order to ensure correct purchases. Balenciaga disapproved of customers who ordered too many models as it showed a lack of discrimination, and he believed that "discerning women . . . only order what is exactly right for them and the lives they lead."[20]

Quality took precedence over number of items in a wardrobe, and Canadian purchases clearly reflect this. It was recognized, however, that this was not a cultural trait of American women. Christian Dior on his first visit to America noted that "the American woman . . . spends more money entirely in order to gratify the collective need to buy. She prefers three new dresses to one beautiful one, and does not linger over a choice, knowing perfectly well that her fancy will be of short duration and the dress which she is in the process of buying will be discarded very soon."[21] This was, of course, exploited by manufacturers and retailers and partially accounts for the American success of couture copies and knock-offs.

The concept of value for money and building a wardrobe that would last was instilled at an early age. Catherine Elliott kept detailed wardrobe accounts and planned all her ensembles and accessories from day to evening, for each summer and winter season from 1937 to 1971. Her accounts clearly document the long-term wearing of her clothes and show that a great deal of very conscious planning went into purchases for each season, which were integrated within her existing wardrobe. Her daughter noted that "while she was under financial restraint for a good many of these years she believed in quality [and] quoted her grandfather, a watchcase manufacturer and importer . . . [as saying,] 'Tiffany is the poor man's friend.'" Mrs Elliott's records demonstrate a process of investment dressing that most women participated in, though few have documented it so meticulously. More usual was to construct similar patterns in one's head or with the assistance of a saleswoman, leaving no permanent record. Mrs Elliott's accounts are even more exceptional in that they traced not only when and where ensembles and individual pieces were worn and when they were updated or altered but also when they were retired from the wardrobe. She also taught her daughter, Flavia Redelmeier, this skill by giving her a dress allowance of $100 a quarter at age twelve. With this, Flavia had to buy her own underwear, stockings, and clothes, though her Branksome Hall private school uniform was not included. She generally purchased all her items at the boutique Joan Rigby, as that was where her mother shopped and the sales staff would work with her and her allowance. Joan Rigby also encouraged a younger clientele by giving 15 to 20 percent off prices to university students.[22]

As discussed, it was common to stagger the purchase of garment types over time in order to afford a couture wardrobe, and the same garments would be worn for years. At Balenciaga, Rose Torno's general rule was to buy one suit a year, one evening dress every two years, and one or two cocktail dresses every three years. Similarly, Rosemary Rathgeb chose models in Paris that would "last," building her couture wardrobe with classics. She actually preferred to buy locally in Toronto because she had more time to buy, could think about individual purchases, and had salespeople who called her to let her know what was available for her taste and lifestyle. For Nancy Boxer, who shopped locally at Creeds, often the determining factor of a purchase was the price. This was because the saleswomen knew her well and would invariably show her clothes that suited her lifestyle and personal taste.[23]

The fashion press perpetuated the dichotomy between the reality of couture consumers making long-term investments in their purchases and the fantasy that these garments were scarcely worn. An interesting 1958 article entitled "For Loyal Fans of the Designer, Old Diors Never Die" illustrates the point. The article focuses on Toronto etiquette and discusses the prestige to be gained by wearing Dior, especially dresses designed by Christian Dior himself, whose last collection was fall 1957. Of the more than 100 Toronto women who wore Dior originals, the article said that most would not "dream of wearing a dress past the season for which it was designed, [yet each] own[s] an especially favoured Dior that they intend to keep for some years."[24] The article promoted the idea that clothes were automatically outdated after a season, but the actual artifacts reveal through their often long, complex biographies that this was simply not true. Even for those who rotated clothes through their wardrobes every few years, the individual items were repeatedly worn. Mary Carr-Harris made one major purchase each year and the following year would buy a different kind of item. She would wear a ball gown approximately twenty-five to thirty times a year for one or two years and then give it to the TSO Rummage Sale. The Royal Ontario Museum collection is not atypical. In fact, most donors only consider giving their most significant clothes to museums, and the wear and alterations in the extant garments were thus not seen as abnormal.

The Canadian women I interviewed were careful that I did not perceive them as spendthrifts or unthinking consumers. Torontonians bought with the intention of making their clothes last and were not about to pay unlimited amounts for their wardrobe. Mary Carr-Harris said, "We bought for our needs."[25] In fact, long-term use of garments was understood by the haute couture houses. Fashion reporter Bettina Ballard commented that when she went to Balenciaga, "He finds it very normal that I should appear in a ten-year-old coat of his."[26] The longevity of couture not only validated the investment but also operated as a testament to the good design and durability of quality fabric and construction. An important aspect of longevity is the technical fact that couture clothes were made with generous seam allowances and deep hems, permitting alterations in order to update, alter, or enlarge the garments at a later date. Women became emotionally and æsthetically attached to their clothes and sought ways to extend their life. This can be seen in a lavish Christian Dior ensemble worn by Nora E. Vaughan, which was let out in the skirt and in the side seams of the jacket to permit longer wear as her figure matured (fig. 6.4). Mrs Vaughan had a large couture wardrobe dating from the 1920s to the 1970s and had no financial need to alter and continue to wear this ensemble, or many others. Through ample fabric allowances, the couture system indirectly acknowledged that its designs would be altered, but this internal aspect of the garments is rarely discussed and was never promoted as a positive marketing strategy.

Canadian notions of value and longevity extended to all garment types, day to evening. Mrs Elliott's second wedding outfit, a Hardy Amies afternoon dress and matching jacket in a subdued taupe colour that she called "cantaloupe," serves as a clear illustration (fig. 6.5). This ensemble was worn with several different hats and accessories from fall 1951 continuously through all seasons, except spring 1957, until fall 1959. In fall 1959, the dress is listed in her active wardrobe column, with a note, "too long." In the winter 1960 list, the dress has moved out of her wardrobe and is entered in another column with the same note, "too long." By winter 1961, it is marked in the "Keep/through [sic] away" column and is not entered again. In other words, this ensemble was worn for fifteen seasons and remained in her wardrobe for nine years.

Even though couture evening garments were often the most expensive purchases, they too were often very much worn. "A formal dress did one fine for years" Judith Wilder commented. Katherine Mackay Stewart, formerly married to Keiller Mackay, the lieutenant-governor, also pointed out the success of a dress when she said, "Evening gowns didn't go out of fashion if they were good."[27] Catherine Elliott had a green taffeta evening dress that she wore every season from spring 1952 until fall 1955, when her wardrobe records refer to it as a "lovely old rag." By spring 1958, the dress has been moved to the "give away" column in her dress accounts. This design was worn, and loved, for eight seasons over four years. Similarly, the formal Norman Hartnell ball gown she called "Waterlily" — the name of the design was "Lily Pond" — she wore every fall season from 1954 to 1959 (figs. 6.6 and 6.7). In her records for winter 1960, she has placed it in the "Carry over, too long" section and by the following winter, it is on her "Keep/through away" list. Both these examples show that extravagance in design for evening clothes was less important than usefulness, which was a highly significant factor for the entire wardrobe of Canadian women. Interestingly, too, even though Mrs Elliott had committed several of her designs to the throw away list, she kept them for sentimental and æsthetic reasons.

For Canadians, "good" design was thus inseparable from lasting value, and further justified the cost of luxury consumption. In fact, long-term wear of evening dress was an elite standard, recognized by Amy Vanderbilt in 1954: "A wise woman never discards an evening or dinner dress that's been becoming to her, no matter how often she's worn it around home. If she goes first class on an ocean liner or cruise ship she will want to dress for dinner most nights, and a well-chosen evening dress five years old can look brand new to people who have never seen it before. Good evening clothes for women approach the uniform and date very slowly."

6.4 Christian Dior beaded satin cocktail and dinner ensemble worn by Nora E. Vaughan, probably modified from the spring 1949 design "Musée du Louvre." The jacket has been let out in the side seams and the skirt altered at the waist in order to extend the wear.

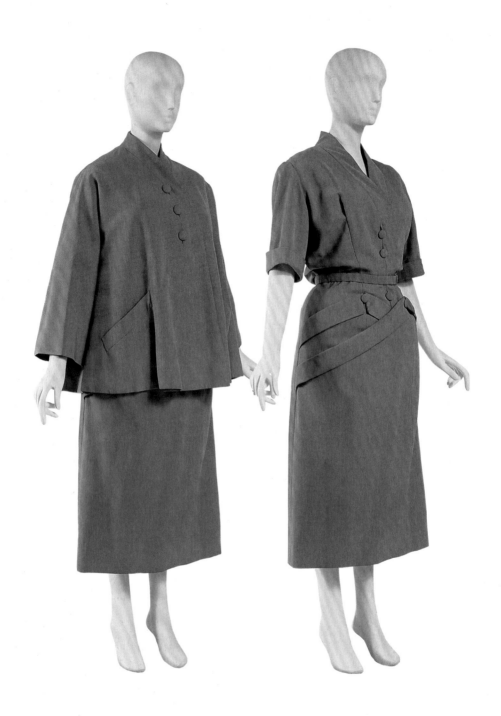

6.5 Fall 1951 Hardy Amies dress and jacket worn by Catherine Elliott for her second wedding (fig. 7.23, p. 277). She wore this ensemble until 1959.

6.6 Fall 1954 Norman Hartnell ball gown "Lily Pond," purchased by Catherine Elliott at Joan Rigby and worn each season until fall 1959.

6.7 Norman Hartnell "Lily Pond" ball gown as shown in *Mayfair* magazine, October 1954, modelled in an appropriate setting. The design was sold at Ogilvy's in Montreal as well as in Toronto.

Such notions of thrift were counselled by Emily Post, who wrote with respect to dinner dress, "It is tiresome everlastingly to wear black on every formal occasion, but nothing looks so well and nothing is so unrecognizable. A very striking dress cannot be worn many times without making others, as well as its owner, feel bored by the sight."[28]

The Canadian penchant for good, conservative couture lasted through the 1950s and was supported by the merchandise available locally. The small numbers of Canadians who shopped directly at the couture houses in Paris, such as Signy Eaton, looked for "dressier" clothes that were not generally seen in Toronto stores. Even in Paris, though, selecting a design that could be worn repeatedly was still important. Sonja Bata, for example, deliberately chose an inconspicuous dress and material so that she would get a lot of use out of her purchase.[29]

Traditional reverence for quality fabric and workmanship has only recently been lost in an age of mass production. Museum collections are filled with garments that have been reused and updated from lavish fabrics. One example in the Royal Ontario Museum is a man's banyan, or dressing gown, made in the 1780s from an early-eighteenth-century French brocaded silk (fig. 6.8). The textile probably dates from before 1730, and its original use was most likely for a women's formal gown. Not only has the expensive textile been recycled fifty years later for a man's garment but it was considered so valuable that it has been used upside down in the back of the banyan as this was the only way to get enough fabric for the design. The garment illustrates the paramount value of textiles and dress, in contrast to our current cultural notions of gender and design. The French haute couture system evolved directly from the tradition of using luxury textiles, and even in the 1950s couture customers continued this historical reverence for reworking rich textiles and fashions in the alterations and mends they made to their garments.

A spring 1949 Schiaparelli evening dress purchased by Lady Eaton at the design house in Paris provides another illustration of the continual wearing of haute couture (fig. 6.9). She was photographed wearing the new gown at the Royal Winter Fair in 1949, and when she wore it again two years later to the state dinner held for Princess Elizabeth in 1951, the dress was most likely the one described in the press as "a pale pink moiré gown with full skirt, [worn with a] diamond and pearl tiara and jewels. She also wore it to the 1951 Hunt Club Supper Dance that was

part of the Royal Winter Fair celebrations just a month after the state dinner. There the very pale pink dress was described as "a white taffeta gown . . . the shirred décolleté with short puffed sleeves, the wide skirt caught up in tiny scallops. With it she wore a diamond tiara and pearl and diamond necklace."[30] This spring evening dress was therefore worn for a minimum of three years, within the same social circles and to the same event. The fact that it was described in the papers two years and five seasons after its design, purchase, and debut — and that it was still considered appropriate — confirms its status-giving properties and fashionability. It also obviously validates the investment.

6.8 This 1780s man's informal dressing gown, or banyan, is made from an early-eighteenth-century French brocaded silk, dating before 1730. The textile may well have been used originally for a women's formal gown.

229

Another example, a Balenciaga cocktail dress, demonstrates the value and longevity of couture purchases even more clearly (fig. 6.10). The dress was designed in 1948. Its original owner may well have acquired it at the design house in Paris, as it shows no signs of alteration in fit. Now in the Royal Ontario Museum, the dress was bought by the donor in a second-hand store in uptown Manhattan in the late 1950s. By that point it had been taken up in the hem and the train to keep up with the fashion of the period. None of the material was cut off on this deep hem, perhaps in an attempt to continue its lifespan should hemlines drop at a later date.[31] The dress was thus worn by two women, the first American and the next Canadian, and remained fashionable over a ten-year period. This is significant, as it specifically illustrates the multifaceted role of haute couture and its long-term function and value as a status-giving commodity within its own fashion system.

6.9 Design sketch for spring 1949 Schiaparelli evening dress worn by Lady Eaton to the Royal Winter Fair in 1949 and again in 1951 to the Hunt Club Supper Dance that was part of the Royal Winter Fair celebrations.

Clothing Maintenance and Storage

Just as purchasing, altering, and updating garments were essential aspects of the wardrobe investment, so too was maintenance. It was standard practice for couture houses to undertake the "maintenance" of any of their own garments at a nominal charge, but this is another facet of the business that the houses, customers, and dress historians have not discussed. Probably it is considered too mundane, detracting from the glamorous promotion of couture. As well, the practice of returning to the couture house of origin to have clothes altered was of course possible only for those women who regularly visited a house. By the 1950s, most couture clients went to department or specialty stores rather than to the design house itself. Alterations were commonly undertaken locally, in the store of purchase. Rose Torno did buy directly at the Paris couture houses but on occasion took her garments to Eaton's for altering. She selected Eaton's as she considered it to have the best alterations department in Toronto. Catherine Elliott took her clothes to Joan Rigby for alteration, and her records include constant notes on alterations, washing, and general refurbishment of her wardrobe.[32]

One of the few records of this activity within a design house are those from the British couture house of Lachasse (Appendix E). Canadian clients' records reveal not only their purchases but also the alterations undertaken by the house over the time a garment was worn. The orders of Mrs Arthur Milner of Toronto and Mrs Plow of Nova Scotia from the mid-1950s to the mid-1960s can be taken as case studies for this type of maintenance. On 7 May 1956, Mrs Milner ordered a black wool suit. It was very likely the same suit that she brought in for alteration on 13 August 1958, two years later. Similarly, on 20 May 1955, Mrs Plow ordered a blue wool dress that was subsequently altered on 9 May 1960, recording a five-year investment that was being extended. The same record notes that a grey jacket was given in for pressing, dyeing the buttons, and putting on a new collar. This may be the suit jacket from her 4 March 1958 purchase, or more probably from her 27 April 1955 "grey suit" purchase, indicating that this jacket was worn between two to five years and that its wear was being extended for several more years' wear. On 18 May 1965, she had a blue suit altered that could have been either of the two she had ordered in May 1959. This documents a garment being worn for six years and still considered worthy of further investment.

6.10 Fall 1948 Balenciaga silk taffeta cocktail dress, model 62, probably custom ordered in Paris, later purchased in a New York City second-hand store and worn until the late 1950s. The garment was shortened but no fabric was cut. This design appeared in a sketch by Eric depicting the dress in the elevator of the haute couture house and was published in both *Vogue*, 1 October 1948, 156 and *L'Officiel de la Haute Couture*, October 1948, 71.

To ensure that the garments did last, great attention was paid to the storage, care, and general maintenance of a good wardrobe. Etiquette books, books on clothing care, and contemporary articles all underlined the concept of protecting your investment. An example of this type of care is reflected in Torontonian Dorothy Boylen's clothing storage, as described in 1956: "Mrs Boylen's third floor dressing room . . . demands a moment of silence from the most blasé. In an air-conditioned, thermostatically-controlled, cedarized room the size of a shop, hang rack upon rack of original gowns from the world's greatest couturiers."[33]

Equal care was taken by Rose Torno, who lived in a custom-designed Forest Hill penthouse. Her wardrobe was organized by garment type in carefully designed wardrobes (fig. 6.11). Nora Vaughan, wife of the vice-president of Eaton's, also had a large wardrobe, and her clothes were stored carefully in garment bags and arranged by colour and type.[34] This allocation of space and care for a wardrobe was recognized by Gertrude Pringle as typical for a wealthy Canadian woman: "A fashionable woman with an ample dress allowance will spend a great deal on her clothes. Hats for all occasions will be a big item, so will furs. Footwear and costume accessories, several evening dresses, at least one dinner dress, suits, sports clothes, afternoon dresses, a negligée for home relaxation, a couple of hostess gowns, housecoats, and several becoming bed jackets, will require a lot of closet space to hold them."[35]

The scale of storage space required a large residence and often a maid to maintain such a wardrobe. Liudja Stulginskas, a Lithuanian refugee, worked as Signy Eaton's upstairs maid from 1950 until her employer's death in 1993. She said that Mrs Eaton would describe what she wanted to wear from her wardrobe, and Liudja would fetch it and lay it out in her dressing room. She would do minor mending for Mrs Eaton, as she was an experienced seamstress, and would offer her opinion on ensembles, if asked.[36] Nevertheless, her main job was the storage and maintenance of Mrs Eaton's wardrobe, which involved trust and mutual respect not only between mistress and servant but also from both of them for the value of the clothes themselves. These were handled as beautiful objects — a collection of very socially significant commodities in Mrs Eaton's life.

This high regard for a wardrobe was emphasized in 1950 by *Harper's Bazaar*, which admonished American women for not maintaining their clothing purchases.

6.11 Rose Torno at her wardrobe, custom designed for her couture suits, in her Forest Hill penthouse. The hangers had eighteen-inch-long handles, a style commonly found in European hotels.

The article lamented that "the lady's maid and the valet have practically disappeared from our lives." It also gave a list of tips for storing and caring for many different types of materials, all in an effort to encourage the "sense to know that the better she looks after them, the longer they will last."[37] The magazine was clearly promoting an understanding of longevity and value understood by Europeans but not considered an American trait, as Americans tended to prefer quantity over quality and did not spend as much on individual items.

The issues of quality and value shed much light on the cultural, social, and financial significance of couture. The value of couture was complex. It was a calculated purchase influenced by price, cultural value, style, taste, and the social prestige of the garment. Torontonians were generally not inclined to frequent, lavish spending on their wardrobes, but made selective expensive purchases with the intention of long and appropriate wear. The family investment in a woman's wardrobe was on average 10 to 20 percent of the annual family income. This was considered a capital cost, necessary to maintain social status and the ability to function within Toronto's annual social season. Couture played a very important part in the wardrobes of elite Toronto women, but for many was only financially and psychologically affordable if augmented with sale items, copies, and dressmaker models. The continual seasonal purchasing and rapid rotation of clothes that have been repeatedly suggested by women's magazines and the fashion industry are a fallacy of couture mythology.

7   THE COUTURE SOCIETY
WARDROBE AS
A MODEL OF TASTE

As we are judged by our appearance, dress is of immense importance in our social and business contacts. Gertrude Pringle, 1949

Couture clothing served the social elite as a badge of membership and gave access to local and international society circles. The etiquette attached to public and private social and fundraising events in Toronto, as elsewhere, required the style and quality inherent in couture to give authority and polish to its wearer (figs. 7.1 and 7.2).

Socially prominent women were given recognition in specifically feminine terms: descriptions of their dress were recorded in the society pages of the local newspapers and recognized nationally by best-dressed lists. Usually this acknowledgment was framed by mention of volunteer work. Volunteerism was an extremely important activity for women during the 1950s, and was incorporated into their daily lives. The social status it gave to the women involved reflected on their entire families. Women not only donated their time but in many cases gave over their homes for events or meetings and their personal possessions to the community shops. Financial support ranged from buying tickets or donating funds to attending teas, balls, fashion shows, fairs, and performances. This participation was often performed while wearing couture clothes. Analyzing taste in dress in conjunction with the activities that socialites undertook while wearing couture provides a context to the purpose, successes, and failures of these designs and the consumption practices associated with them.

The Wardrobe and Etiquette

The etiquette of socially correct clothing and its attendant complexities were derived from eighteenth- and nineteenth-century court circles. The potential horror of making

7.1 Spring 1950 Balenciaga lace cocktail or dinner dress, model 172. A capelet worn over the shoulders made this a more modest ensemble for cocktails. Without the capelet, the dress becomes appropriate for later in the evening. See fig. 1.2, p.15.

7.2 Fall 1955 Dior red faille cocktail dress "Zémire." The boned bodice and multiple petticoats are all firmly placed in the dress to guarantee that the wearer will look impeccable. The three-quarter-length sleeves and skirt length were perfectly appropriate for cocktail wear. See fig. 0.4, p. 5.

a faux pas by appearing in incorrect clothing or accessories was a real concern that persisted into the 1950s. Some mechanisms designed to prevent this have already been discussed: knowledgeable sales assistants would guide one's taste; and fashion shows served as etiquette demonstrations. Many Canadian women inherited a knowledge of what was suitable and tasteful from their mothers. Rose Torno's interest in and knowledge of good clothing was gained from her mother, who taught her to "buy one good dress and wear it with authority." She bought couture from the 1930s until the mid-1970s.[1]

To be correctly dressed for the occasion required planning. Catherine Elliott's detailed wardrobe accounts have already been discussed. This level of organization required a regular pattern of shopping and seeing what was available, as her daughter describes:

She had her own saleswoman, Miss O'Halloran, at Eaton's College St millinery, she bought shoes at Eaton's Downtown (Mrs Carrington), shopped The Room at Simpson's, had her hair cut and manicures at the Arden Salon at Simpson's, managed by her cousin's schoolfriend Helen Brown, maintained her deposit account at Eaton's . . . and charge account at Simpson's . . . Shoes also at Owens and Elmes, then at Vanity's. Vanity Fair (Eaton's) brand underwear. Liked Eaton's for fundamentals, Simpson's fashion accessories like handbags and gloves. She comparison shopped routinely, criss-crossing Queen Street in search of her needs. Routine — park at Eaton's College St, take the courtesy bus to Eaton's downtown [Queen Street], do her list, occasionally meeting family or friends for lunches at the Arcadian Court [Simpson's], the Georgian Room ("the Gorging Room"), or the Round Room, at Eaton's College Street.[2]

Ruth Frankel was also very conscious of her appearance, especially in the many volunteer roles she undertook. She was noted for always being well dressed and was on the 1952 *Toronto Telegram* best-dressed list. She planned what to wear to meetings, and in fact had to do so as she was not a standard size and needed lead time to have things made up for her. She advised those who wished to be active and productive volunteers that "to be well groomed for the occasion is essential." While Mrs Frankel undoubtedly learned her social graces from her mother, and passed them on to her daughter, others relied on books, magazines, and newspapers.[3]

The numerous etiquette books published from the 1940s to 1960s attest to the social demand for detailed instructions about correct social behaviour and dress.[4]

They discussed the overall wardrobe as well as the clothing types required for different occasions. These books were aimed at an upper-middle-class woman who did not undertake paid work, though books written by the end of the 1950s tend to include business wardrobes for professional working women.

The first etiquette book written specifically for Canadians was by Gertrude Pringle and appeared in 1932. The preface explains the need for a particular dictum for Canada: "The books which have been available are not entirely suitable because they are by American writers. While American etiquette is of course founded on certain basic rules of good-breeding, it differs in many instances from social usage in Canada — this country leans more to English ways . . . Why not use English works on etiquette? To this the answer is they are much too general . . . They entirely ignore many of the small details."[5] This opinion was supported by the Toronto Reference Library, which initiated a 1949 edition because it received several etiquette-related questions a day.[6] Gertrude Pringle noted in the preface to the later edition that "interest in etiquette is on the increase."[7] She devoted a full chapter to the significance and general rules of dress. Further details were to be found in chapters relating to specific occasions. Pringle, like her American counterparts Emily Post and Amy Vanderbilt, stressed that the most important requirement was appropriateness of dress for the occasion. British etiquette books also stressed this point and noted that "'taste' is a notoriously difficult thing to define . . . Roughly speaking, clothes which are in 'good taste' are those which not only suit us, but suit the occasions for which we want them."[8] As documented in interviews, this was the single most significant concern for Torontonians. Appropriateness implied a sophisticated understanding of the social milieu.

Etiquette books flourished on the anxiety felt by many women, often newer members of elite society who were afraid of showing social ignorance. Postwar economic growth in Canada brought financial success to many who then needed guidance to manage the social situations to which they had gained admittance. Many women used Emily Post and Amy Vanderbilt as references for correct manners and dress. Etiquette books were one safe reference, but particularly useful at a local level were newspapers and Canadian fashion magazines.

Women also often sought advice and confirmation from friends in the same social circles. Julia Ruby Lean, who was not brought up in Toronto society, would sometimes discuss a dress and its suitability for a particular social occasion with a woman friend if she had any concerns about her selection. The same friend also "taught" her how to shop for the season, introducing her to the elite shops and sales assistants. June McLean would sometimes talk over her dress with a friend or ask her hostess what the guests would be wearing.[9] Etiquette books repeated that it was perfectly correct to ask the hostess for advice if you were in doubt about what to wear.[10] It was also the duty of the hostess to make the type of occasion clear in the invitation, as the dress code was implied by the formality of the invitation itself. If one was in doubt, however, the rule was to underdress. This point was reiterated by Emily Post as well as by those interviewed.[11]

Society News, Fashion Magazines, and Best-Dressed Lists

In the world of smart society, clothes represent not only our ticket of admission but our contribution to the effect of a party.[12]

Toronto's female social leaders during the early 1950s tended to be prominent and active in volunteer work, and they were accorded public recognition largely through press reports. The very real importance attached to their dress is clearly reflected in the society columns of the daily newspapers, which constantly reported women's events, focusing on who attended or was going to attend, and what they wore or were going to wear. Often these details supplanted a description of the event itself. The text was often accompanied by a photograph or was itself the caption of a photograph. Clothing was given the majority of copy, characterized by colour, textile, and often designer. If the designer's name was not known, or not given to the reporter, a dress might be identified by country of origin or else as an import, as the main interest to the reporter and the reader was news about couture. These descriptions signified the importance of fashion in establishing prestige and fuelled competition among women. A successful dress that generated press attention served as a symbol of participation in an event.

The following example from 1950 is typical of the period: "Mrs E.J. Meager of Oakville in a brown English original suit . . . Mrs Charles Pitts looked stunning in her handsome new blue mink jacket over a navy wool Dior original fashioned on the oblique line . . . Mrs Egmont Frankel, who spent the summer on the Continent, had fashion's favourite — the Bright Look — with her brilliant royal blue wool costume she wore a crimson hat."[13] Such detailed descriptions appeared almost daily throughout the postwar period. Not only could readers follow the social leaders and events, but at every opportunity they were given the chance to learn about the most fashionable styles worn in their city. The women who were consistently featured in the newspaper were clearly identified with their couture wardrobe and acquired high social status at both a local and a national level. Society women were role models in style and etiquette, while the descriptions of occasions and fashions acted as a lesson in protocol for Canadians in general.

One measure of approved Canadian glamour and taste was the creation of best-dressed lists. The original list was created in 1940 by New York publicist Eleanor Lambert when the German occupation of Paris forced the haute couture houses to stop their practice of annually listing their most fashionable clients.[14] Candidates were selected from international circles. The first Canadian list was taken from a poll and published by the woman's magazine *New Liberty* in January 1948. While the New York list was exclusively concerned with style, the Canadian list asked the judges, who were the editors of the national daily newspaper women's pages, to nominate women from "ten walks of life."[15] Categories included the fashion field, public life, the arts, advertising, modelling, publishing, radio, sport, the young set, and club women. The last category was filled by Mrs Ryland New, national president of the "formidable" Imperial Order of Daughters of the Empire. The socialite, and particularly the active volunteer, was thus considered a professional who took her role seriously, even though she did not work for pay, and the list was designed to emphasize that role. *New Liberty* received 100 submissions from across Canada. Thirty were Torontonians, twenty-nine Montrealers, and the remaining forty-one were scattered in cities from Vancouver to Halifax. The requirement that the judges base their assessment on more than dress style speaks volumes for the conservative, understated Canadian system, which had to validate interest and success in fashionable dress. All the women selected were portrayed as professionals, a point that simultaneously justified the expense of their dress and was reinforced by it. In fact, couture or luxury dress was regarded as part of the reason for their success.

Over the 1950s, the approach taken in the best-dressed list changed. In contrast to the earlier, highly specific categories, by 1950 the judges were allowed to choose women from any background. All the winners were married and most were mature women.[16] By 1955, the criteria for the "annual round-up of Canada's 10 best-dressed women" in *Liberty* magazine had changed again, "with a twist . . . only the younger business and professional women were chosen for the honor list."[17] All ten were working for pay, none was identified as a committee member or a housewife, and most were involved in the arts and media such as radio, television, magazines, fashion, or stage. This move marked a shift toward media celebrities and paid professional women serving as role models for Canadian women, rather than unpaid, wealthy, professional committee women. The women's pages of the newspapers were now aimed at a larger, middle-class suburban readership.

The need to measure Canadians against other Canadians and, what was more important, against their international counterparts, is reflected in the other best-dressed lists that emerged over the period. The *Toronto Telegram* ran a "best-dressed in Toronto list," starting in 1952 (figs. 7.3 and 7.4).[18] Once on the list, a woman could not be nominated again, necessitating new members annually. The 1962 "Hall of Fame" list was drawn from each of the previous ten years, with one woman selected from each year. It included Signy Eaton, Dorothy Boylen, Katherine Mackay, and Nora Vaughan.

In 1956, *Mayfair* responded to the 1955 New York nominations, which did not include a Canadian, by putting forward the name of Mme Yves Bourassa of Montreal as a candidate for the international list. The editorial "question[ed] the methods of any poll, which in preparing a world-wide list of 179 candidates, could fail to recognize the eligibility of even one Canadian . . . *Mayfair* believes that Canada has as many well-dressed women, per capita, as any country in the world." In the following issue, the magazine then published portraits of Canadian women whom it believed qualified, including Torontonian Katherine Mackay, wife of the lieutenant-governor.[19]

Fashion magazines played an important part in describing the latest styles and their social implications. Carmel Snow's seasonal reports from Paris for *Harper's*

7.3 *Toronto Telegram* 1953 best-dressed list. The list included Eaton's fashion co-ordinator Dora Matthews (centre left), noted as "always looking as attractive as one of the models in the fashion shows she directs." Clayton Burton (bottom right), wife of Simpson's president, was noted for her "tailored suits [that] have interesting detail." Dorothy Boylen (top left), in her Christian Dior design "Palmyre," was known for her "fabulous collection of beautiful evening gowns."

Mrs. M. J. Boylen

Canada Pictures
Lady Kemp →

Betty Anne Rough ↑
← Mrs. Dana Porter

Ballard & Jarrett
Mrs. Dora Matthews

Best-Dressed Women

Once again The Telegram presents its annual list of Toronto's ten best-dressed women.

Compiling this list is probably the most difficult task our judges have to do in a year, because there are so many well-dressed women in this city. Only two phases of the job made it a little easier for them. Ten women were automatically eliminated from the judging before they made up our best-dressed list last year. Secondly, the judges have again been promised the protection of anonymity so that they will not have to spend the next year trying to explain to their wives if they are not on the list.

Yet, our judges are all men and their choice both this year and last show that they are men of taste and discrimination—and that they consider the beauty of clothes and their suitability for any given occasion.

Ballard & Jarrett
Mrs. Fred Porter

Ballard & Jarrett
Mrs. Alan Skaith

Ballard & Jarrett
Mrs. Benjamin Luxenberg

← Mrs. E. P. Taylor

Mrs. Edgar Burton →

7.4 Fall 1952 Christian Dior design "Palmyre," worn by Dorothy Boylen and probably bought at Simpson's or Holt Renfrew. This may have been a bonded model. The Dior design was worn by several women on the international best-dressed list, including Wallis Simpson, Marlene Dietrich, and Mrs Charles Chaplin. A cocktail-length version is in the collection of the Palais Galliera, Paris.

Bazaar provided detailed information on the latest fashions. Styles were described in a similar manner to the way in which they were presented in a collection, by social usage and time of day. American *Vogue* regularly featured a fictional matron, Mrs Exeter, who acted as a role model for mature women. Her lifestyle was never explicitly described. She attended teas and luncheons and generally followed the schedule of an active society club woman. Mrs Exeter gave advice on correct dress in terms of style and quality: "*Vogue's* heroine of fifty-odd, Mrs Exeter, never sacrifices appearances for the sake of price." Similarly, 1949 *Harper's Bazaar* occasionally had a column entitled "At My Age . . ." for women "fifty and up" that offered wardrobe advice such as: "One perfect tailored suit with two sets of perfect details is a better buy than several inexpensive outfits."[20] The magazines acknowledged that older women were the target market for couture clothing. Mature figures had the most to gain from quality clothing that was well made and masked physical imperfections. Furthermore, older women were financially secure, so had time to devote to their lives as club women and society hostesses. The press and magazines, directly and indirectly, reinforced ideas of appropriate dress for the occasion. That couture clothing represented the pinnacle of correctness was undisputed.

The Couture Wardrobe

A moderate wardrobe, that is to be adequate to its wearer's every need, must be chosen carefully. Everything that is bought should be in harmony with the rest of the clothes.[21]

Since so much hinged on being seen in the appropriate dress, building a correct wardrobe, purchase by purchase, was essential for social success. This has already been discussed in terms of Catherine Elliott's lists and the requirements of value and longevity, and the point was reiterated during interviews as well as in etiquette books and fashion magazines. A co-ordinated wardrobe was advocated for all social levels but was particularly stressed for those on a limited budget.[22]

Colour harmony, as well as style, was always considered in terms of the entire wardrobe. Elizabeth Bryce commented, "It seems to me we spent a lot of time shopping and thinking about things. Finding the right shoes and getting them dyed the right colour. The idea of ensemble dressing." The advice given in 1960 was similar to that of ten years before: "The economical way to be well dressed at all times is to choose two basic colours, such as navy blue and gray or black and brown, so that the main accessories . . . can be worn with both. A third colour to accent either outfit may be introduced in scarves, jewellery and minor accessories."[23]

Often the nucleus of a woman's "professional" (i.e., married) wardrobe began with her trousseau. Its size would depend on the bride's future role and on her parents' financial circumstances. Rationing prevented women who were married during or just after the war from having large trousseaux, and postwar the importance of the trousseau began to diminish. The impact of the New Look in 1947 had radically changed fashion and made recent fashion purchases obsolete. To safeguard the wardrobe investment, fashion authorities began to advise against purchasing too much or choosing high-fashion designs that, it was feared, would quickly become *démodé*. In 1949, an article in a local Toronto newspaper on this subject stated that a typical trousseau consisted of four to five "carefully selected outfits" and stressed that two afternoon dresses — one a print, one plain — a cocktail gown for the "fussiest" dress, and quality in lingerie was preferred over quantity in general. By 1956, American etiquette advisor Frances Benton suggested that the trousseau wardrobe should be considered to last for a year and not much more because it would get outdated. Canadian women expected to wear their trousseau items for as long as possible, however, and a year would have been considered an absolute minimum.[24]

One of the first considerations when planning a purchase was the time of day and type of occasion when the garment would be worn. Morning dress encompassed activities such as shopping, committee meetings, and perhaps a luncheon. A socially active committee woman would often have to dress in the same ensemble until tea time, as she would be attending consecutive events that precluded going home to change. Dress for the morning was commonly a wool suit with silk blouse, or a woollen dress with matching coat or jacket, and a set of matching accessories that would include a hat, gloves, handbag, and perhaps a scarf and umbrella. Joan Rosefield Lepofsky wore her bonded Chanel suits so often that though the jackets and skirts survive, the more delicate silk blouses are worn out. Suits were especially important for meetings, and it was noted that "the assured clubwoman dresses like a successful businesswoman, in smart suits, simple and becoming wools or cottons according to the season, with the proper accessories . . . for daytime wear."[25]

THE NEW MOUNT SINAI HOSPITAL

Highlights

Volume 4, No. 2   Toronto, Ont., November, 1956

Some of the members of the Ball Committee of the
Women's Auxiliary as they plan for the

SECOND ANNUAL ANNIVERSARY BALL

Thursday, November 29   Royal York Hotel

Ruth Frankel favoured just such a formula. A dress and matching jacket, or a custom-made suit with the jacket lined in the same material as the blouse, was typical of her style. She was quoted for her nomination to the 1952 *Toronto Telegram* best-dressed list as saying that her selections in dress were made "with the thought that she may wear them at a meeting," as she was so active on various committees.[26] The 1955 list included Winifred Bell, who commented that "suits were almost a uniform" as she worked for the Junior League and the Red Cross and also had daily meetings. On the same list was Mrs Arthur Soles, "one of the busiest women in Toronto . . . an officer in nearly all the Jewish welfare organizations and the Red Cross," who also favoured suits and well-tailored dresses for all her meetings.[27] Thus, the link between being well dressed and working professionally as a volunteer was clearly made and sanctioned by the press. The stylistic and social conformity of suits for such occasions is confirmed in a 1956 photograph of the New Mount Sinai Hospital Women's Auxiliary committee members (fig. 7.5). Most are wearing suits, and a few women have on sleeved dresses. A 1953 photograph of Canadian Cancer Society members demonstrates the same point (fig. 7.6).

As the day progressed, clothing became more formal. Afternoon dress was either the same as morning dress or a little dressier, though unlike the prewar styles,

7.5 Members of the Ball Committee of the New Mount Sinai Hospital Women's Auxiliary attending a planning meeting, 1956. The women are dressed in smart day wear and overwhelmingly conform to the social etiquette that approved of suits.

hemlines remained the same from morning until cocktails. Details about success-ful dress for this time of day were offered by Gertrude Pringle: "Afternoon dress is always worn at teas and afternoon receptions. The hat is kept on, and at a large party the gloves also." Emily Post called the hours between one and six o'clock the time for "important" day dresses and suggested "worsteds or dull silks made with tailored simplicity."[28]

Princess Elizabeth's 1951 trip to Toronto raised concerns about appropriate dress. Her visit encompassed a civic reception, a private luncheon at Queen's Park, and a state dinner on Saturday night, all of which required different dress. For those invited to any of these functions, errors were forestalled by an interview published in the newspaper with Helen Lawson, wife of the lieutenant-governor. She was

7.6 Members of the Canadian Cancer Society planning for the fall 1953 meeting. From left to right are Mrs H.B. Keenleyside, Mrs F.F. McEachern, and Mrs O.S. Hollinrake. They are dressed in suits that serve as professional working attire.

asked about correct dress and outlined the different requirements. For the civic reception she said that "afternoon dress is correct and this would include dressy suits or dress-maker style wool dresses." For the luncheon, "Mrs Lawson is asking the young women to wear pretty afternoon dresses, rather than wool suits or tailored dresses . . . Hats will be worn of course . . . White gloves are a must for those being presented . . . Neither at the dinner or luncheon is there any rule against wearing black." In order to clarify any doubts about what would be appropriate, socialites were photographed in their ensembles prior to the events (fig. 7.7).[29]

The material and the *décolleté* of the design were the two most important factors in determining the suitability of a garment for an occasion. For instance,

7.7 Three Toronto socialites "discuss the most flattering angle for the little veil on [a] hat," prior to a luncheon they will attend in honour of Princess Elizabeth in October 1951. The women are identified by their volunteer work, from left to right: Mrs R. Fred Porter Jr, chairman of the Junior League Cerebral Palsy Training Centre; Mrs Robert Dale-Harris, member of the Junior League and the Women's Opera Concert Committee of the Royal Conservatory; and Mrs Peter Osler of the Junior League, a regular volunteer at hospital clinics.

Christian Dior

44 - COCOTTE

Robe après-midi, pied de poule
garnie velours noir.

N° 6

Reproduction de modèle interdite

Mona Campbell wore a black silk Dior dress in the afternoon. Long sleeves made the design appropriate for daytime, though because it was silk she considered it a little "dressy" and thus appropriate for afternoon. For festive late day events such as bridal showers or special teas, sleeved dresses in velveteen or wool crepe were also considered appropriate.[30] None of these had low necklines.

The race track was traditionally a place to show off the new season's fashions, and the local newspapers always reported them. In the late 1940s, Joan Rosefield Lepofsky wore her dramatic Dior original "Cocotte," from the spring 1948 collection, to the King's Plate races, with a black Hattie Carnegie hat and black shoes that were cut high with white uppers, like spats. The drama of the dress is its bustle, which suited the standing activities of the race track, while the basic design of the dress, tailored in wool houndstooth with long sleeves, perfectly suited the festive daytime requirements (fig. 7.8). Mrs Lepofsky later removed the bustle and continued to wear the dress for several more years. For the same occasion in the late 1950s, she wore another Dior, a peach linen dress with three-quarter-length sleeves. Similarly, Mary Carr-Harris wore a silk dress and a large straw hat in the spring, while in the winter of 1951, Rosemary Rathgeb chose a light wool suit, silk shirt, and fur stole.[31]

The etiquette of cocktail dresses was more complicated than that of late day dressing. The time of the cocktail party determined the elaborateness of the dress.

7.8 Design sketch for spring 1948 Christian Dior model "Cocotte." This design was worn by Torontonian Joan Rosefield Lepofsky to the race course with a black Hattie Carnegie hat and a tightly rolled black umbrella. She bought it as a bonded model.

Although a cocktail dress was always daytime length, a cocktail party often preceded another event, so consideration had to be given to dress that would suit both occasions. For late afternoon cocktails, Signy Eaton wore a black silk Givenchy suit that was subtly embroidered with flowers trimmed with a centre sequin. The decoration of the suit and the silk material made it suitable for late afternoon and early evening wear. On a New York trip in 1962, however, she selected a silk dress with a matching coat by Givenchy for afternoon cocktails at an art opening, followed by a dinner at the Museum of Modern Art. The sleeveless dress and the brocaded silk woven with metallic thread contributed to the increased formality of this ensemble over that of the suit. Nonetheless, she did not consider the dress and coat ensemble dressy enough for a truly formal dinner.[32] An elegant off-white satin Fath cocktail dress was selected by Mrs Lepofsky for a formal photograph with her children, who were dressed in the same colour, thus underscoring the importance of this family (fig. 7.9). The subtleties of these distinctions were central to the successful socialite in the 1950s.

Events held after cocktails demanded increased formality in dress. The more formal and ceremonial the dinner, the more elaborate the dress. A dinner dress was described by Gertrude Pringle in the following way: "A dinner dress is a half-low [in the neckline] evening dress; it is sometimes made with sleeves . . . It has not

7.9 Toronto socialite Joan Rosefield Lepofsky with her children, in a fall 1955 off-white satin design by Jacques Fath.

the elaboration of the ballroom frock, the skirt of which is especially designed for dancing." For semi-formal dinner parties at private homes, or out at public restaurants, dresses with sleeves and shallow necklines were acceptable.[33]

The nuances of clothing etiquette were clearly reflected in Signy Eaton's comments on appropriate dress for different occasions. In her opinion, it was acceptable to wear colour for a dinner in one's own home, but for dinners out it was better to wear black and dark colours. Her two-piece Dior dress "Nocturne" was such a dinner dress (fig. 7.10). Its black silk velvet trimmed with iridescent beading created a rich ensemble in colour and tone, and the short sleeves and V-neck suggest *décolleté* without actually exposing the shoulders, neck, or bust. Interestingly, the same design was worn by her American counterpart, Mrs I. Magnin, also the wife of a department store president.[34] The Canadian tendency to wear darker colours in order to be understated in public is borne out by others. Joan Rosefield Lepofsky would wear her 1951 black silk taffeta Balenciaga for going out to dinner (fig. 7.11). This dress had a matching bolero-style jacket that made it versatile for formal and informal occasions.[35]

In contrast to her dark Dior, Mrs Eaton's beaded Balmain sheath was worn for dinner parties she held in her own home, and she and the press considered it a successful dress, probably because the style is simple and all the detail is in the beading (fig. 7.12).[36] She wore the dress as hostess for a Christmas party, even though it was designed as a spring cocktail design, again underscoring that Canadian couture consumers favoured garments that could be worn outside of a single season or occasion and would have longevity in the wardrobe.

Dress for theatre was similar to that for dinner. Joan Rosefield Lepofsky considered her sleeveless Jean Dessès, of black silk taffeta draped in a lattice effect across the bodice, perfect for dinners and the theatre.[37] For the opening night of the theatre season, however, more spectacular dress was appropriate. Such an occasion was described in 1958: "[At the] Royal Alexandra [Theatre] last night . . . top designers of the fashion world were represented . . . Mrs Ian Macdonell wearing a Balenciaga in white satin beautifully embroidered in pale blue and gold thread . . . Mrs Mona Band was in slim sheath designed by Guggenheim, its grey brocade sprinkled with tiny jet beads and matching coat banded by black broadtail." Socialite Mona Band's dress was a knee-length Italian original by Mingolini Guggenheim that

7.10 Two-piece fall 1948 Christian Dior dress "Nocturne," of black silk velvet with iridescent beading, worn by Signy Eaton for dinners out of her home.

7.11 Spring 1951 black silk taffeta Balenciaga dress, worn by Joan Rosefield Lepofsky for dinners out. Its matching jacket made it more versatile.

7.12 Spring 1950 beaded Balmain sheath, worn by Signy Eaton for dinner parties she held in her own home.

she dubbed her "caviar dress" because of its black, clustered beading.[38] The short length was also chosen by Betty Cassels for the opening performance of the ballet season. Mrs Cassels was on the *Toronto Telegram* best-dressed list in 1960, and was at that time president of the Toronto branch of the National Ballet Guild. Her attendance and appearance were very important as she was performing a professional role that night. She took some guests out to dinner before the performance and afterward entertained some of the performers at a private club. She selected a Marty of Switzerland coat and dress ensemble, comprising a draped knee-length pink silk chiffon sheath and pink silk and gold brocade coat (fig. 7.13).[39]

Formal dinners necessitated even more elaborate dinner or evening dress than just described. This was usually floor length and more *décolleté* than a semi-formal dress. For the state dinner in honour of Princess Elizabeth in 1951, Mrs Lawson explained that "evening dress is required for the dinner . . . For the women this does not necessarily mean a ball gown with deep *décolletage*, though most of the dresses will be floor length."[40] A few days later, Katherine Mackay appeared in the *Globe and Mail* newspaper in "a striking Parisian Ballgown of black lace over

7.13 Betty Cassels wears the draped knee-length pink silk chiffon sheath from her Marty of Switzerland coat and dress ensemble, c.1960, purchased at Eaton's Ensemble Shop. See fig. 4.8, pp.112–13 for the original dress.

white satin" that she would be wearing to the state dinner, thereby staking out her design and demonstrating correct etiquette. Some of the other guests who would be attending the functions were also photographed prior to the event (figs. 7.14 and 7.15). Clayton Burton wore a black velvet strapless Oleg Cassini gown, Margaret Godsoe chose a French dress of pale grey net overlaid with black lace, and Signy Eaton decided on a Balenciaga sheath of black lace embroidered with ribbon.[41] Helen Band wore a British design that was also noted in the *Toronto Telegram* as being "one of the most attractive of Hartnell's slender styles," and perhaps was also considered most appropriate for the occasion as Norman Hartnell was a

7.14 These two photographs were published together in the *Globe and Mail*, 12 October 1951, to illustrate the "beautiful evening gowns" that would be worn to a state dinner in honour of Princess Elizabeth and the Duke of Edinburgh. Mrs J. Keiller MacKay, left, wears "a striking Parisian ballroom gown of black lace over white satin, the full gathered skirt accented by a deep border of black velvet." Mrs Paul Martin, right, wife of the French consul, wears a "gown of deep iris taffeta, wide skirted and gracefully draped."

royal dressmaker (figs. 7.16 and 7.17).[42]

Formal dinners that were not state occasions also required floor-length dresses. For a dinner before the Royal Winter Fair, followed by a supper dance after the Fair events, Clayton Burton chose a draped green chiffon Jean Dessès (fig. 7.18), while Ethel Harris chose her bonded floor-length white lace Pierre Balmain dress trimmed with sequins (see fig. 2.10, p. 67).[43] Correspondingly, for a 1954 New Year's Eve dance at the Royal York Hotel, Mrs Benjamin Luxenberg wore a "luscious magnolia satin gown made by Balenciaga."[44] Yet not all of these elaborate dresses in rich textiles would have been considered formal enough for a ball.

Ball gowns were usually the most dramatic pieces in any wardrobe. They were also the most revealing, and usually had full skirts for ease of dancing and to enhance graceful movements. The types of gowns worn ran the gambit from understated elegance, such as the Fath dress Signy Eaton wore to the Hunt Club

7.15 Mrs Hiram McCallum, wife of Toronto's mayor, and her daughter, Dorothy McCallum, "pose in the graceful gowns" before the state dinner, 13 October 1951. "Mrs McCallum's gown of powder blue and silver brocade is cut on princess lines. Miss McCallum wears lustrous sky blue satin with very wide crinolined skirt and a splash of bright flame blossoms at the waist."
7.16 (opposite) Simpson's advertisement for "Moonlight Masterpieces," 11 September 1951. The Norman Hartnell design shown in fig. 7.17 is illustrated centre left. The Jacques Griffe design illustrated centre right is also part of the Royal Ontario Museum collection.

MOONLIGHT MASTERPIECES

From Our Designers' Collection

The evening scene shows a renaissance of magnificence with but the occasional young dress stopped short above a ballroom floor. You'll see gowns of fabulous foliage where layer upon layer of skirt is encrusted with beading or mock jewels... you'll see sunbursts of color flashing from opalescent white to Jean Desses' new "bluebird" right through to the deep beauty of black. Many gowns are showing slightly less decollete, more extravagance of skirt, more meeting of several fabrics at once. As dramatic contrast to the general bouffance, watch for lines of stark excitement as you'll see in our serpentine black velvet by Lanvin of Paris, or for gowns of regal bearing as in our Hardy Amies purple velvet. Simpson's has the gowns that cast the most important evening shadows... now in our designers' collection.

Simpson's

From Left to Right the Significant Evening Gowns Sketched:
by **Castillo** of Paris... the regal line... spectacular white satin etched with sequins.
by **Hartnell** of London... the narrow trend... sophisticated lemon-green tucked sheath.
by **Jacques Griffe** of Paris... of colorful importance—wine rouge ball gown.
by **George Bailey** of New York... jewel-encrusted petals of bronze lace-appliqued velvet over pleated chiffon.
The beautiful fashions sketched are typical of the designers' originals being shown in Simpson's Fall Fashion Revue "Designers' Collection", September 10th to 15th.

267

7.17 This fall 1951 Norman Hartnell tucked crepe gown, worn by Helen Band to the state dinner, was commented on by the press. The dress had been shown by Simpson's at the Canadian National Exhibition earlier in the season.

7.18 Draped green chiffon dress by Jean Dessès worn by Clayton Burton, November 1953, to the Royal Winter Fair and the following supper dance. The design was published in *L'Officiel de la Haute Couture*, June 1953, 113.

7.19 Fall 1953 Jacques Fath ball gown of ice-blue satin, worn by Signy Eaton to the Hunt Club Ball. The design was published in *Harper's Bazaar*, September 1953, 232.

Ball (fig. 7.19), to a more dramatic, red-and-black halter neck British design by Victor Steibel that was worn by Mona Campbell to the Ballet Ball in 1953, or the made-to-order Pierre Balmain worn by Grace Gooderham to the Artillery Ball in 1956 (fig. 7.20).[45] Etiquette books constantly reiterated that one should "select clothes appropriate to the life you lead. The wildly inappropriate garment is usually the mistake of youth, before the discipline of taste and budget has had time to sink in. Although the temptation may be strong, even in maturity, to purchase the dress that would be a knockout for a unique occasion and completely out of key the rest of the time, unless you're rich, don't succumb."[46] For Canadians, even ball gowns could be ostentatious. Signy Eaton wore her Rodriguez, which she purchased at Eaton's in Toronto, to a ball in London, but she considered it "too much" and uncomfortable (fig. 7.21). Because it was designed as "a knockout," she felt that it was too dramatic and therefore inappropriate. In other words, Signy Eaton, a model for other Canadian women, considered it more elegant to be dressed subtly when out in public, reinforcing the maxim that it was always more tasteful to be under- than overdressed. This is contrary to the advice offered by Americans Emily Post and Margery Wilson, who wrote, "A woman of tact wears her prettiest frocks to other people's houses; and wears her less decorative ones when she is hostess."[47]

7.20 Fall 1956 Pierre Balmain ball gown "Agéna," made to order in Paris for Grace Gooderham, who wore it to the Artillery Ball for her daughter's debut that year. See also fig. 0.1, p. 2, and fig. 2.6, pp. 56–7.

7.21 Spring 1953 Rodriguez ball gown, purchased by Signy Eaton at Eaton's Toronto store and worn to a ball in London. See also fig. 4.11, p.116.

In addition to its regular events, the season was punctuated with special occasions when a particular kind of dress outside of the standard wardrobe was prescribed. Debutante events, weddings, funerals, and maternity clothing fell into this category, though maternity dresses were not usually considered in terms of couture. Toronto debutantes usually purchased their coming-out dresses at the leading stores where their mothers shopped for their own clothing. Anne C. Smith, daughter of Mrs and Mr Edgar Burton, the president of Simpson's, had her dress custom made at Simpson's (fig. 7.22). Economy was practised on debutante dresses as they had a very limited lifespan. Judith James, for example, wore the same dress to her debut in 1954 that her sister had a few years earlier.[48]

The bridal dress was a unique garment that did not necessarily follow the fashionable styles of the day. It was common, as it is still, for these to be made to order for the bride, and bridal salons in department stores played a key role. A second

7.22 Toronto debutantes in 1948. Anne Burton, second from left in the back row, is wearing a made-to-order dress from Simpson's couture salon.

wedding, such as that of Catherine Elliott to John A. Wilson in 1951, necessitated a particular understanding of etiquette since it required a mature design without virginal white or long veil. Mrs Elliott was married during the day and wore an imported Hardy Amies couture wool dress with matching jacket, and a hat trimmed with a veil, which was smart and suitable for day (fig. 7.23).[49]

Wedding guests also had to consider their attire. In 1949, Gertrude Pringle suggested that "women guests at a wedding, whether it takes place in the morning or afternoon, wear an elaborate toilet of the type suitable for a large afternoon reception." By the end of the 1950s, Claire Wallace suggested evening clothes for an evening wedding, and street-length or floor-length afternoon dress "as long as the

7.23 Catherine Elliott on her second wedding day, fall 1951, in her Hardy Amies couture wool dress with matching jacket (fig. 6.5, pp. 224–5), and a red hat trimmed with a veil that she bought at local boutique Joan Rigby.

guest is not overdressed" for a formal daytime wedding. This advice was confirmed by Joan Rosefield Lepofsky, who thought that for Jewish evening weddings, formal evening dresses were appropriate. Sally Brenzel also wore long dresses to evening weddings, and Zelda Hersenhorn wore a bonded floor-length Jacques Heim to a wedding in the early 1960s.[50]

For funerals, a good black suit or dress was required, and a hat. These were usually day clothes that were already part of the wardrobe. By the 1960s, though black was still considered de rigeur for the widow, friends and relatives could wear sombre colours.[51]

The requirements of a travel wardrobe also followed etiquette codes, and these changed with new methods of transportation. Crossing the Atlantic by boat took about a week and involved dress for shipboard occasions. A strict rule when travelling first class was that all dinners were formal except for the first night, and on the last night there was a big party. It was recommended that clothes be worn as if "for shopping in town in the morning . . . This 'morning shopping rule' holds for all train travel here or abroad and for debarking or going on board a ship in any but the smallest port . . . [This applies to] all travel that begins and ends in a city of any size."[52] For the actual sea voyage and the trip, Rose Torno would take simple tailored dresses for lunches, suits, cocktail ensembles, dinner clothes for intimate dinners, and usually one ball gown. The social aspect of the boat was an important part of the trip and had to be considered along with the events planned at the destination. Concern was even directed to the luggage. Rose Torno noted that at that time, "luggage was made to order, to hang up clothes and store clothes on shipboard, a flat case for lingerie and accessories, a shoe case and hat case."[53] Generous luggage allowances permitted one to take the required large wardrobe.

Etiquette expert Millicent Fenwick suggested that once on board ship, one should consider the boat a country club and dress accordingly. She suggested two weights of coat and hat, a couple of silk print dresses, a wool sports suit, afternoon dress, and evening dress. Margery Wilson strongly advocated a lace dress for travelling as it was resistant to wrinkles. She went on, "Clothes obviously purchased to be worn on a ship are in bad taste. Things with anchors or steering wheels on them should be let severely alone. The seasoned traveller of good taste . . . wears sports clothes in the daytime and a dinner dress at night." Wearing older clothes

from the wardrobe for ship travel was an established tradition, though Gertrude Pringle considered it outdated by 1949: "Once women thriftily used their oldest clothing for a sea voyage, but not so now. There may not be many frocks in the traveller's wardrobe, but they will be smart." Whatever the choice, it had to be of good quality, and that quality served to ensure that the garment would be fashionable.[54]

The subject of appropriate travel dress was tackled in 1953 by the society magazine *Mayfair*, which published an article to assist those going to Britain by ship for the coronation. Recommended for embarkation was a "dark city suit" designed by Christian Dior–New York. Listed for the entire trip were two wool suits, a coat that could also be worn for evening, a pink sweater set that matched the lining of one of the wool suits, a navy wool jersey jacket to go with a white crepe dress and a white pullover and skirt, four pairs of shoes, a bathing suit for the ship's pool, and a formal, short or waltz-length dinner dress.[55]

The postwar shift from boat to air travel brought with it newly invented conventions for dress. Regular transatlantic commercial flights were still new, and by the early 1950s airline advertising was just beginning, as seen in a BOAC Stratocruiser to Britain advertisement in *Mayfair* (fig. 7.24). Airline marketing stressed the comfort, luxury, and socializing that had been associated with boat travel: "Here in 'living room' comfort you enjoy the cocktail hour with stimulating conversation and companions . . . then as a guest of B.O.A.C., a delicious full-course dinner including wine and liqueurs. Finally, if you wish, a full-size

7.24 BOAC advertisement for air travel in "'living room' comfort," April 1952.

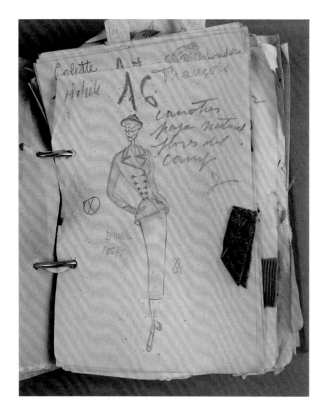

sleeper berth at only a slight extra charge." Illustrations depict the two floors of the plane, the downstairs lounge, dressing rooms, and a photograph of two couples enjoying cocktails in a lounge complete with bartender. The limitations of luggage when travelling by air necessitated a small and tightly co-ordinated wardrobe, not only for the actual voyage but for the whole trip.[56] Highly recommended were wrinkle-resistant and understated garments: "Travel clothes are conservative clothes, quality clothes." Adaptability was key: "The clothes for tomorrow's flight must be as chic as, if not indistin-guishable from, their resident contemporaries . . . They may be worn from dinner to theatre to plane. They must be adaptable."[57]

Rose Torno remembers taking the "Parisienne" plane from New York to Paris. Only one garment was needed for the voyage, a daytime ensemble. She wore a grey wool two-piece Balenciaga suit made for her at the salon in 1950 (figs. 7.25 to 7.27). Her choice perfectly reflects that espoused by the etiquette books: "Dressing for a long airplane trip . . . one should wear clothes that are more obviously sturdy and unmussable. A gray flannel suit, a small, close-fitting hat, shoes with heels of medium height, a good, warm overcoat of tweed or fur-lined wool." When Rose Torno began

7.25 Design house sketch and fabric swatch of the Balenciaga suit shown in figs. 7.26 and 7.27. **7.26** (opposite left) Rose Torno took the "Parisienne" plane from New York to Paris and wore her grey wool flannel two-piece spring 1950 Balenciaga suit, which had been made for her in Paris. She considered it "perfect." **7.27** (opposite right) Design house photograph of the spring 1950 Balenciaga suit that was reproduced exactly as designed for Rose Torno. She too wore it with gloves, hat, and appropriate handbag.

Balenciaga
25 Avril 1950

1 6

281

to fly, she had to pack with air regulations in mind and could not accommodate the same wardrobe as she had fitted in her steamer trunks. She would travel with an itinerary and pack accordingly, having been told in advance by her hostesses the sort of events that were to be arranged.[58]

The importance of having appropriate clothing for airplanes was such that Norman Hartnell designed a travel ensemble in 1957 specifically for the purpose. It was described as an "easy fitting, tailored topcoat with patch pockets large enough to hold passports, tickets and other such documents."[59] That couturiers were designing for flights was a clear indication of the increased use of airlines and the demand for a new style of correct dress.

The recurring theme of stylistic conformity and quality in dress was emphasized by all the etiquette books and magazines. Quality took precedence over the number of items in a wardrobe, and was also seen as a safeguard against outdatedness. These intrinsic notions of quality and value greatly influenced the building and maintenance of wardrobes.

Torontonian Taste in Couture

To be at all outstanding in dress now requires distinct originality and exceptional taste.[60]

The interplay of factors that determined the market for couture reveals a distinctly Torontonian taste. Canadian taste was regulated and filtered by professionals — Paris *vendeuses*, store buyers, and sales assistants — who exerted a considerable influence on what fashions were ultimately seen, purchased, and worn. Commercial choices of couture were made for two audiences: private clients; and the general public, which was kept up to date with current design trends through elaborate fashion shows. Couture was marketed as the height of advanced style, serving as a role model for all fashion design. Theatrical, attention-getting designs were chosen for fashion shows to show off the cosmopolitan sophistication of the store. Canadian retailers were acutely aware of the cultural value of displaying couture within fashion shows that were seen by thousands of women. Their interpretation of couture designs and presentation of co-ordinated ensembles unquestionably acted as a barometer for a feminine, English-Canadian standard of approved good taste and demonstrated correct Canadian etiquette. By contrast, store purchases for a private client were considered in terms of the individual and her role in society.

Local merchants' comprehension of a Canadian, and specifically Torontonian, taste has been illustrated throughout this book. The example of Eaton's fashion co-ordinator, Dora Matthews, ordering Paris designs in fabrics more suited to Canadian taste, not the "itchy doormat" fabric, testifies to her identification of a taste very distinct from that of Paris. Analogously, Holt Renfrew ordered a Dior cocktail dress in a colourful blue taffeta instead of in black as shown on the runway model, and thought it necessary to move the pockets on a Balenciaga suit from the skirt to the jacket, resulting in a more conservative look (see figs. 3.6 and 3.7, pp. 80–1). In 1955, fashion reporter Olive Dickason remarked that Canadian manufacturers were "Canadian-izing the new fashions . . . as Canadians prefer toned down versions of extreme Paris styles . . . more casual than what is found in originals." This was in contrast to American consumers, who were inclined to buy copies that were closer to the Paris design.[61] Emily Post wrote that Americans tended to overdress and that to be overdressed "is to be vulgar and merely conspicuous," while *Vogue's Book of Etiquette* put it more bluntly, saying, "It is in extremely bad taste to wear clothes in public that depart wildly from the accepted norm."[62] By contrast, Canadian understatement was a recognized characteristic. It was discussed on national television when Rosemary Boxer asked Harold Sniederman, owner of a sportswear shop, to compare the style of Canadian and American women. Sniederman said of Canadian women, "I think they are more conservative; I think they dress better."[63]

Finally, the Toronto consumer imposed her own taste on all these preselected goods. Her taste was formed in conjunction with the requirements of the social season and Canadian cultural notions of value. To make the decision to buy a garment, a woman would want to feel flattered by the design and to have the requirements of appropriateness, longevity, and value met in terms of price, exclusivity, and design. The Canadian taste for understatement and long-term value is demonstrated by Catherine Elliott's wardrobe. She did not shop in Paris but relied on the preselected taste of Toronto buyers, and especially on the local specialty shop Joan Rigby, as well as patronizing local dressmakers. She was an active committee woman, serving as a member of the Garden Club and the Girl Guide Council. She was also a member of the old Toronto society and had inherited the tradition of her mother, who had dressed in leading designers' fashions.[64] Her taste embraced tailored suits, such as a Sybil Connolly (fig. 7.28). She wore her second wedding dress — the taupe wool

7.28 Catherine Elliott's Sybil Connolly daytime coat and suit of handwoven tweeds. The suit has been let out in the skirt and jacket. She wore the coat from 1959 to 1965 with a taupe suit accessorized with black or brown suede shoes and bag and later a green suit with violet velvet hat. The suit dates from 1965 and was worn until 1967 with both green and brown accessories.

dress and jacket ensemble by Hardy Amies seen in fig. 6.5 (pp. 224–5) — for years. She preferred British designers, who were not known for dramatic styles, and this extended into her choice of evening wear by Norman Hartnell (see fig. 6.6, p. 226). Her taste was for well-made, conservative styles that would last, reinforcing the importance of serviceability and longevity for Torontonians.

Joan Rosefield Lepofsky's wardrobe was composed of a quantity of imported bonded couture models and did embrace some lavish designs. The 1948 Dior bustle dress that she wore to the races was a bonded model and certainly one of the more striking Paris models produced at the time. Her very dramatic Jean Dessès evening gown, "Sciabe," she only wore once or twice as it was so noticeable and also because the hobble skirt design made it difficult to walk in (fig. 7.29).[65] Her bonded Chanel suits were much worn, however, demonstrating Torontonian taste for understatement.

The couture wardrobe of Toronto socialite Signy Eaton reveals many typical aspects of couture worn in Toronto. She was an important member of the old elite Toronto circle, playing a prominent sociocultural role as wife of the president of Eaton's department store, a member of the Junior League, and an active member of the Art Gallery of Toronto. She was keenly aware of the impact of her dress, which was often reported in the press. Her constant nomination to the best-dressed lists and place within the Hall of Fame established by the *Toronto Telegram* testify to the correctness of her taste and also to the certainty that she was a role model for other Canadians, though she told me she dressed for herself. Mrs Eaton first dressed in Paris couture in 1933 and continued do so into the 1960s, when she would travel to Europe with her husband, who was conducting business. The bulk of her extant wardrobe in the Royal Ontario Museum, though predominantly evening wear, demonstrates her selections from the top European couturiers — Balmain, Dior, Fath, Givenchy, and Hartnell — as well as from more obscure names such as the Italian house Villa & Co. and the Spaniard Rodriguez. She also purchased bonded models, even though she did not recall doing so (fig. 5.12, pp. 158–9).[66] The nuances of Canadian clothing etiquette are clearly reflected in Mrs Eaton's many comments

7.29 Dramatic fall 1948 Jean Dessès evening gown "Sciabe," of iridescent velvet and beaded trim. Joan Rosefield Lepofsky bought the dress on sale after it had been shown at the Canadian National Exhibition by Simpson's but wore it only once or twice. The design was sketched for *Mayfair* magazine, October 1948, 84.

on appropriate dress for different occasions. The social importance of wearing "good" and "correct" clothes cannot be overstated, and its significance was directly reflected in the time spent shopping, dressing, and maintaining a couture-based wardrobe, an important point that has been largely disregarded and unvalidated, as scholar Daniel Miller has noted.[67]

Margaret Maynard, in her work on Australian dress, discusses the balancing act of being fashionable, but not too fashionable, which was also encountered by the Australian elite in the nineteenth century. She writes of the "constant tension between the concern for maintaining a suitable stylish appearance and trying to avoid the shame of vulgarity," and the "extremely narrow line marking the difference between being finely dressed, thus achieving social visibility, and seeming to be overdressed."[68] Insecurity in dress and etiquette, and particularly the fear of appearing in public in an overly dressy costume, seems to have been a constant and recurring colonial anxiety. Canadians consistently chose a conservative tack that emulated British sartorial taste, summed up by the English couturier Hardy Amies, who said, "It has always been rather bad taste in England to be obviously expensively dressed, especially among society people."[69]

There was an informal Canadian consensus that to be too fashionable was in fact, un-Canadian. This self-effacing stance was cautioned against in 1954 by a "British expert . . . a professor of political science at Cambridge University" who was visiting Canada and thought that "a lack of extravagant self-esteem is all to the good — there is enough of that for all North America on constant tap south of the border. But it can be overdone. There is a danger that a modest man or a modest nation may be taken at face value."[70]

By the early 1960s, however, a change was evident. Canadians accepted styles that were increasingly interchangeable with European and American models. Not only had the importance of couture originals drastically dwindled but English-Canadian taste in couture had become less distinct, replaced by an emerging international taste in fashion. It also needs to be remembered that during the 1950s, American manufacturers and stores influenced elite Canadian taste indirectly by reselling bonded models and directly by widely disseminating copies adapted for the North American market. There were certainly some similarities in the two markets, as demonstrated by sales of Christian Dior–New York models in both countries. The

1950 Christian Dior–New York model "Avenue Montaigne," for example, sold 121 copies throughout North America and was considered perfectly appropriate for Canadian taste (fig. 7.30 and Table 2, pp. 184–5).

The couture dress of elite Toronto women from 1945 to 1960, however, can be seen as part of the development of English-Canadian postwar cultural identity. Historically, there has been no iconographic form of dress to represent Canada, or Canadianness, despite regional symbols of English-Canadian dress such as Scottish tartans and kilts and Québécois *habitant* dress, as exemplified by the *capote* and *ceinture fléchée*. Yet during the 1950s, couture clothing worn in Canada did act as a recognizable form of "national" dress for elite women and was also what the majority of women aspired to wear. Dressed in couture, elite women moved in international circles as cultural ambassadors, and through their dress achieved what the 1949–51 Massey Report, a study of Canadian culture, called for: "the promotion abroad of a knowledge of Canada [that] is not a luxury but an obligation."[71] Canadian women wearing couture served the nation in this capacity.

A European model of couture suited English Canadians, as it reinforced their distance from American customs and aligned them with their traditional European and English roots. Couture was the most desirable form of dress, as it provided a visual social entrée into elite social circles. It was easily recognized and instantaneously accepted as beyond reproach, as long as it conformed to the occasion. Couture was one of the clearest symbols that the wearer understood codes of behaviour.

During the 1950s, the roles of the elite were clearly based on gender and class. Men dominated public and political life, while women orchestrated the private lives of their families and their social circle. Couture wardrobes symbolized and highlighted the status of the social elite and implied that the wearers were knowledgeable cultural and social professionals who practised connoisseurship in many fields. Couture operated as a professional working uniform.

Couture provided a standard for national sartorial taste, influencing large numbers of Canadian women at far wider social levels than the small number of couture clients. Elite Torontonian women were not avant garde in their couture dress. Their consumption simply conformed to an internationally accepted standard, adjusted to national and then personal taste. Distinguishing their dress was a uniquely Canadian discrimination imposed on their selections at all stages of design,

7.30 Spring 1950 Christian Dior–New York model 711, "Avenue Montaigne," named after the street on which the house of Dior was located. This is one of 121 copies sold in North America at the wholesale cost of $110. This ensemble was worn by Mrs Saul Silverman and purchased at Holt Renfrew in Toronto. The label shown in fig. 4.15, p.119 is from this garment.

production, merchandising, and purchase. Understatement, discretion, and notions of socio-economic value epitomized Toronto women's couture style and consumption patterns in the postwar years.

In 1952, British fashion journalist Alison Settle wrote, "Fashion is, after all, the most successful . . . I'd be inclined to say, the only really successful . . . form of internationalism."[72] Couture signified European elitist sociocultural economic power and values to an international constituency. This book has set out to study couture consumption in a way that treats it as a continually evolving aspect of modern culture rather than as a fixed and universal social function.[73] Consumption is a central element of contemporary societies and must play an important role in attempts to understand their nature. I hope that my work has both problematized and illuminated the designs and the lives of those who participated in the production, reception, and consumption of couture during the 1950s — when these beautifully designed and crafted clothes were worn and enjoyed by so many North American women.

Toronto Boutiques Selling Couture, Copies, and High-Priced Ready-to-Wear, 1945–63

Billye Vincent Shop

Billye Vincent had five daughters, whom she supported when her husband became ill. She got a job selling clothing at Miller's during the 1930s and became the buyer for Simpson's St Regis Room before the war. After the war, she opened her own business, Billye Vincent, on Bay Street and ran it until the mid-1950s, when she retired due to poor health. *Source*: Elsa Jenkins.

Jean Pierce

Jean E. Pierce was born in Regina, née Stewart. Her first job was with Simpson's for three years, after which she worked for the Saskatchewan Wheat Pool. She moved to Toronto and in the early 1950s opened Pierce-Caldwell, a gift shop selling designer merchandise on Bloor Street. The location was taken over by Rodolphe. Pierce opened a clothing store on Eglinton Avenue in 1956, taking over an existing dress shop, Lillian Ritchie. She bought couture in Europe as well as from American and Canadian manufacturers. Everett Staples worked for her as a designer under the label "Everett Staples for Jean Pierce." *Source*: Jean E. Pierce.

Joan Rigby

The shop was owned and operated by Joan Rigby and her husband. She designed her own line of manufactured suits and dresses, and also had an in-house designer and an alterations department. The shop sold fashions and accessories and held the licence for Jaeger during the early 1950s. The business opened in approximately 1943 at 54 Bloor Street West. In 1951, she moved to a new location, 104 Bloor Street West, until 1967, when she moved to 118 Cumberland. During late the 1940s and 1950s, the sales staff included Lee Allen, Frankie Axeford, Maggy Bennet, Barbara Cook, Mrs Dawe, Ardith Gardiner, Connie James, Miss Johnson, Mary Knight, Jane Murray, Joyce Scott, Bev Scripture, Doris Senior, and Helen Stimpson. Connie James came from Cameron Jeffries and ran the gloves and hosiery department. *Sources*: Helen Stimpson, Joyce Scott, Flavia Redelmeier.

Simon Ramm

Simon Ramm sold ready-to-wear, imported couture, and copies. The shop was less expensive than Travers Fox. The business was located at 40 Bloor Street East in the 1940s. In 1950, it moved to 751 Yonge Street, just north of Bloor, and in the early 1960s expanded to 779–781 Yonge Street. *Source*: *Metropolitan Toronto City Directory*.

Towne and Country Wear

Ruth McDougal, the owner of Towne and Country Wear, took custom orders, but primarily sold high-priced ready-to-wear. Tailor Domenico Vassallo, who had worked in Simpson's custom-order room, worked for her. Her sister, Alison Stock, made hats from her workroom on Gerrard Street. Towne and Country Wear opened at 46 Avenue Road in 1940, moved to 111 Bloor Street West by 1946, and to 232 Bloor Street West by 1949. Joan Rigby bought her out in the early 1950s. *Sources*: Flavia Redelmeier, June McLean.

Travers Fox

The shop was owned and operated by Travers Fox, who did the buying. He sold imports and high-priced ready-to-wear, purchased with specific clients in mind. The shop never made custom orders but had an alterations department of approximately eight women. Sales staff did not receive a commission. The store opened in the late 1940s at 1179 Bay Street and remained in business until the mid-1960s. *Source*: Agnes "Nan" Allen.

APPENDIX B   **Toronto Retail Prices of Second-Hand Couture,
1951–60**

Store	Designer or provenance	Garment	Original price	2nd-hand price	Reference
1951					
Opportunity Shop		Suit		$10	*Globe and Mail*, 1 February 1951, 11
Opportunity Shop		Suits		$10 to $20	*Telegram*, 14 February 1951, 13
1955					
Opportunity Shop	English, French			$3–10	*Telegram*, 23 March 1955, 27
1958					
Opportunity Shop	Sybil Connolly	Suit		$35	V. Denton, "On and Off the Avenue," *The Key*, May 1958, 40
Opportunity Shop	Hardy Amies	Suit		$35	V. Denton, "On and Off the Avenue," *The Key*, May 1958, 40
1959					
Opportunity Shop	Worth	Evening dress	$400	$67	*Globe and Mail*, 22 January 1959, 22
1960					
139 Shoppe	Schiaparelli	Suit	$300	$27	Mary Walpole, "Around Town," *Globe and Mail*, 17 February 1960, 15
139 Shoppe	Koupy	Coat	$155	$49	Mary Walpole, "Around Town," *Globe and Mail*, 17 February 1960, 15
139 Shoppe		Coat	$255	$50	Mary Walpole, "Around Town," *Globe and Mail*, 17 February 1960, 15
139 Shoppe		Theatre coat	$275	$70	Mary Walpole, "Around Town," *Globe and Mail*, 28 September 1960, 13
139 Shoppe	"Couturier designed for a large woman"	Theatre dress, black	$250	$40	Mary Walpole, "Around Town," *Globe and Mail*, 28 September 1960, 13
139 Shoppe	Jean Dessès	[Evening dress]	$375	$60	Mary Walpole, "Around Town," *Globe and Mail*, 28 September 1960, 13
139 Shoppe	Balenciaga	Dinner dress	$375	$50	*Globe and Mail*, 14 December 1960, 14
139 Shoppe	Philip Hulito	Evening dress	$400	$50	*Globe and Mail*, 14 December 1960, 14
139 Shoppe		[Cocktail dress]	$275	$70	*Globe and Mail*, 14 December 1960, 14
Symphony Band Box	Balenciaga	Day dress	$295	$42	*Globe and Mail*, 12 October 1960, 14
Symphony Band Box	Maggy Rouff	Day dress	$150	$45	*Globe and Mail*, 12 October 1960, 14
Symphony Band Box		Wedding guest dress		$30	*Globe and Mail*, 12 October 1960, 14

Note: Prices are rounded to the nearest dollar. All figures in Canadian currency. The value of a dollar over the period, put in terms of average Canadian currency value as of the end of 2000, varies as follows: 1950 = 8 cents; 1955 = 7 cents; 1960 = 6 cents; 1965 = 5.5 cents.

APPENDIX C Toronto Retail Prices of European Couture and Boutique Imports, 1950, 1955, 1960

Store	Designer or provenance	Garment	Retail price	Sale price	Reference
Couture, 1950					
Billye Vincent	Molyneux	Cocktail dress	$149	$90	*Globe and Mail*, 28 November 1950, 15
Billye Vincent	France	Dinner dress	$95	$50	*Globe and Mail*, 28 November 1950, 15
Billye Vincent	Molyneux	Evening dress	$159	$90	*Globe and Mail*, 29 November 1950, 15
Creeds	Europe	Day and evening wear	Up to $250	Half-price or less	*Globe and Mail*, 6 January 1950, 12
Creeds	England	Suit	$95		*Globe and Mail*, 31 January 1950, 14
Creeds	England	Coat	$95		*Globe and Mail*, 5 September 1950, 14
Creeds	England	Suit	$95		"You'll wear chatting over tea, scouring for Antiques . . ." *Globe and Mail*, 18 September 1950, 19
Creeds	France	Evening dress and jacket	$125		*Globe and Mail*, 30 October 1950, 19
Creeds	France	Coats, suits, dresses [bonded models?]	$195 to $350	Half price or less	*Globe and Mail*, 7 November 1950, 13[1]
Eaton's	France	Wool day dress	$75		*Globe and Mail*, 3 February 1950, 30
Eaton's	France	Day dress and vest	$135		*Globe and Mail*, 3 February 1950, 30
Eaton's	France	Dinner dress and jacket	$145		*Globe and Mail*, 3 February 1950, 30
Eaton's	France	Taffeta afternoon dress	$95		*Globe and Mail*, 3 February 1950, 30
Eaton's	Holland	Coats	$40, $60		*Globe and Mail*, 16 February 1950, 28
Eaton's	England	Coats	$70 to $95		*Globe and Mail*, 16 February 1950, 28
Eaton's	England	Coat	$110		*Globe and Mail*, 6 September 1950, 28
Eaton's	Digby Morton	Tweed suit	$295		*Globe and Mail*, 6 September 1950, 28
Eaton's	Georges Boutet of Paris	Wool day dress	$115		*Globe and Mail*, 6 September 1950, 28
Eaton's	Maison Meyer of Paris	Wool cocktail dress with jacket	$125		*Globe and Mail*, 6 September 1950, 28
Eaton's	Switzerland	Embroidered and beaded ball gown, with jacket[2]	$195		*Globe and Mail*, 6 September 1950, 28
Holt Renfrew		Cocktail/dinner dress	$65 to $110	$47	*Globe and Mail*, 17 November 1950, 14
Joan Rigby	Hardy Amies	Suit	$110		*Globe and Mail*, 25 October 1950, 12
Morgan's	England	Suit	$150		*Globe and Mail*, 25 October 1950, 12

Simpson's	Paris, London, Sweden, New York, and from top Canadian designers	Coats	$65 to $595	$55 to $295	Fashion show dispersal, St Regis Room, *Globe and Mail*, 4 March 1950, 14
Simpson's	Paris, London, Sweden, New York, and from top Canadian designers	Suits	$125 to $350	$110 to $275	Fashion show dispersal, St Regis Room, *Globe and Mail*, 4 March 1950, 14
Simpson's	Paris, London, Sweden, New York, and from top Canadian designers	Dresses	$55 to $750	$48 to $450	Fashion show dispersal, St Regis Room, *Globe and Mail*, 4 March 1950, 14
Simpson's	Paris, London, Sweden, New York, and from top Canadian designers	Evening dresses	$90 to $1,295	$80 to $450	Fashion show dispersal, St Regis Room, *Globe and Mail*, 4 March 1950, 14
Simpson's	Paris, London, Sweden, New York, and from top Canadian designers	Bride/ bridesmaid dresses	$175 to $395	$135 to $325	Fashion show dispersal, St Regis Room, *Globe and Mail*, 4 March 1950, 14
Simpson's	Madeleine Casalino	Coat	$195		*Globe and Mail*, 8 September 1950, 14
Simpson's	Madeleine Casalino	Jet-trimmed black suit	$165		*Globe and Mail*, 8 September 1950, 14
Simpson's	Rue de la Paix	Wool suit	$110		*Globe and Mail*, 8 September 1950, 14
Simpson's	Mainbocher	Coat	$110		*Globe and Mail*, 8 September 1950, 14
Simpson's	England	Coat	$115		*Globe and Mail*, 8 September 1950, 14
Simpson's	England	Embroidered coat	$195		*Globe and Mail*, 8 September 1950, 14
Simpson's	England, by Silhouette de Luxe	Suit	$110		*Globe and Mail*, 8 September 1950, 14
Simpson's	France, England, New York, Canada	Coats	$145 to $550	$135 to $395	*Globe and Mail*, 8 September 1950, 14
Simpson's	France	Suit	$110		*Globe and Mail*, 8 September 1950, 14
Simpson's	France, England, New York, Canada[3]	Suits	$110 to $875	$65 to $675	*Globe and Mail*, 16 September 1950, 14
Simpson's	France, England, New York, Canada[3]	Late day, evening wear	$100 to $2,800	$90 to $550	*Globe and Mail*, 16 September 1950, 14
Simpson's	France, England, New York, Canada[3]	Wedding gowns	$285 to $1,750	$225 to $750	*Globe and Mail*, 16 September 1950, 14
Simpson's	Paris, London, New York	Evening gowns	$60 to $295		*Globe and Mail*, 24 October 1950, 14
Simpson's	Madeleine Casalino	Late day dress	$195		*Globe and Mail*, 28 December 1950, 12

Boutique, 1950

Eaton's	Amies Boutique	Coat	$195		*Globe and Mail*, 10 November 1950, 14
Morgan's	Amies Boutique	Suit	$165		*Globe and Mail*, 19 October 1950, 13

Couture, 1955

Billye Vincent	Italy	Suit	$250	$125	*Globe and Mail*, 10 February, 1955, 15
Billye Vincent	Import	Cocktail dress	$139	$15 to $69	*Globe and Mail*, 10 February 1955, 15
Billye Vincent	Import	Wool day dress	$250	$125	*Globe and Mail*, 10 February 1955, 15
Creeds	England	Suit	$150		*Globe and Mail*, 27 January 1955, 15
Creeds	England	Suit with two skirts, pencil and pleated	$85		*Globe and Mail*, 17 February 1955, 15
Creeds	Original models		$150+		*Globe and Mail*, 18 September 1955, 14
Creeds	Rouff, Raphael, Heim, and others	Coats, suits, day dresses, cocktail dresses	$195 to $275		*Globe and Mail*, 30 September 1955, 18
Creeds	England	Suit	$85	$69	*Globe and Mail*, 4 October 1955, 15
Creeds	England	Suit	$85		*Globe and Mail*, 31 October 1955, 17
Creeds	France, Italy, Fath, Rouff, Balmain, and others	Coats	$195 to $275	One-third to one-half off regular price	*Globe and Mail*, 31 October 1955, 17
Creeds	France, Italy, Switzerland	Evening	$135+		*Globe and Mail*, 3 November 1955, 14
Creeds		Coats	$135 to $150	$99 to $105	*Globe and Mail*, 17 November 1955, 14
Creeds	France, Italy[4]	Coats, suits, dresses	$250 to $295	$150 to $195	*Globe and Mail*, 1 December 1955, 19
Creeds	France, Italy		$225 to $350	Half price	*Globe and Mail*, 12 December 1955, 19
Eaton's	Switzerland	Suit	$125		*Globe and Mail*, 18 January 1955, 30
Eaton's	Switzerland	Suit	$150		*Globe and Mail*, 18 January 1955, 30
Eaton's	Switzerland	Suits	$90 to $95		*Globe and Mail*, 18 January 1955, 30
Eaton's	Switzerland	Spring day suit	$119		*Globe and Mail*, 18 January 1955, 30
Eaton's	Holland	Wool tweed suit	$110		*Globe and Mail*, 18 January 1955, 30
Eaton's	France	Suit	$125		*Globe and Mail*, 18 January 1955, 30
Eaton's	Holland	Coat	$75		*Globe and Mail*, 7 March 1955, 40
Eaton's	Holland	Suit	$99		*Globe and Mail*, 7 March 1955, 40
Eaton's	Sybil Connolly	Suit	$125		*Globe and Mail*, 7 March 1955, 40
Eaton's	Holland	Wool coat	$70 to $95		*Globe and Mail*, 17 March 1955, 48
Eaton's	Casa da Silva	Cocktail dress[5]	$195		1955 spring fashion show program, F229-135-4, file 2, T. Eaton Records, AOO[6]

Eaton's	Marty of Switzerland	Pink cotton brocade suit	$150	1955 spring fashion show program, F229-135-4, file 2, T. Eaton Records, AOO
Eaton's	Marty of Switzerland	Yellow dotted net over white cocktail/ evening dress	$225	1955 spring fashion show program, F229-135-4, file 2, T. Eaton Records, AOO
Eaton's	Madeleine Casalino	Grey flannel suit with fur trim	$250	1955 fall fashion show program, F229-135-4, file 1, T. Eaton Records, AOO[7]
Eaton's	Madeleine Casalino	Black ninon and lace tunic cocktail dress	$175	1955 fall fashion show program, F229-135-4, file 1, T. Eaton Records, AOO
Eaton's	Michael of London	Suit [matches next entry]	$99	1955 fall fashion show program, F229-135-4, file 1, T. Eaton Records, AOO
Eaton's	Michael of London	Tweed coat [matches previous entry]	$99	1955 fall fashion show program, 136-4, file 1, T. Eaton Records, AOO
Eaton's	Hardy Amies	Suit	$125	1955 fall fashion show program, F229-135-4, file 1, T. Eaton Records, AOO
Eaton's	Hardy Amies	Tweed day dress	$125	1955 fall fashion show program, F229-135-4, file 1, T. Eaton Records, AOO
Eaton's	Marty of Switzerland	Blue silk damask evening dress	$225	1955 fall fashion show program, F229-135-4, file 1, T. Eaton Records, AOO
Eaton's	Marty of Switzerland	Ocelot coat trimmed with black dyed Alaska seal	$1,995	1955 fall fashion show program, F229-135-4, file 1, T. Eaton Records, AOO
Eaton's	Marty of Switzerland	Late day dress	$125	1955 fall fashion show program, F229-135-4, file 1, T. Eaton Records, AOO
Eaton's	Marty of Switzerland	Evening dress and matching coat	$295 and $225	1955 fall fashion show program, F229-135-4, file 1, T. Eaton Records, AOO
Eaton's	Marty of Switzerland	Pale periwinkle blue ninon, draped, jewelled, and embroidered bodice	$195	1955 fall fashion show program, F229-135-4, file 1, T. Eaton Records, AOO
Eaton's	Sweden	Yellow wool short coat and skirt	$125	1955 fall fashion show program, F229-135-4, file 1, T. Eaton Records, AOO
Eaton's	Schibili	Black wool coat and slim skirt ensemble	$150	1955 fall fashion show program, F229-135-4, file 1, T. Eaton Records, AOO
Eaton's	Schibili	Navy wool crepe cocktail dress with jacket for day	$150	1955 fall fashion show program, F229-135-4, file 1, T. Eaton Records, AOO

Eaton's	Sybil Connolly	Pale blue handwoven Irish tweed	$125		1955 fall fashion show program, F229-135-4, file 1, T. Eaton Records, AOO
Eaton's		Beaded evening sheath	$295		*Globe and Mail*, 12 October 1955, 16
Eaton's	Imports, one of a kind		$50 to $295	One-third to one-half off	*Globe and Mail*, 23 November 1955, 10
Eaton's	Macola of Switzerland	Beaded ball gown	$325		*Globe and Mail*, 29 December 1955, 32
Eaton's	Marty of Switzerland	Silk organza ball gown, beaded bodice	$295		*Globe and Mail*, 29 December 1955, 32
Eaton's	Brussels	Beaded evening dress	$250		*Globe and Mail*, 29 December 1955, 32
Holt Renfrew	Christian Dior	Wool spring dress	$195		*Globe and Mail*, 10 February 1955, 14
Holt Renfrew	Christian Dior	Suit	$185		*Globe and Mail*, 23 February 1955, 12
Holt Renfrew	Christian Dior	Suit	$175		*Globe and Mail*, 23 February 1955, 12
Holt Renfrew		Wool suit	$80		*Globe and Mail*, 17 March 1955, 22
Holt Renfrew		Faille suit	$85		*Globe and Mail*, 17 March 1955, 22
Holt Renfrew	England	Lined knitted suit	$95		*Globe and Mail*, 4 October 1955, 14
Holt Renfrew	Import	Debutante dresses	$75 to $150		*Globe and Mail*, 31 October 1955, 16
Holt Renfrew	Christian Dior[8]	Coats, suits, dresses		$95 to $395	*Globe and Mail*, 2 November 1955, 12
Holt Renfrew	Christian Dior	Day dress	$135		*Globe and Mail*, 17 November 1955, 14
Morgan's	Switzerland	Strapless ball gown	$275		*Canadian Jewish Review* 37, 51 (16 September 1955): 162
Simon Ramm	England	Tweed suits	$75 to $110	$58, $68	*Globe and Mail*, 20 October 1955, 14
Simon Ramm	Import	Silk afternoon dresses and after-five cocktail dresses	$55 to $145	$28 to $73	*Globe and Mail*, 7 November 1955, 16
Simon Ramm		Coats	$90 to $249	$59 to $119	*Globe and Mail*, 29 December 1955, 10
Simon Ramm	Italy, France, and England	Wool day suits	$65 to $115	$33 to $59	*Globe and Mail*, 29 December 1955, 10
Simon Ramm	Import	Cocktail dresses	$60 to $135	$29 to $69	*Globe and Mail*, 29 December 1955, 10
Simon Ramm	Import	Evening dresses	$95 to $250	$59 to $124	*Globe and Mail*, 29 December 1955, 10
Simon Ramm	England and France	Tweed suits	$95 to $175	$49 to $88	*Globe and Mail*, 29 December 1955, 10
Simpson's	Import	Theatre costume[9]	$135		*Globe and Mail*, 4 February 1955, 14
Simpson's	Import	Theatre costume	$125		*Globe and Mail*, 4 February 1955, 14
Simpson's	Holland	Coats	$55 to $70		*Globe and Mail*, 3 September 1955, 14

Simpson's	Madeleine Casalino	Coat with leopard collar	$195	*Globe and Mail*, 6 September 1955, 16
Simpson's	Europe	Suit	$165	*Globe and Mail*, 6 September 1955, 16
Simpson's	England	Suits	$70	*Globe and Mail*, 6 September 1955, 16
Simpson's	Scotland	Suits	$60	*Globe and Mail*, 6 September 1955, 16
Simpson's		Ball gown and stole	$210	*Globe and Mail*, 12 October 1955, 16
Simpson's	Simone of London	Beaded satin ball gown	$325	*Globe and Mail*, 2 November 1955, 19
Simpson's	England	Suit	$150	*Globe and Mail*, 2 November 1955, 19
Simpson's		Suit and three-quarter-length jacket	$140	*Globe and Mail*, 2 November 1955, 19
Simpson's	France	Three-quarter-length lace evening dress	$195	*Globe and Mail*, 29 December 1955, 32

Boutique, 1955

Eaton's	Heim Boutique	Three-quarter-length rayon brocade evening dress	$175	*Globe and Mail*, 29 December 1955, 32
Holt Renfrew	Hardy Amies Boutique	Suit	$165	*Globe and Mail*, 24 January 1955, 14
Morgan's	Hardy Amies Boutique	Day dress	$85	*Globe and Mail*, 8 September 1955, 28
Simpson's	Hardy Amies Boutique	Tweed suit	$99	*Globe and Mail*, 6 September 1955, 16

Couture, 1960

Creeds	France	Dress and jacket suit	$165	*Globe and Mail*, 10 March 1960, 14
Creeds	Hardy Amies	Dress and jacket suit	$175	*Globe and Mail*, 17 March 1960, 15
Creeds	Pierre Cardin	Tweed "walking suit" with seven-eighths-length coat and skirt	$265	*Globe and Mail*, 22 March 1960, 12
Creeds	Switzerland	Wool day dress and jacket suit	$115	*Globe and Mail*, 29 March 1960, 12
Creeds	Europe	Dress and coat[10]	$225	*Globe and Mail*, 31 March 1960, 14
Eaton's	Pierre Cardin	Coat and skirt	$275	1960 spring fashion show program, F229-135-4, file 2, T. Eaton Records, AOO
Eaton's	Pierre Cardin	Black-and-white tweed suit with white silk collar	$225	1960 spring fashion show program, F229-135-4, file 2, T. Eaton Records, AOO
Eaton's	Jean Dessès	Navy blue crepe suit with cross-over jacket	$175	1960 spring fashion show program, F229-135-4, file 2, T. Eaton Records, AOO

Eaton's	Jacques Griffe	Suit	$225		1960 spring fashion show program, F229-135-4, file 2, T. Eaton Records, AOO
Eaton's	Guy Laroche	Short evening dress	$250		1960 spring fashion show. F229-135-4, file 2, T. Eaton Records, AOO
Eaton's	Jeanne Lanvin	Evening tunic dress of beige Chantilly lace	$195		1960 spring fashion show. F229-135-4, file 2, T. Eaton Records, AOO
Eaton's	Simone of London	Evening dress[11]	$395		1960 spring fashion show. F229-135-4, file 2, T. Eaton Records, AOO
Eaton's	Marty of Switzerland	Cocktail dress	$150		1960 spring fashion show. F229-135-4, file 2, T. Eaton Records, AOO
Eaton's	Marty of Switzerland	Evening dress	$250		1960 spring fashion show. F229-135-4, file 2, T. Eaton Records, AOO
Eaton's	Pierre Cardin	Coat	$225		*Globe and Mail*, 22 February 1960, 36
Eaton's	Switzerland	Late day/ cocktail dress	$175		*Globe and Mail*, 3 March 1960, 48
Eaton's	Lanvin/Castillo	Coat	$195		*Globe and Mail*, 18 March 1960, 28
Eaton's		Coat	$99		*Globe and Mail*, 31 March 1960, 44
Eaton's	Marty of Switzerland	Cocktail dress and coat[12]	$450		*Globe and Mail*, 2 September 1960, 32
Eaton's	Jacques Griffe	Black wool coat	$295		*Globe and Mail*, 13 September 1960, 34
Eaton's	Jacques Griffe	Wool sheath late day dress	$195		*Globe and Mail*, 13 September 1960, 34
Eaton's	England	Dress and jacket with Persian lamb collar	$250		*Globe and Mail*, 13 September 1960, 34
Eaton's	Marty of Switzerland	Re-embroidered lace cocktail dress	$195		*Globe and Mail*, 7 October 1960, 38
Eaton's	Marty of Switzerland	Beaded, sequinned ball gown	$395		*Globe and Mail*, 31 October 1960, 40
Eaton's	Europe/US?	Ball gown and coat	$595		*Globe and Mail*, 31 October 1960, 40
Eaton's	Pierre Balmain	Ball gown	$595		*Globe and Mail*, 15 November 1960, 12
Holt Renfrew	Import	Evening dresses	$350		*Globe and Mail*, 6 October 1960, 24
Julius Simon	Imported fabric	Suits	$95 to $175	$68 to $118	*Globe and Mail*, 27 October 1960, 14
Morgan's	Nicole of Sweden	Reversible coat	$119		Mary Walpole, "Around the Town," *Globe and Mail*, 23 March 1960, 13
Morgan's	France	Coats	$70 to $225		Mary Walpole, "Around the Town," *Globe and Mail*, 23 March 1960, 13
Morgan's	Hardy Amies	Wool crepe day dress	$95		*Globe and Mail*, 13 October 1960, 19
Morgan's	Hardy Amies	Wool crepe day dress	$110		*Globe and Mail*, 13 October 1960, 19

Morgan's	Robita of Mayfair	Cocktail dress and jacket	$150		*Globe and Mail*, 17 October 1960, 15
Morgan's	Europe	Theatre suit	$195		*Globe and Mail*, 17 October 1960, 15
Morgan's	Robita of Mayfair	Evening dress	$225		*Globe and Mail*, 16 November 1960, 19
Simon Ramm	Europe	Suits	$115 to $149	$70 to $99	*Globe and Mail*, 20 October 1960, 14
Simon Ramm	Europe	Coat	$95 to $295	$59 to $155	*Globe and Mail*, 29 December 1960, 10
Simon Ramm	Europe	Formal gowns	$75 to $195	$38 to $98	*Globe and Mail*, 29 December 1960, 10
Simpson's	Marty of Switzerland	Silk damask cocktail dress	$250		*Globe and Mail*, 20 February 1960, 12
Simpson's	France	Grey wool suit	$110		*Globe and Mail*, 10 September 1960, 12
Simpson's	Europe	Cocktail dress	$235		*Globe and Mail*, 10 September 1960, 12
Simpson's	Nina Ricci	Beaded white silk cocktail sheath dress	$225		*Globe and Mail*, 10 September 1960, 12
Simpson's	Marty of Switzerland	Ball gown	$295		*Globe and Mail*, 13 September 1960, 14
Simpson's	Grès	Coat	$225		*Globe and Mail*, 16 September 1960, 12
Simpson's	Europe	Silk brocade ball gown	$210		*Globe and Mail*, 21 October 1960, 16
Simpson's	Europe	Pleated crepe ball gown	$295		*Globe and Mail*, 21 October 1960, 16
Simpson's	Nina Ricci	Ball gown	$325		*Globe and Mail*, 21 October 1960, 16

Boutique, 1960

Eaton's	Jean Dessès	Cocktail dress	$225	*Globe and Mail*, 23 September 1960, 32
Eaton's	Pierre Balmain, Florilège	Cocktail dress	$195	*Globe and Mail*, 15 December 1960, 34
Holt Renfrew	Hardy Amies Boutique	Day dress	$125	*Globe and Mail*, 17 February 1960, 15
Holt Renfrew	Hardy Amies Boutique	Suit	$125	*Globe and Mail*, 28 March 1960, 15
Holt Renfrew	Dior–London	Suit	$250	*Globe and Mail*, 1 September 1960, 15
Holt Renfrew	Heim Boutique	Coats, suits	$75+	*Style*, 7 September 1960, 7
Holt Renfrew	Givenchy Boutique	Dresses	$50+	*Style*, 7 September 1960, 7
Holt Renfrew	Givenchy for Miss Renfrew[13]	Two-piece day dress	$65	*Globe and Mail*, 17 October 1960, 15
Holt Renfrew	Givenchy for Miss Renfrew	Dress and jacket	$80	*Globe and Mail*, 17 October 1960, 15
Holt Renfrew	Givenchy for Miss Renfrew	Coat dress	$50	*Globe and Mail*, 17 October 1960, 15
Morgan's	Hardy Amies Boutique	Suit	$165	*Globe and Mail*, 19 October 1950, 13
Simpson's	Heim Boutique	Coat	$195	*Globe and Mail*, 10 September 1960, 12
Simpson's	Nina Ricci	Cocktail sheath	$250	*Globe and Mail*, 13 September 1960, 14

Notes: The category of "couture" is used in its broadest sense. The terminology of advertisements was varied and imprecise, and prices are sometimes the best indicator of the type of clothing promoted. The focus of the advertisements was largely on provenance. Prices are rounded to the nearest dollar. All figures in Canadian currency. The value of a dollar over the period, put in terms of average Canadian currency value as of the end of 2000, varies as follows: 1950 = 8 cents; 1955 = 7 cents; 1960 = 6 cents; 1965 = 5.5 cents.

[1] "Spectacular opportunity — an extraordinary sale of exclusive French originals from the most famous Paris couturiers."

[2] This ball gown and its accompanying stole were from Zurich, in "shot sari silk in bronze-green embroidered, beaded and brilliant sewn." It was advertised with a $250 Hattie Carnegie suit and a $150 New York cocktail dress.

[3] Included designs by Dior, Dessès, Fath, Piguet, Ricci, Alwynn, Griffe, Amies, Trigère Rosenstein, Cassini, Reig, and leading Canadian designers.

[4] "This outstanding group represents practically every top name in French and Italian haute couture."

[5] The skirt of this two-piece cocktail ensemble sold for $195 and the top for $29.95. See Figure 4.7, p.110, ROM 962.21.3ab, worn by Dora Matthews. It was described as having a "full cotton skirt . . . hand painted in gold and printed with flowers" in Eaton's 1955 spring fashion show program.

[6] Fifteen designs by Sybil Connolly, Irene Gilbert, Jacques Fath, Christian Dior, Pierre Balmain, Jean Dessès, and Givenchy were included in the spring 1955 Eaton's fashion show program but prices were not listed, presumably because they were very expensive.

[7] Nineteen designs by Sybil Connolly, Norman Hartnell, Digby Morton, Givenchy, Jean Dessès, Pierre Balmain, Jacques Fath, and Michael Sherard were described in the fall 1955 Eaton's fashion show program but prices were not listed.

[8] "Original models by Christian Dior shown last Thursday . . . sponsored by the Women's Committee of the Art Gallery of Toronto."

[9] This lace sheath was advertised for the Opera Festival, 25 February to 12 March 1955.

[10] "Stained glass print dress with its own monotone coat . . . Swiss silky surfaced, homespun-weave wool."

[11] This floor-length black faille gown with jewelled embroidery insets can be compared to one found in the Royal Ontario Museum, ROM 970.358.13.

[12] This beaded strapless dress and coat came in a size 14, "deep chocolate brown silk peau de soie."

[13] Designed in France by Givenchy and made in Canada as an exclusive with Miss Renfrew.

APPENDIX D Toronto Retail Prices of Couture Copies and Adaptations, 1950, 1955, 1960

Store	Designer or provenance	Garment	Retail price	Sale price	Reference
1950					
Creeds	France	Dress	$40		*Globe and Mail*, 18 January 1950, 11
Creeds	France	Dress	$40		*Globe and Mail*, 24 January 1950, 10
Eaton's	Christian Dior	Coat	$60		*Globe and Mail*, 2 February 1950, 28
Eaton's	Christian Dior	Coat	$50		*Globe and Mail*, 22 February 1950, 26
Eaton's	Fath	Coat	$50		*Globe and Mail*, 22 February 1950, 26
Eaton's	Piguet	Cape	$25		*Globe and Mail*, 22 February 1950, 26
Holt Renfrew	Fath	Rayon spring dress	$40		*Globe and Mail*, 14 February 1950, 10
Holt Renfrew	Christian Dior[1]	Coat	$150		*Globe and Mail*, 18 April 1950, 14
Holt Renfrew	Balenciaga	Suit	$125		*Globe and Mail*, 20 April 1950, 14
Holt Renfrew	Holt's adaptation from original Hardy Amies model	Suit	$110		*Globe and Mail*, 24 April 1950, 14
Holt Renfrew	Paris	Fur-lined fleece coat	$235		*Globe and Mail*, 11 September 1950, 17
Holt Renfrew	Balenciaga	Suit	$110		*Globe and Mail*, 25 September 1950, 18
Holt Renfrew	Paris	Holt Renfrew designed suit	$55		*Globe and Mail*, 2 October 1950, 18
Joan Rigby	Import	Three-quarter-length jacket	$79		*Globe and Mail*, 10 March 1950, 11
Joan Rigby	Import	Suit	$115		*Globe and Mail*, 16 March 1950, 13
Morgan's	Hardy Amies	Coat	$165		*Globe and Mail*, 25 October 1950, 12
Morgan's	Fath	Crepe afternoon dress	$53		*Globe and Mail*, 1 November 1950, 15
Morgan's	Fath	Suit	$55		*Globe and Mail*, 1 November 1950, 15
Simpson's	New York copies of Paris originals	Coats	$100 to $195		*Globe and Mail*, 11 October 1950, 14
1955					
Creeds	Balenciaga	Suit and blouse	$110		*Globe and Mail*, 5 September 1955, 15
Creeds	Balenciaga	Coat	$210		*Globe and Mail*, 21 September 1955, 15
Creeds	Pierre Balmain[2]	Coat	$175		*Globe and Mail*, 21 September 1955, 15
Creeds	France, Italy	Coat	$195 to $275	One-third to one-half off original price	*Globe and Mail*, 31 October 1955, 15

Creeds	England	Suit	$85	One-third to one-half off original price	*Globe and Mail*, 31 October 1955, 17
Holt Renfrew	England	Suit	$80		*Globe and Mail*, 4 February 1955, 12
Holt Renfrew	Holt's own reproduction of English model	Suit	$85		*Globe and Mail*, 8 February 1955, 12
Holt Renfrew	France[3]	Suit	$55		*Globe and Mail*, 2 October 1955, 18
Holt Renfrew	Christian Dior, Fath, Simonetta, Veneziani	Coat	$115 to $175		*Globe and Mail*, 14 October 1955, 15
Morgan's	France	Coat	$110		*Globe and Mail*, 3 February 1955, 12
Morgan's	France	Suit	$95		*Globe and Mail*, 3 February 1955, 12
Morgan's	Hardy Amies	Suit	$110		*Globe and Mail*, 30 March 1955, 13
Morgan's	Balenciaga	Worsted or French faille suit	$85		*Globe and Mail*, 30 March 1955, 13
Morgan's	Michael of London	Tweed or grey flannel suit	$110		*Globe and Mail*, 31 March 1955, 13
Morgan's	Antonelli	Coat	$100		*Globe and Mail*, 14 October 1955, 24
Morgan's	Michael of London	Coat	$100		*Globe and Mail*, 14 October 1955, 24
Morgan's	Hardy Amies	Coat	$110		*Globe and Mail*, 14 October 1955, 24
Morgan's	Hardy Amies	Coat	$115		*Globe and Mail*, 3 November 1955, 13
Simpson's	Davidow	Bianchini silk tweed suit and blouse	$225		*Globe and Mail*, 1 February 1955, 23
Simpson's	Hardy Amies	Coat with lamb collar and braid	$189		*Globe and Mail*, 7 October 1955, 12
Simpson's St Regis Room	Hardy Amies	Coat with braid but without fur trim	$115		*Globe and Mail*, 7 October 1955, 12
Simpson's	Givenchy	Coat	$100		*Globe and Mail*, 7 October 1955, 12
Simpson's	John Cavanagh	Wool tweed suit	$95		*Globe and Mail*, 7 October 1955, 12
Simpson's	Balenciaga	Blin and Blin cashmere suit	$115		*Globe and Mail*, 7 October 1955, 12
Simpson's	Fath	Dyed Blin and Blin cashmere suit with nutria trim	$169		*Globe and Mail*, 7 October 1955, 12
Simpson's	Ronald Patterson	Dress	$50		*Globe and Mail*, 7 October 1955, 12
Simpson's	Balenciaga	Black and white tweed dress	$80		*Globe and Mail*, 7 October 1955, 12
Simpson's	Pierre Balmain	Forstmann wool dress	$90		*Globe and Mail*, 7 October 1955, 12
Simpson's	Norman Hartnell	Black velvet and silk evening dress	$95		*Globe and Mail*, 7 October 1955, 12

1960

Eaton's	Nina Ricci[4]	Coat	$125		Eaton's 1960 spring fashion show program, F229-135-4, file 2, T. Eaton Records, AOO
Eaton's	Originala[5]	Blue wool coat	$300		Eaton's 1960 spring fashion show program, F229-135-4, file 2, T. Eaton Records, AOO
Eaton's	Originala	Double-breasted coat with leopard collar	$395		Eaton's 1960 spring fashion show program, F229-135-4, file 2, T. Eaton Records, AOO
Eaton's	Givenchy	Wool walking suit	$100		*Globe and Mail*, 23 September 1960, 32
Eaton's	Nina Ricci	Coat with fox fur trim	$229		*Globe and Mail*, 6 October 1960, 52
Eaton's	Balenciaga	Coat	$100		*Globe and Mail*, 6 October 1960, 52
Eaton's	Guy Laroche	Wool crepe day dress	$45		*Globe and Mail*, 6 October 1960, 52
Eaton's	Pierre Cardin	Two-piece day dress	$65		*Globe and Mail*, 6 October 1960, 52
Eaton's	Heim	Wool jersey day dress	$35		*Globe and Mail*, 6 October 1960, 52
Eaton's	Givenchy	Suit	$100		*Globe and Mail*, 6 October 1960, 52
Eaton's	Nina Ricci	Cocktail dress	$70		*Globe and Mail*, 6 October 1960, 52
Eaton's	Marty of Switzerland	Cocktail dress	$195		*Globe and Mail*, 7 October 1960, 38
Eaton's	Simonetta and Carose	Cocktail dress	$95		*Globe and Mail*, 26 October 1960, 22
Eaton's	Originala	Coat with mink trim	$495		*Globe and Mail*, 4 November 1960, 34
Holt Renfrew	Holt Renfrew reproductions of haute couture models	Coat	$140		*Globe and Mail*, 13 October 1960, 17
Holt Renfrew	Holt Renfrew reproductions of haute couture models	Coat with fur trim	$200 to $300		*Globe and Mail*, 13 October 1960, 17
Holt Renfrew	Couture	Suits	$100 to $120		*Globe and Mail*, 13 October 1960, 17
Morgan's	Fabiani	Cocktail dress	$60		*Globe and Mail*, 6 October 1960, 32
Simon Ramm	France	Suits[6]	$95 to $129	$79	*Globe and Mail*, 24 March 1960, 18
Simpson's	Jean Dessès, by Marcassite	Black silk cocktail dress	$175		*Globe and Mail*, 13 September 1960, 14
Simpson's	Nina Ricci	Coat with fur trim	$249		*Globe and Mail*, 7 October 1960, 16
Simpson's	Lanvin/Castillo	Coat	$99		*Globe and Mail*, 7 October 1960, 16
Simpson's	Balenciaga	Coat	$99		*Globe and Mail*, 7 October 1960, 16

Simpson's	Simonetta	Suit with pleated skirt	$95	*Globe and Mail*, 7 October 1960, 16
Simpson's	Givenchy	One-shoulder cocktail dress	$65	*Globe and Mail*, 7 October 1960, 16
Simpson's	Jean Patou	Silk cocktail dress	$70	*Globe and Mail*, 7 October 1960, 16
Simpson's	Nina Ricci	Day dress	$65	*Globe and Mail*, 7 October 1960, 16

Notes: Prices are rounded to the nearest dollar. All figures in Canadian currency. The value of a dollar over the period, put in terms of average Canadian currency value as of the end of 2000, varies as follows: 1950 = 8 cents; 1955 = 7 cents; 1960 = 6 cents; 1965 = 5.5 cents.

[1] According to the *Globe*, Holt Renfrew imported the model of "Allegro," Dior's best coat, and made reproductions.

[2] "French adaptions of original models . . . hand-made from French tweeds, by a French tailor."

[3] "Suits made in Paris . . . HR's artist in Paris sketched the two stunning models . . . The suits are in perfectly proportioned American sizes."

[4] "A copy of a black silk moiré coat by Nina Ricci with a cabbage rose."

[5] The original designer is unknown, but Originala was a manufacturer known for high-end European knock-offs.

[6] Made from Italian fabrics, Le Sur and Rodier French textiles, and Linton tweeds.

Canadian Client Records from the London Couture House of Lachasse, 1954–66

	Currency exchange rate of Canadian dollar to pounds sterling				
Year	$ to £	Year	$ to £	Year	$ to £
1945	4.45	1955	2.75	1965	3.01
1950	3.04	1960	2.72		

Mrs Plow

AAD 6-10-1989, P195
PLOW Government House
1/ HQ Eastern Command, Royal Artillery Park, Halifax
2/ Silver Birches Nova Scotia, Bank of Nova Scotia, Halifax

1955			[£.s.d]	
2895	April 27	Grey wool suit 24	27.4.0	
2897	April 21	Grey/mauve tweed suit	52.10.0	
2963	May 20	Blue wool dress 35	44.2.0	
		Air freight	2.00.0	£165/16-

1958			[£.s.d]	
7748	Mar 4	Grey suiting suit 56	71.8	

1959			[£.s.d]	
5168	Mar 26	Altering grey suit 139	5.15.6	
9276		Beige/white print suit dress/jkt	96.12.0	
9277	25	Navy worsted suit	73.10.0	
9334	May 29	Navy suiting suit 171	58.16.0	£175.17.6

1960			[£.s.d]	
1068	May 10	Blk dress 162	71.8.0	
6994	9	Alt[ering] blue wool dress 162	4.4.0	
6995	5	New Gro collar/re dyeing		
		buttons/press grey jacket	2.12.6	£78.4.6

1965			[£.s.d]	
8003	May 21	Grey ribbed wool suit 92 gns [guineas] 169		
5758	18	Alt[ering] blue suit 24 gns	96.12	
			25.4	£121.16-

1966			[£.s.d]	
8034	Nov 4	4 buttons inc[luding] postage	3.0.2	

Mrs Milner

Sheet 107, AAD 6-4-1989
Mrs Arthur Milner, 11 Castlefrank Drive, Toronto, Ontario
(rec by Mrs Victor Blundel)

1954			[£.s.d]	
1601	April 16	Blue/pink checked suit	54.12.0	

AAD 6-10-1989, M-P Ledger, M235
Mrs Arthur Milner, 11 Castlefrank Drive, Hyde Park Hotel

1955			[£.s.d]	
2717	April 14	Green tweed suit 17	60.18.0	
		4 new set of buttons for		
		light check suit	1.11.6	£62.9.6
1956			**[£.s.d]**	
5062	May 7	Black wool suit 71	67.04.1	
5063	May 7	Pink wool suit	65.02.0	£132.6.0
1957			**[£.s.d]**	
6666	May 15	Green check coat 58	86.2.0	
		Green tweed suit 63	78.15.0	£164.17.0
	May 17	By cash $450.00		160.18.1
	14			3.11.6
				7.5
1958			**[£.s.d]**	
4042	Aug 11	Pressing brown check skirt 23	12.06.0	
46	15	Alt[ering] grey skirt 23	3.03.0	
3941	Aug 13	Alt[ering] blk wool suit 23	12.12.0	
3942		Alt[ering] blk silk suit	5.05.0	
			17.17.0	
1960			**[£.s.d]**	
728	April 7	Beige wool suit 149	75.12.0	70.18.5
	April 9	By cash $200		4.12.0
1961			**[£.s.d]**	
8674	May 5	Short yellow/beige cord		
		overcoat 335	3.13.6	
2541	12	Tan/blk fleck wool suit 335		
		Peach nylon chiffon skt 17	77.14.0	
2560	Aug 7			
			25.04.0	106.11.6
1965			**[£.s.d]**	
7719	April 9	Lime/fawn check wool suit,		
		80 gns 142	84.00.0	

Note: Appendix reproduces exact layout of the client records. It is not always possible to match item and price precisely.

Source: Lachasse records, AAD 6-1989, Archive of Art and Design, National Art Library, London.

APPENDIX F **People Discussed or Interviewed**

Allen, Agnes (Nan) Saleswoman at Toronto boutique Travers Fox for twenty-three years and later for Ira-Berg. Interview by author, Toronto, Canada, 20 April 1993.

Bata, Sonja (Mrs Thomas J. Bata) Wife of chairman of Bata, the shoe company. Listed under her own entry in *The Canadian Who's Who* from 1979 on. Interview by author, Toronto, Canada, 22 August 1990.

Berg, Russel Owner of Toronto boutique Ira-Berg, which sold high-priced ready-to-wear from the 1930s to the 1990s. Interview by author, Toronto, Canada, 19 November 1990.

Boxer, Nancy (Mrs Richard J. Boxer) Joined the Junior League in 1946; volunteered in hospitals and the Opportunity Shop; Royal Ontario Museum Members Volunteer Committee 1960 chairman; Garden Club member. Interview by author, Toronto, Canada, 6 December 1990.

Boxer, Rosemary. See *Feick, Rosemary.*

Boylen, Dorothy (Mrs Matthew James Boylen) Wife of mining engineer/executive. Named to 1953 *Toronto Telegram* best-dressed list; 1962 Hall of Fame; 1953 and 1954 *Liberty* best-dressed lists. Daughter Elaine on 1960 *Toronto Telegram* list.

Bradshaw, Marian (Mrs J.E. Bradshaw) Attended Bishop Strachan School. Royal Ontario Museum Members Volunteer Committee member; Garden Club board member. Editor of *Canadian Collector.* Interview by author, Toronto, Canada, 25 July 1991.

Brenzel, Sally (Mrs L.A. Brenzel) Daughter of Mrs Ethel and Mr Henry Greisman, daughter-in-law of dress manufacturer and wholesaler Brenzel Imports, Toronto. Toronto Symphony Junior Women's Committee president; New Mount Sinai Hospital Women's Auxiliary member; Royal Ontario Museum Members Volunteer Committee member; Hadassah member. Interview by author, Toronto, Canada, 22 March 1991.

Bryce, Elizabeth (Mrs Douglas B. Bryce) Royal Ontario Museum Members Volunteer Committee and Textile Endowment Fund Committee founding member; Garden Club member; Holman School president; chairman of the board of the YMCA Metro Nursery School. Interview by author, Toronto, Canada, 5 November 1991.

Bunnett, Mary S. (Mrs George E. Bunnett) Attended Molton College boarding school. Sister of *Frances M. Weir*; wife of a Simpson's executive. Junior League member; Junior Cradleship Crèche member. Interview by author with Frances M. Weir, Toronto, Canada, 6 June 1991.

Burait, Madame Mannequin, then *vendeuse*, now administrator at Nina Ricci, Paris. Interview by author, Paris, France, 24 April 1991.

Burton, Clayton (Mrs Edgar G. Burton) American wife of Simpson's department store president. Wimodausis member; Toronto Symphony Women's Committee president, vice president, and member. Named to the 1953 *Toronto Telegram* best-dressed list; nominated for the 1951 *Liberty* best-dressed list. Daughters *Anne C. Smith* and Mary Alice Stuart. Interview by author, Toronto, Canada, 22 August 1990.

Campbell, Mona (Mrs Kenneth Laidlaw), née Mona Morrow Wife of John Band during 1940s and 1950s. Opera and Concert Committee member; National Ballet Guild member; 37 Club member (debutante in 1937); Royal Ontario Museum Board of Trustees. Dover Industries Limited president and director, listed under her own entry in *The Canadian Who's Who*, 1991, and named Officer of the Order of Canada, 1996. Interview by author, Toronto, Canada, 24 January 1991.

Carr-Harris, Mary (Mrs A.R. Carr-Harris) Toronto Symphony Women's Committee president and member; Ladies Hunt Club member. Named to 1957 *Toronto Telegram* best-dressed list. Interview by author, Toronto, Canada, 15 January 1991.

Cassels, Betty (Mrs Patrick Cassels) Attended Havergal College. Wife of general manager of frozen food company. National Ballet Guild member and 1961 president; Junior League member. Named to 1960 *Toronto Telegram* best-dressed list. Interview by author, Toronto, Canada, 29 October 1992.

Chelot, Florette Balenciaga *vendeuse* from 1939 to the early 1960s. Interview by author, Paris, France, 3 May 1991.

Chicoye, Madame Philippe Venet *vendeuse.* Interview by author, Paris, France, 9 December 1991.

Crase, Martha S. (Mrs George H. Crase) née Stewart Attended Hatfield College, an Anglican boarding school; studied architecture at University of Toronto, 1943. Daughter of a civil engineer and executive of Imperial Oil. Interview by author, Toronto, Canada, 5 June 1991.

Crawford, John Reed. British milliner; studied millinery in Paris in 1950; began a business in London in 1954, selling in England and to Neiman Marcus and Bloomingdales in the United States; an associate of the Incorporated Society of London Fashion Designers from 1961; closed 1972. Interview by author, London, England, 26 November 1991.

Curry, Leonora. British fashion editor of *Fashions and Fabrics*, an export magazine. Interview by author, London, England, 18 May 1992.

Dollery, Eveleen Fashion and beauty journalist and editor at *Chatelaine* magazine for approximately thirty years; editor for *Cosmetics Beauty Guide*. Interview by author, Toronto, Canada, 25 September 1991.

Eaton, Signy (Mrs John David Eaton) Wife of Eaton's department store president. Art Gallery of Toronto Women's Committee member; Junior League member. Nominated to 1948 and named to 1952 *Liberty* best-dressed list; 1952 *Toronto Telegram* best-dressed list; 1962 Hall of Fame. Interview by author, Toronto, Canada, 11 July 1991.

Elliott, Catherine Canfield (Mrs Leighton Elliott, later Mrs John A. Wilson) Toronto Welfare Council president; Girl Guides of Canada district commissioner; YWCA National Council member. Named to 1950 *Liberty* best-dressed list. Daughter *Flavia Redelmeier.*

Epstein, Madeleine (Mrs A.A. Epstein) From New York, where her father was a clothing manufacturer; wife of radiologist. Hadassah member and chair; New Mount Sinai Women's Auxiliary member; Jewish Federation of Greater Toronto member; Variety Club member. Interview by author, Toronto, Canada, 22 October 1991.

Feick, Rosemary "Posy" Chisholm (Mrs William Feick Jr) Better known in Toronto as Rosemary Boxer. Attended Bishop Strachan School; Academy of Radio Arts, 1946. Wife of Donald Boxer, 1946. Worked at CBC television and CFRB radio; at *Mayfair* as fashion editor; later at *Chatelaine*; editor-in-chief for *Canadian Home Journal*; Simpson's fashion show commentator and television fashion commentator during 1950s; opened beauty salon in October 1955. Named to 1952 *Toronto Telegram* best-dressed list. Interview by author, New York, US, 1 July 1991.

Fleming, Dorothy Attended Bishop Strachan School. Top Canadian fashion model; Eaton's model; opened Dorothy Fleming School for Models in Toronto, 1950s. Named to 1960 *Toronto Telegram* best-dressed list. Interview by author, Toronto, Canada, 17 November 1991.

Frankel, Ruth (Mrs Egmont Frankel) Graduated in law from Chicago. Canadian Cancer Society president and founder; Ontario Cancer Treatment and Research Foundation Board of Governors member; Ontario Cancer Institute Board member; Opera and Concert Committee member; Toronto Symphony Women's Committee member; Art Gallery of Toronto Women's Committee member. Named to 1952 *Toronto Telegram* best-dressed list. Daughter *Joyce Kofman.*

Goad, Diana L. (Mrs J. Lawrence Goad) Attended Havergal College, University of Toronto. Wife of investment dealer. Art Gallery of Toronto Junior Women's Committee member and 1959–60 president; CNIB volunteer; Junior League member. Interview by author, Toronto, Canada, 26 February 1991.

Godsoe, Margaret (Mrs J. Gerald Godsoe) Wife of British American Oil Company vice president, Toronto Board of Trade president, QC. Junior League 1946 president; Art Gallery of Toronto Women's Committee founding member and 1965–7 president; Opera and Concert Committee member; Royal Conservatory of Music member; National Ballet Guild member. Interview by author, Toronto, Canada, 13 March 1991.

Gooderham, Grace (Mrs George M. Gooderham) Debutante in 1920s. Wimodausis member; Art Gallery of Toronto Women's Committee member. Named to 1952 *Toronto Telegram* best-dressed list. Daughter Susan on 1958 *Toronto Telegram* list. Interview by author, Toronto, Canada, 27 February 1991.

Goodman, Andrew Bergdorf Goodman, New York, president. Interview by author, New York, US, 7 March 1991.

Harris, Ethel (Mrs W.C. Harris) Wife of chairman of Harris and Partners Ltd. Royal Ontario Museum Members Volunteer Committee member; Art Gallery of Toronto Women's Committee member. Named to 1955 *Toronto Telegram* best-dressed list. Daughter-in-law *Patricia Harris.*

Harris, Patricia (Mrs William B. Harris) Daughter-in-law of *Ethel Harris.* Junior League member; Royal Ontario Museum Members Volunteer Committee and Textile Endowment Fund Committee member. Interviews by author, Toronto, Canada, 22 November 1990, 17 March 1992, 20 April 1993.

Hersenhoren, Jeanie (Mrs Samuel Hersenhoren), née Gibbard) Daughter of Ontario furniture manufacturer; wife of first violinist and conductor, Toronto Symphony Orchestra. Canadian Cancer Society member; Cuisine Club member; Toronto Symphony Women's Committee member. Nominated to 1948 *New Liberty* and 1950 *Liberty* best-dressed lists. Interview by author, Toronto, Canada, 4 March 1991.

James, Judith Attended Bishop Strachan School; debutante in 1954. Daughter of Doris Morrow. Junior League member. Interview by author, with Judy Ridout, Toronto, Canada, 28 March 1991.

Jansons, Velga Toronto dressmaker, originally from Latvia. Interview by author, Toronto, Canada, 23 March 1993.

Jenkins, Elsa Daughter of *Billye Vincent*. Manager of Women's Activities at the Canadian National Exhibition; formerly feature and fashion editor at *Style* and fashion writer for *Globe and Mail*. Named to 1958 *Liberty* best-dressed list. Interview by author, Toronto, Canada, 8 October 1991.

John, Marion (Mrs Postlethwaite), Worked in Eaton's Fashion Bureau; Royal Ontario Museum Members Volunteer Committee and Textile Endowment Fund Committee member. Interview by author, Toronto, Canada, 4 July 1993.

King-Wilson, Norma Owner of second-hand clothing store Shoppe D'Or, taken over from grandmother, *Vera Victoria Morrison*. Interview by author, Toronto, Canada, 11 June 1991.

Kofman, Joyce (Mrs Oscar S. Kofman) Attended Branksome Hall, Smith College. Daughter of *Ruth Frankel*. Canadian Cancer Society Junior Committee member; Toronto Symphony Junior Women's Committee founding member; Art Gallery of Toronto Women's Committee member; National Ballet Guild member. Interview by author, Toronto, Canada, 4 June 1991.

Lean, Julia Ruby (Mrs Saul Lean) Wife of Morris Ruby, magazine publisher, in the 1950s. Hadassah member; Forest Hill School Board president; National Ballet Guild member. Interview by author, Toronto, Canada, 31 May 1991.

Lepofsky, Joan Rosefield Attended Forest Hill Collegiate. Father in oil business. Interview by author, Toronto, Canada, 18 September 1990.

Levitt, Ann Daughter of Alvin Walker; sister of *Barbara Shavick*. Interview by author, Toronto, Canada, 21 July 1997.

Liska, Rodolphe Toronto couturier, member of Association of Canadian Couturiers. Interviews by author, Toronto, Canada, 16 August 1991, 13 December 1993.

Lumley, Peter Hope Public relations consultant, specializing in fashion industry; worked with members of Incorporated Society of London Fashion Designers. Began working for Hardy Amies in 1947. Interview by author, London, England, 3 December 1991.

McGillawee, Joy A. (Mrs Ross McGillawee) Wool Bureau of Canada president. Named to 1956 *Toronto Telegram* best-dressed list. Interview by author, Toronto, Canada, 22 July 1992.

Mackay, Katherine. See *Stewart, Katherine Mackay*

McLean, June (Mrs W.F. McLean) Wife of Board of Bank of Commerce (now CIBC) member and Canada Packers president. Victoria Day Nursery member; Rosedale United Appeal chair; Red Cross member during war; Art Gallery of Toronto Women's Committee member; Arthritis Society member. Interview by author, Toronto, Canada, 15 March 1991.

McNabb, Barbara Newspaper editor of business import and merchandise magazine *Current Publications Limited*. One of the first female Canadian business editors. Interview by author, Toronto, Canada, 4 February 1991.

Martin, Cecily (Mrs Camis Martin) Wife of Peter S. Osler in 1950s. 37 Club member (debutante in 1937); Junior League member; Garden Club member. Interview by author, Toronto, Canada, 7 June 1991.

Morison, Margaret R. Eaton's employee, worked with Dora Matthews and J.A. Brockie in the Merchandise Display and Sales Promotion Office. Interview by author, Toronto, Canada, 19 July 1990.

Morrison, Vera Victoria (Mrs David Sykes) Founder and owner of the 139 Shoppe, later known as Shoppe D'Or. See *Norma King-Wilson*.

O'Connor, Ollie (Mrs Martin O'Connor) See *Ollie Smythe*.

Oualid, Danielle Jean Patou *vendeuse*. Interview by author, Paris, France, 24 April 1991.

Parkin, Jeanne (Mrs John Parkin) Attended Bishop Strachan School, University of Toronto. Daughter of Mr N.B. Warmith, KC; wife of architect and principal in John B. Parkin Associates during 1950s. Art Gallery of Toronto

Women's Committee member; Art Gallery of Toronto Purchase Committee chair. Interview by author, Toronto, Canada, 11 August 1993.

Pierce, Jean E. Toronto boutique owner. Interview by author, Toronto, Canada, 20 January 1991.

Rathgeb, Rosemary (Mrs Charles I. Rathgeb) née Clarke Originally from Montreal. Wife of Canadian Comstock Ltd. president. Art Gallery of Toronto Women's Committee member; Children's Aid Society member; Junior League member. Interview by author, Toronto, Canada, 20 February 1991.

Redelmeier, Flavia (Mrs J.H. Redelmeier) Attended Branksome Hall, University of Toronto. Daughter of *Catherine Elliott*. Royal Ontario Museum Board of Trustees and Members Volunteer Committee member; Garden Club member; Girl Guides of Canada member. Interview by author, Toronto, Canada, 12 December 1990.

Rhind, Elizabeth (Mrs John Arthur Rhind) Daughter of G.E. Green; wife of insurance executive. West End Crèche member; Junior League 1959 vice president, 1961–3 president; Art Gallery of Toronto Women's Committee member; Royal Ontario Museum volunteer. Interview by author, Toronto, Canada, 12 February 1991.

Ridout, Judy Attended Bishop Strachan School; refused to be a debutante. Interview by author, with Judith James, Toronto, Canada, 28 March 1991.

Rigby, Joan Boutique owner whose clients included *Catherine Elliott, Flavia Redelmeier, Ethel Harris*.

Robertson, Mary Louise (Mrs William S. Robertson) Telephone interview by author, 2 November 1990.

Rockett, Beverley (Mrs Paul Rockett) Attended Dorothy Fleming School for Models. Fashion model for Toronto couturiers Cornelia, Tibor de Nagay, Federica; later fashion photographer. Interview by author, Toronto, Canada, 2 June 1991.

Rodolphe. See *Liska, Rodolphe.*

Rogers, Peta London fashion model in the late 1940s for Peter Russell, Hardy Amies, Digby Morton, among others. Interview by author, London, England, 11 December 1991.

Rouët, Jacques Manager at House of Christian Dior, Paris. Interview by author, Paris, France, 29 April 1991.

Satz, Irene Buyer at Ohrbach's, New York. Interview by author, New York, US, 16 September 1990.

Scott, Joyce Saleswoman at Joan Rigby boutique, Toronto. Interview by author, with Helen Stimpson, Toronto, Canada, 20 March 1991.

Shavick, Barbara (Mrs Leonard Shavick) Daughter of Alvin Walker; sister of *Ann Levitt*; wife of *Leonard Shavick*. Interview by author, Montreal, Canada, 2 January 1999.

Shavick, Leonard Holt Renfrew president and son-in-law of Alvin Walker, president during 1950s. Telephone interview by author, 8 April 1991.

Smith, Anne C. Attended Branksome Hall, University of Toronto; debutante in 1949. Daughter of *Clayton Burton* and Edgar Burton, Simpson's president; eloped in 1950. Toronto Symphony Junior Women's Committee member; Junior League member. Interview by author, Toronto, Canada, 6 June 1991.

Smythe, Ollie (Mrs Martin O'Connor) Buyer at Eaton's Ensemble Shop. Interview by author, Toronto, Canada, 4 October 1990; interview by author, with Ida Hewett and Lucille Gauthier, Toronto, Canada, 14 September 1990.

Steele, Margery (Mrs Bruce Steele) Buyer at Simpson's St Regis Room. Interview by author, Toronto, Canada, 7 November 1990.

Stewart, Katherine Mackay (Mrs Charles B. Stewart) Formerly wife of Colonel the Honourable J. Keiller Mackay, 1957–63 lieutenant-governor of Ontario. Queensway Hospital volunteer; member of the Board of Governors of Women's College Hospital; member of the Board of Regents of Mount Allison University. Named to 1958 *Toronto Telegram* best-dressed list; 1962 Hall of Fame. Interview by author, Toronto, Canada, 14 March 1991.

Stimpson, Helen Saleswoman at Joan Rigby boutique, Toronto. Interview by author, with Joyce Scott, Toronto, Canada, 20 March 1991.

Stohn, Suzanne A. (Mrs John D. Stohn) Daughter of Mrs Max Haas, who was president of the National Ballet Guild. Junior League member; Art Gallery of Toronto Junior Women's Committee member. Interview by author, Toronto, Canada, 18 February 1991.

Stulginskas, Liudja Upstairs maid to *Signy Eaton*. Telephone interview by author, 18 April 1993.

Suddon, Alan Clothing collector; head of the Fine Arts Department of Toronto's Metro Central Reference Library until his retirement in 1980. Interview by author, Toronto, Canada, 22 January 1993.

Torno, Rose (Mrs Noah Torno) Admitted to the Bar in Alberta. Wife of business executive. New Mount Sinai Hospital Women's Auxiliary founder and first president; served with Canadian Red Cross National Headquarters during the Second World War; Council of Jewish Women member; Toronto Symphony Women's Committee member; Art Gallery of Ontario life member. Named to 1954 *Toronto Telegram* best-dressed list. Listed under own entry in *Who's Who in Canadian Jewry*. Interview by author, Toronto, Canada, 26 July 1990.

Vaughan, Nora E. (Mrs O.D. Vaughan) Wife of Eaton's vice-president. Named to 1960 *Toronto Telegram* best-dressed list; 1962 Hall of Fame.

Venet, Philippe Paris couturier; assistant designer for Schiaparelli, 1951–3; master tailor for Givenchy, 1953–62; opened own house in 1962. Interview by author, Paris, France, 9 December 1991.

Vincent, Billye Buyer at Simpson's St Regis Room. Opened own boutique in her name. Daughter *Elsa Jenkins*.

Weir, Frances M. (Mrs John G. Weir) Attended Molton College boarding school. Sister to *Mary S. Bunnett*. Junior League member; Junior Cradleship Crèche member. Interview by author, with Mary S. Bunnett, Toronto, Canada, 6 June 1991.

Weld, Harriet "Sis" Bunting Attended McGill University, Montreal; debutante in 1953. Daughter of stockbroker Alfred Bunting. Junior League member; Junior Opera Committee member; Crest Theatre board member. Interviews by author, Toronto, Canada, 30 January 1992, 20 January 1994.

Wilcox, Vivian Fashion reporter for *Mayfair* and *Style*. Interview by author, Toronto, Canada, 11 October 1990.

Wilder, Judith R. (Mrs William P. Wilder) Attended McGill University, Montreal. Daughter of Helen Ryrie, of Ryrie-Birks, and of Edward Bickle, Wood Gundy Securities director and vice president; wife of investment executive. Art Gallery of Toronto Women's Committee member; Queen Elizabeth Hospital committee member. Interview by author, Toronto, Canada, 18 March 1991.

Wildgoose, Norma Eaton's model, worked for Toronto manufacturers and local couturiers Olivia of Hamilton, Robert Irwin, Angelina, Tibor de Nagay. Interview by author, Toronto, Canada, 22 October 1991.

NOTES

Authorship and title of periodical articles is not always given in the original.

Introduction

[1] J. Ash, "Memory and Objects," in *The Gendered Object*, ed. Pat Kirkham (Manchester and New York: Manchester University Press, 1996), 219.

[2] There are numerous books on this subject, and many are listed in the bibliography.

[3] Daniel Miller has written that "analysis of artefact must begin with the most obvious characteristic . . . This factor may provide the key to understanding its power and significance in cultural construction." Miller, *Material Culture and Mass Consumption* (Oxford: Basil Blackwell, 1987), 98–9.

[4] For the theory of conspicuous consumption, see Thorstein Veblen, *The Theory of the Leisure Class* (1899; reprint, New York: Penguin Books, 1979).

[5] John A. Walker, *Design History and the History of Design* (London: Pluto Press, 1990), 174.

[6] See Regina Lee Blaszczyk, *Imagining Consumers: Design and Innovation from Wedgwood to Corning* (Baltimore, MD: Johns Hopkins University Press, 2000), for a recent and interesting discussion of this from the perspective of the mass-market manufacturers and retailers of china and glassware in North America.

[7] Joy Parr has addressed the issue of taste and consumption of domestic goods in the postwar period in Canada, in *Domestic Goods: The Material, the Moral, and the Economic in the Postwar Years* (Toronto: University of Toronto Press, 1999).

[8] Authors writing in the 1950s and '60s have described the workings of the haute couture system for stores and manufacturers. See Celia Bertin, *Paris à la mode: A Voyage of Discovery*, trans. Marjorie Deans (London: Victor Gollancz, 1956); Didier Grumbach, *Histoires de la mode* (Paris: Seuil, 1993); Jeanette A. Jarnow and Beatrice Judelle, *Inside the Fashion Business* (New York: John Wiley and Sons, 1965), 89–128; Anny Latour, *Kings of Fashion*, trans. Mervyn Savill (London: Weidenfeld and Nicolson, 1956); Bernard Roshco, *The Rag Race: How New York and Paris Run the Breakneck Business of Dressing American Women* (New York: Funk and Wagnalls, 1963).

[9] John A. Porter, *The Vertical Mosaic: An Analysis of Social Class and Power in Canada* (Toronto: University of Toronto Press, 1965); Peter C. Newman, ed., *Debrett's Illustrated Guide to the Canadian Establishment* (Agincourt, ON: Methuen Publishers, 1983); W.G. Runciman, *A Treatise on Social Theory* (Cambridge and New York: Cambridge University Press, 1983).

[10] Canada, Department of Labour, Women's Bureau, *Married Women Working for Pay in Eight Canadian Cities* (Ottawa: Department of Labour, Women's Bureau, 1958), 34, 45; Kathleen D. McCarthy, "Parallel Power Structures: Women and the Voluntary Sphere," in *Lady Bountiful Revisited: Women, Philanthropy and Power*, ed. McCarthy (New Brunswick, NJ: Rutgers University Press, 1990).

[11] This has recently been done for the trade in second-hand clothes from Europe to Zambia. See Karen Tranberg Hansen, *Salaula: The World of Second-hand Clothing and Zambia* (Chicago: University of Chicago Press, 2000).

[12] Igor Kopytoff, "The Cultural Biography of Things: Commoditization As Process," in *The Social Life of Things*, ed. Arjun Appadurai (Cambridge: Cambridge University Press, 1986), 67–8.

[13] Jules David Prown, "Mind in Matter: An Introduction to Material Culture Theory and Method," *Winterthur Portfolio* 17, 1 (1982): 1–2.

[14] Miller, *Material Culture*, 154–5.

[15] There was an enormous growth in Toronto's total population from 687,457 in 1941 to 1,824,481 by 1961. Canada, Dominion Bureau of Statistics, *Census of Canada, 1941* (Ottawa: E. Cloutier, Printer to the King, 1944–50), Table 15; Canada, Dominion Bureau of Statistics, Census Division, *Census of Canada, 1961* (Ottawa: Queen's Printer, 1962), Table 1.

[16] Over the 1945–60 period, the North American market was more unified in the sense that American and Canadian dollar values were far closer than they are today, and fluctuated within a narrow range against one another. The pound sterling was at an average value of Cdn$4.45 in 1945, but from 1950 to 1965 was closer to an average of Cdn$3.

[17] Eaton's closed in 1999 and reopened under Sears in late 2000.

Chapter 1: The Paris Couture Structure

[1] See Peter Thornton, *Baroque and Rococo Silks* (London: Faber and Faber, 1965); Lesley Ellis Miller, "Silk Designers in the Lyons Silk Industry, 1712–1787" (PhD

diss., Brighton Polytechnic, 1988); Lesley Ellis Miller, "Paris-Lyon-Paris: Dialogue in the Design and Distribution of Patterned Silks in the Eighteenth Century," in *Luxury Trades and Consumerism in Ancien Régime Paris: Studies in the History of the Skilled Workforce*, ed. R. Rox and A. Turner (Aldershot: Ashgate Publishing, 1998), 139–67.

[2] Diana de Marly, *Worth: Father of Haute Couture* (London: Elm Tree Books, 1980); Elizabeth Ann Coleman, *The Opulent Era: Fashion of Worth, Doucet and Pingat* (London: The Brooklyn Museum in association with Thames and Hudson, 1989). Nancy Troy is currently pursuing very interesting work that links the promotion of the couture salon to that of the formal academic painting salon. Troy, "Fashion As Art/Art As Fashion," (Teezel Lecture series "Couture and Culture: Fashion and the Marketing of Modernism, c. 1880–1918" University of Toronto, 11 March 1997).

[3] For more on this history see Diana de Marly, *The History of Haute Couture, 1850–1950* (London: B.T. Batsford, 1980), 106–7, 195–7; Marjorie Dunton, "La Chambre syndicale," in *Couture: An Illustrated History of the Great Paris Designers and Their Creations*, ed. Ruth Lynam (New York: Doubleday and Company, 1972), 40–9; Didier Grumbach, *Histoires de la mode* (Paris: Seuil, 1993), 15–72; Mary Brooks Picken and Dora Loues Miller, *Dressmakers of France: The Who, How and Why of French Couture* (New York: Harper and Bros., 1956), 9–18; Jeannette A. Jarnow and Beatrice Judelle, *Inside the Fashion Business* (New York: John Wiley and Sons, 1965), 89–128.

[4] Jarnow and Judelle, *Inside the Fashion Business*, 89–90.

[5] Dunton, "La Chambre syndicale," 40.

[6] See sticker marked "AVIS TRÈS IMPORTANT" that cites this law on several documents issued by the Chambre syndicale de la couture parisienne in the Christian Dior Archives, Paris.

[7] D. Gorin, secrétaire général de la Chambre syndicale, "Dépôt des modèles," memorandum, 25 July 1950, Christian Dior Archives, Paris. The design shown in fig. 1.2 is in the Royal Ontario Museum, ROM 964.241. 3abcd, as a gift of Mrs Graham Morrow.

[8] Décision, 23 January 1945, F12/10505, Archives nationales, Paris. For reproduction of the regulations, see annexe 2 in Grumbach, *Histoires de la mode*, 31.

[9] In 1952, it was suggested that the jury be made up of four representatives from the couture industry, four from the textile industry, and one from the administration. Madeleine Godeau, secrétaire générale de la Chambre syndicale, to M. Laventent, Ministre de l'Industrie, 16 January 1952, F12/10504, Archives nationales, Paris.

[10] Classification Couture-Création, 1954–5, F12/10505, Archives nationales, Paris.

[11] Commission de classement et de contrôle Couture-Création to Chambre syndicale, Jury report, 11 October 1949, F12/10503, Archives nationales, Paris. Henri Hirsch of Léda, 59 Faubourg St Honoré and 29 Ave. Marginy, makers of "manteaux de pluie" since 1925, were refused Couture-Création status in 1952 and requested a special category, "imperméable création," 28 July 1952, F12/10504, Archives nationales, Paris. Lola Prusac, 93 Faubourg St Honoré, maker of sport-tricot and a member since 1942, appealed the denial of Couture-Création status in 1952. See Lola Prusac to Chambre syndicale, 22 August 1952, F12/10504, Archives nationales, Paris.

[12] Statistics from Gilles Lipovetsky, *The Empire of Fashion: Dressing Modern Democracy*, trans. Catherine Porter (Princeton, NJ: Princeton University Press, 1994), 58.

[13] Grumbach, *Histoires de la mode*, 27–31; Dominique Veillon, *La mode sous l'Occupation: Débrouillardise et coqutteries dans la France en guerre (1939–1945)* (Paris: Documents Payot, 1990).

[14] Bernard Roshco, *The Rag Race: How New York and Paris Run the Breakneck Business of Dressing American Women* (New York: Funk and Wagnalls, 1963), 134.

[15] Danielle Oualid, interview by author, Paris, France, 24 April 1991.

[16] The only new houses to open after Christian Dior in 1947 were Pierre Cardin in 1950, Hubert de Givenchy in 1952, and Yves Saint Laurent in 1962. See Valérie Guillaume, *Jacques Fath* (Paris: Adam Biro, 1993), 36–8.

[17] Centro de Promoción de Diseno y Moda, *España, 50 Anos de Moda* (Barcelona: Aduntemante de Barcelona Area de Cultura, 1988), 282. The Italian collective showing took place on 12 February 1951 at Villa Torregiani, Florence. Marchese Batista Giorgini invited American buyers and the foreign press. Bonizza Giordani Aragno, *40 Years of Italian Fashion, 1940–1980* (Rome: The Made in Ltd., 1983), introduction, unpaginated. Information about the Association of Canadian Couturiers is found in Alexandra Palmer, "The Myth and Reality of Haute Couture: Consumption, Social Function and Taste in Toronto, 1945–1963" (PhD diss., University of Brighton, 1994), 1:188–209.

[18] Alison Adburgham, "The Weather in the Salons," reprinted from *Harper's Bazaar* (June 1960), in Alison Adburgham, *View of Fashion* (London: Allen and Unwin, 1966), 15.

[19] See Caroline Rennolds Milbank, *New York Fashion: The Evolution of American Style* (New York: Harry N. Abrams, 1989); Sarah Tomerlin Lee, ed., *American Fashion* (New York: The Fashion Institute of Technology, 1975); Beryl Williams, *Fashion Is Our Business* (New York: J.B. Lip-

pincott, 1945). There is no scholarship to date on Rae Hildebrand, Alfandri, or other Canadian manufacturers.

[20] Alison Settle, "Paris Gambles on Luxury Modes: 30 Yard Dresses Cost £265," A Woman's Viewpoint column, *Observer* (London), 10 August 1947, A47.29, Alison Settle Archives, University of Brighton.

[21] Edmonde Charles-Roux, *Théâtre de la mode* (New York: Rizzoli, 1991).

[22] Lou Taylor, "Paris Couture, 1940–44," in *Chic Thrills: A Fashion Reader*, ed. Juliet Ash and Elizabeth Wilson (London: Pandora Press, 1992), 135–42. For information on Canada's wartime clothing and textile policy, see S.G. Turnbull Caton, "Government Control and Canadian Civilian Clothing during World War II," *Ars Textrina* 22 (1994): 175–92; S.G. Turnbull Caton, "Fashion Marches On: A Canadian Snapshot of the Second World War," *Canadian Home Economics Journal* 44 (Fall 1994): 167–9.

[23] Dora Miller, Appendix to Bernice G. Chambers, *Fashion Fundamentals* (New York: Prentice-Hall, 1947), 471, 474.

[24] Public Relations, J.A. Brockie files, F229-151-5, file 143, T. Eaton Records, Archives of Ontario, Toronto (hereinafter AOO). Mr Brockie was a long-term employee of Eaton's. His two important jobs were as head of Toronto's Merchandise Display and Sales Promotion Office from 1936 to 1951 and as first manager of the new Public Relations Office from 1951 to 1962, when he retired.

[25] Gwenda Thompson, "Paris Spring Collections," *Mayfair*, April 1945, 27–9, 101. Figures 1.3 and 1.4 also appeared in this issue.

[26] There are many general overviews of this history, but the first serious discussions are more recent. See Veillon, *La mode sous l'Occupation*; Taylor, "Paris Couture, 1940–44"; Lou Taylor, "'Coquelicots, Marguerites, et Bleuets': An Analysis of Vichyist Imagery in the Design of Fashion Fabrics, 1940–44" (paper presented at "Textile Sample Books Reassessed: Commerce, Communication, and Culture," a conference held by the Centre for the History of Textiles and Dress, Winchester School of Art, University of Southampton, 29–30 June 2000). To understand the German perspective, see the interesting work by Irene Guenther, "Nazi 'Chic'? German Politics and Women's Fashions, 1915–1945," *Fashion Theory: The Journal of Dress, Body and Culture* 1, 1 (1997): 29–58.

[27] "Paris Couturiers Predict Spring Trends," *Mayfair*, April 1945, 98.

[28] The dress is made of apricot lace and silk chiffon. 1-945-14-00300, Seneca Fashion Resource Centre, Seneca College of Applied Arts and Technology, Toronto, Canada.

[29] For more on the early couture trade, see Coleman, *The Opulent Era*, 32–43, where she discusses the distribution of Worth designs.

[30] Minutes of Sales and Promotion Committee meeting, 17 July 1945, F229-151-4, T. Eaton Records, AOO.

[31] Ibid., 31 July 1945.

[32] Dora Matthews, "Unpublished memoirs" (Documentary Files, Textile and Costume Section, Royal Ontario Museum, manuscript), 32.

[33] Hardy Amies, *Just So Far* (London: Collins, 1954), 120.

[34] Ibid., 139.

[35] Clayton Burton, interview by author, Toronto, Canada, 22 August 1990; Ollie Smythe, interview by author, Toronto, Canada, 4 October 1990.

[36] See Christian Dior internal correspondence, 1 July 1949, concerning dates of presentations for fall 1949, Christian Dior Archives, Paris. The collection was shown first on 8 August at 5:30 p.m. to Grands Magasins, US; on 9 and 10 August at 3:00 p.m., to Manufacturiers, US; on 11 August at 3:00 p.m., to Manufacturiers à l'Europe; and on 12 August at 3:00 p.m., to French buyers.

[37] Barbara Stevenson, "Devalued Franc Attracts Buyers to Paris," *Saturday Night*, 28 February 1948, 22.

[38] Staff Superintendent's Office, Winnipeg, to Merchandise Display and Sales Promotion Office, Toronto, memorandum, 8 May 1944, F229-151-6, file 170, T. Eaton Records, AOO.

[39] Agenda, Advertising and Merchandise Display Conference, Winnipeg, 20 March 1944, F229-151-6, file 170, T. Eaton Records, AOO.

[40] *Simpson's Staff News*, p. 1, F229-151-5, file 134, T. Eaton Records, AOO. The show was held on 6 March 1945 at 3:25 p.m. and 8:30 p.m. Fairweather and Northway's did not carry haute couture and are therefore not discussed here.

[41] The show was held 3 October 1945 at 3:15 p.m. and 8:15 p.m. Program, F229-151-3, file 75/2, T. Eaton Records, AOO.

[42] In 1946, *Mayfair* announced the first originals being shown in Canada since the war. The designs were credited as available at Eaton's, "with the exception of Molyneux and Hardy Amies originals which are at Morgan's, Montreal." "Paris and London Originals," *Mayfair*, May 1946, 86–7.

[43] The show was held on Friday, 30 November 1946, in Eaton's Georgian Room. It was part of the British export drive associated with the "Britain Can Make It" exhibition, as was noted in an undated and unidentified newspaper clipping attached to this file. F229-151-1,

file 4/2, T. Eaton Records, AOO. For more on the Lucie Clayton modelling school, see Harriet Quick, *Catwalking: A History of the Fashion Model* (London: Hamlyn, 1997), 65. Quotation from "Ideas for Article on History of Fashion Shows and Models at Eaton's," F229-162-41, T. Eaton Records, AOO.

[44] Minutes, 3 February 1948, F229-151-4, file 118, T. Eaton Records, AOO.

[45] "Canadian Revenue at Its Peak," *The Ambassador: The British Export Journal for Textiles and Fabrics*, no. 7 (1946): 125.

[46] "First Postwar Spring 'Collection' Arrives from Paris," *Globe and Mail*, 26 March 1946, 13.

[47] "Heirloom Beauty for the Day of Days," *Mayfair*, May 1946, 80. The wedding dress is in the Royal Ontario Museum collection, ROM 975.80.1a,b. Nancy Boxer recalled the reaction to this dress in an interview by author, Toronto, Canada, 6 December 1990.

[48] Advertisement, *Globe and Mail*, 9 March 1946, 14; "10 Style Commandments Laid Down by Swarthout," *Globe and Mail*, 15 March 1946, 14.

[49] Advertisement for Lucien Lelong originals, *Globe and Mail*, 9 September 1946, 14; for Jacques Fath see Mary E. James, "Elegance and Femininity Feature Simpson Fashions," *Globe and Mail*, 17 September 1946, 13. Simpson's may have had a few more Paris dresses, but only two were identified. "Around the World Fashion," Simpson's fashion show program, 16–21 September 1946, collection of the author, with sincere thanks to David Livingstone. See also advertisements, *Globe and Mail*, 9 September 1946, 14; 10 September 1946, 14; 11 September 1946, 14; 13 September 1946, 14; 14 September 1946, 14; 19 September 1946, 13.

[50] *Flash*, 7 October 1949, 10–11, F229-141-0-177, T. Eaton Records, AOO; advertisements, *Globe and Mail*, 17 September 1946, 26; 18 September 1946, 26; 19 September 1946, 30; *The Key*, October 1946, 5.

[51] Advertisement, *Globe and Mail*, 8 March 1947, 26.

[52] Eaton's advertisement, *Mayfair*, April 1947, 53.

[53] The "blue book" was *The Torontonian Society Blue Book and Club Membership Register*, published from 1920 to 1946 to function as a local who's who. Helen Beattie, "From Paniers to Bustles, '47 Styles Truly Chic," *Globe and Mail*, 6 March 1947, 12.

[54] An advertisement in the *Globe and Mail*, 15 September 1947, 30, illustrates ten Paris models. See also "Fashion Presents Decisive, Dramatic Changes," fashion show program, 15–19 September 1945, Paris originals, day dresses, suits, day-into-evening, and formal dresses sections, F229-135-4, file 1, T. Eaton Records, AOO.

[55] "Horse Show at 19th Royal Winter Fair Draws Large Crowd from across Canada," *Mayfair*, February 1948, 35–7; Palmer, "The Myth and Reality of Haute Couture."

[56] Stevenson, "Devalued Franc Attracts Buyers," 22.

[57] Canada, Dominion Bureau of Statistics, *Department Store Sales and Stocks, 1941 to 1948*, DBS Reference Papers no. 4 (Ottawa: Dominion Bureau of Statistics, 1949), Tables 2 and 3.

[58] Quoted in "Some Contemporary Comments on Dior: The 'New Look' — A Canadian Footnote," compiled by Alan Suddon, *Costume Society of Ontario Newsletter* 7, 3 (1977): 2, reprinted 27, 1 (1997): 9.

[59] "What's Happened to the New Look? In Paris Only the Models Can Afford It," *New Liberty*, 28 February 1948, 8.

[60] "'Flash' Goes to a Fashion Show," *Flash*, 15 September 1947, 4–5, F229-141-0-175, T. Eaton Records, AOO.

[61] Dora Matthews, "Unpublished memoirs," 34.

[62] "Overture to Fashion" script, fall 1947, F229-151-5, file 152, T. Eaton Records, AOO.

Chapter 2: The Purchase of Haute Couture by Private Clients

[1] Jennifer Jones, "*Coquettes* and *Grisettes*: Women Buying and Selling in Ancien Régime Paris" in *The Sex of Things: Gender and Consumption in Historical Perspective*, ed. Victoria de Grazia with Ellen Furlough (Berkeley and Los Angeles: University of California Press, 1996), 34, 28–9, and 25–53.

[2] See Elaine Ableson, *When Ladies Go A-Thieving: Middle-Class Shoppers in the Victorian Department Store* (New York: Oxford University Press, 1989).

[3] The film *Mrs 'Arris Goes to Paris*, based on a story by Paul Gallico, clearly illustrates this in a charming fashion. Paul Gallico, *Mrs 'Arris Goes to Paris* (New York: Doubleday, 1958); *Mrs 'Arris Goes to Paris*, 1992, television movie, Accent Films in association with Novo Films and Corymore Productions.

[4] As well, the more prestigious the house, the higher the *caution*, which differed from house to house though it was supervised by the Chambre syndicale. Florette Chelot, who was a *vendeuse*, gave the information about Balenciaga in an interview by the author, Paris, France, 3 May 1991. While conducting research in Paris, I tried to obtain an invitation to a fashion presentation at the house of Lacroix through the Canadian cultural attachée. This was unsuccessful and — from the reaction of the secretary who had been charged with obtaining the invitation — laughable.

[5] Posy Chisholm Feick, interview by author, New York, US, 1 July 1991.

[6] Mona Campbell, interview by author, Toronto, Canada, 24 January 1991.

[7] Signy Eaton, interview by author, Toronto, Canada, 11 July 1991.

[8] Sally Brenzel, interview by author, Toronto, Canada, 22 March 1991; Harriet "Sis" Bunting Weld, interview by author, Toronto, Canada, 30 January 1992; Patricia Harris, interview by author, Toronto, Canada, 22 November 1990.

[9] The term *vendeuse* is feminine, and the gendered role of the profession is so strong that it was used for salesman Mr Peter Crown, who worked at two houses in London, Peter Russell and Lachasse. Peter Hope Lumley, interview by author, London, England, 3 December 1991.

[10] Mary Brooks Picken and Dora Loues Miller, *Dressmakers of France: The Who, How and Why of French Couture* (New York: Harper and Bros., 1956), 23. This definition was verified by Mme Burait, at Nina Ricci, during an interview, Paris, France, 24 April 1991. See also Celia Bertin, *Paris à la mode: A Voyage of Discovery*, trans. Marjorie Deans (London: Victor Gollancz, 1956), 55–70.

[11] Picken and Miller, *Dressmakers of France*, 23.

[12] Ginette Spanier, *It Isn't All Mink* (New York: Random House, 1959), 207.

[13] One way to preserve this type of ephemeral documentation is to donate the records to a museum or archive with the caveat that they not be made public until a requested date, thus ensuring the privacy of all those still living. The Lachasse records are available at AAD 6-1989, Archive of Art and Design, National Art Library, London.

[14] M-P ledger, Mrs A. Milner, Account M235, AAD 6-10-1989 and Account M235, Sheet 107, ADD 6-4-1989, Archive of Art and Design, National Art Library, London.

[15] Bernard Roshco, *The Rag Race: How New York and Paris Run the Breakneck Business of Dressing American Women* (New York: Funk and Wagnalls, 1963), 156.

[16] Christian Dior, *Talking about Fashion: Christian Dior As Told to Élie Rabourdin and Alice Chavane*, trans. Eugenia Sheppard (New York: G.P. Putnam's Sons, 1954), 106–7.

[17] Bertin, *Paris à la mode*, 59.

[18] Picken and Miller, *Dressmakers of France*, 23.

[19] Correspondence between author and Véronique Wiesinger, curator, Musée national de la coopération franco-américaine au Château de Blérancourt, 22 July and 15 September 1992. Thanks to Mrs Dupasquier, chief curator of the Musée national de la Légion d'Honneur et des ordres de chevaliers, for this contact. Information

was also obtained from Clayton Burton, interview by author, Toronto, Canada, 22 August 1990; Mme Chicoye, interview by author, Paris, France, 9 December 1991.

[20] Clayton Burton, interview.

[21] After the war, the commission was 10 percent at the house of Jacques Fath. Mme Chicoye was a *vendeuse* at Fath at that time. Mme Chicoye, interview.

[22] Anonymous, interview by author, Paris, France, 1991.

[23] Clayton Burton, interview.

[24] Mme Chicoye, interview.

[25] Ibid.; Philippe Venet, interview by author, Paris, France, 9 December 1991; Mary Carr-Harris, interview by author, Toronto, Canada, 15 January 1991. Laura Bacon probably used other houses too.

[26] Mary Carr-Harris, interview.

[27] "Dictator by Demand," *Time*, 4 March 1957, 34.

[28] Mme Burait, interview. She was a mannequin at Nina Ricci during the 1950s and has continued to work for the house. Fig. 2.1 from *Mayfair*, October 1951, 51.

[29] Rose Torno, interview by author, Toronto, Canada, 26 July 1990. The only samples available to try on were those made for the fashion shows and made to measure for the individual mannequins attached to the house.

[30] Sonja Bata, interview by author, Toronto, Canada, 22 August 1990.

[31] Rose Torno, interview.

[32] Grace Gooderham, interview by author, Toronto, Canada, 27 February 1991.

[33] Nonetheless, another dress of this design exists in the collection of the Museum of Fine Arts, Houston. John Vollmer, *Dressed to Celebrate: Evening Wear in the Twentieth Century* (Houston: Museum of Fine Arts, 1988), 9, cat. no. 18. The Royal Ontario Museum dress ROM 981. 206.3 is missing the moss green silk stole that is shown in the Pierre Balmain sketch, p. 273.

[34] "Start of a Season: Toronto's Brilliant Artillery Ball," *Mayfair*, January 1957, 30.

[35] Grace Gooderham, interview.

[36] Colin Campbell, "Consumption and the Rhetoric of Need and Want," *Journal of Design History* 11, 3 (1998): 235–46.

[37] Rosemary Rathgeb, interview, Toronto, Canada, 20 February 1991.

[38] William Leach discusses these ideas in various chapters of *Land of Desire: Merchants, Power and the Rise of a New American Culture* (New York: Vintage Books, 1993).

[39] Susan Porter Benson, *Counter Cultures: Saleswomen, Managers, and Customers in American Department Stores*

1890–1940 (Urbana and Chicago: University of Illinois Press, 1986), 81; Cynthia Jane Wright, "'The Most Prominent Rendezvous of the Feminine Toronto': Eaton's College Street and the Organization of Shopping in Toronto, 1920–1950" (PhD diss., OISE, University of Toronto, 1993), 139–43; Gail Reekie, *Temptations: Sex, Selling and the Department Store* (Sydney: Allen and Unwin 1993), 12.

[40] Margery Steele, interview by author, Toronto, Canada, 7 November 1990.

[41] Ollie Smythe, interview with Ida Hewett and Lucille Gauthier by author, Toronto, Canada, 14 September; and interview by author, Toronto, Canada, 4 October 1990.

[42] Ollie Smythe, interviews; Margery Steele, interview; Helen Stimpson and Joyce Scott, interview by the author, Toronto, Canada, 20 March 1991.

[43] Joyce Scott and Helen Stimpson, interview.

[44] Marsha Rovan, "Lexy," *Creeds, The Magazine* (Holiday 1987): 39.

[45] Joyce Carter, "Memories Recalled at Party," *Globe and Mail*, 1 November 1988, C6

[46] Ollie Smythe, interview.

[47] Joyce Scott and Helen Stimpson, interview.

[48] Clayton Burton, interview.

[49] Edmund Creed, author's questionnaire, 21 April 1992.

[50] Helen Stimpson, interview.

[51] "Pins and Needles: The Case of the Altering Circumstances," *Flash*, 18 September 1950, 9, F229-141-0-178, T. Eaton Records, Archives of Ontario, Toronto.

Chapter 3: Buying and Merchandising European Couture in Toronto

[1] Quotation from Jeanine Locke, "Canadian Society," *Chatelaine*, April 1958, 79. For more on women's groups and the Toronto social season see Alexandra Palmer, "The Myth and Reality of Haute Couture: Consumption, Social Function and Taste in Toronto, 1945–1963" (PhD diss., University of Brighton, 1994). I am currently researching the Toronto social season during the early twentieth century, and this will be discussed in a future publication. Fig. 3.1 from "Silver-Star Carpet and Silver-Laden Trees at League Ball," *Toronto Telegram*, 4 December 1954, 27; fig. 3.2 from *Globe and Mail*, 2 November 1956, 16.

[2] Cynthia Jane Wright discusses the competition between the two stores in "'The Most Prominent Rendezvous of the Feminine Toronto': Eaton's College Street and the Organization of Shopping in Toronto, 1920–1950" (PhD diss., OISE, University of Toronto, 1993). Also see Allan

G. Burton, *A Store of Memories* (Toronto: McClelland and Stewart, 1986); C.L. Burton, *A Sense of Urgency: Memoirs of a Canadian Merchant* (Toronto: Clarke, Irwin and Company, 1952). For haute couture as cultural capital, see Pierre Bourdieu, *Distinction: A Social Critique of the Judgement of Taste*, trans. Richard Nice (Cambridge, MA: Harvard University Press, 1984), 12.

[3] For an example, see Jeanne Lanvin dinner dress, c. 1913, ROM 965.53.1. Paul Poiret was invited to Toronto by Eaton's in 1913.

[4] Wright, "The Most Prominent Rendezvous," 136–7. Eaton's was forced into bankruptcy in 1999. Simpson's was founded in 1872 by Robert Simpson and bought out by the Hudson's Bay Company in 1991.

[5] Holt Renfrew was founded in 1837 in Quebec City by W.S. Henderson, an Irishman and dealer in fur caps and hats. In 1852, he sold out to his brother, John, in Montreal, who sent G.R. Renfrew and V.H. Marcou to Quebec City to manage the business there. In 1860, the firm became known as Henderson, Renfrew, and Company. By 1901, the Holt Renfrew and Company name was established. The first Toronto branch was opened in 1889 and it is still in business today. See William S. Boas, *Canada, Post-War Possibilities* (Montreal: William S. Boas and Company, 1948); John William Ferry, *A History of the Department Store* (New York: Macmillan, 1960), 326–8. Creeds opened in 1915 and filed for voluntary bankruptcy in November 1990.

[6] The Toronto branch opened on 11 October 1950 at 56 Bloor Street East. Morgan's was founded in 1845 under the name Smith and Morgan. In 1852, David Smith sold his share to Henry Morgan, who entered into partnership with his brother, James, to create Henry Morgan and Company. Ferry, *A History of the Department Store*, 317. The opening is described in Margaret Cragg, "Outfit Women Top-to-Toe at New Morgan Store," *Globe and Mail*, 11 October 1950, 12. Fig. 3.4 from *Mayfair*, September 1953, 8.

[7] "New Bid for Suburbia Sales: Morgan's Will Give Night Shopping a Whirl," *Financial Post*, 20 November 1954, 5; "How to Win Suburban Sales: Morgan's Two-Rule Policy Sparks Growth, Profits," *Financial Post*, 20 August 1955, 23; "Orbital Retailing Guide for New Morgan Store," *Globe and Mail*, 17 August 1955, 10; James Bryant, *Department Store Disease* (Toronto: McClelland and Stewart, 1977), 139.

[8] Advertisement, *Globe and Mail*, 15 October 1949, 14; Might Directories, *Metropolitan Toronto City Directory*, 1952 (Toronto: McLaren Micropublishing, 1952).

[9] In 1945, the buyers or commissionaires were paid a salary and also got a 2 to 3 percent commission on their sales.

Former saleswomen Helen Stimpson and Joyce Scott, interview by author, Toronto, Canada, 20 March 1991.

[10] Jeanie Hersenhoren, interview by author, Toronto, Canada, 4 March 1991; Elsa Jenkins, interview by author, Toronto, Canada, 8 October 1991; advertisement, *Mayfair*, October 1948, 126.

[11] Jean E. Pierce became very important in the 1960s for encouraging and promoting new Canadian designers. Julius Simon had two shops that sold couture and high-end ready-to-wear as well. The first, the midtown branch, opened in 1934 on Bay Street, moved to Yonge Street in 1938, reappeared in 1943 on Bloor Street, and moved across the road in 1954. A second store opened in 1958 on Lawrence Avenue, in the north end of the city. Simon Ramm opened on midtown Bloor Street in 1940, announced a new store opening on Yonge Street just north of Bloor in 1950, and moved farther north up Yonge in 1964. All three stores continued business into the 1960s.

[12] Jean E. Pierce, interview by author, Toronto, Canada, 20 January 1991.

[13] Ibid.; Celia Bertin, *Paris à la mode: A Voyage of Discovery*, trans. Marjorie Deans (London: Victor Gollancz, 1956), 51–5.

[14] Joseph A. Barry, "Semi-Annual Paris Openings Dramatic Affairs for Designers, Buyers," *Globe and Mail*, 6 March 1951, 15. Further, the rules and regulations set out by the Chambre syndicale detail the ongoing control of which buyers were allowed to see the collections and the fees charged to each. Christian Dior Archives, Paris.

[15] They were also charged a fee for their buyers' cards, which were issued by the Chambre syndicale. In the fall 1950 season, this fee was 500 francs. Chambre syndicale to haute couture houses, "Relations avec les acheteurs," memorandum, June 1950, Christian Dior Archives, Paris.

[16] Jeannette A. Jarnow and Beatrice Judelle, *Inside the Fashion Business* (New York: John Wiley and Sons, 1965), 93, 157.

[17] Chambre syndicale, "Instructions sur la carte d'acheteur français pour la saison Automne–Hiver 1947," memorandum, July 1947, Christian Dior Archives, Paris; D. Gorin, secrétaire général de la Chambre syndicale, "Conditions de vente," memorandum, 23 July 1948, Christian Dior Archives, Paris.

[18] An internal memorandum by J. Rouët notes that the minimum fees in 1949 for "Grands Magasins, détaillants, couturiers de tous pays" were 100 francs for the Collection Haute Couture and 40 francs for the Collection Mode. For "manufacturiers, confectionneurs américains," the minimum was 350 francs for the Collection Haute Couture and 40 francs for the Collection Mode. For "manufacturiers, confectionneurs des autre pays," it was 100 francs for the Collection Haute Couture and 40 francs for the Collection Mode. J. Rouët to Christian Dior personnel, 1 July 1949, Christian Dior Archives, Paris. See also Olive Dickason, "Paris and London Fashions Are Quickly Copied Here," *Globe and Mail*, 8 September 1955, 17. An unidentified and undated news clipping, "Dior Raises Buyer Deposit for Showings," discusses that Dior "has raised the buyer's deposit . . . to 100,000 francs for retailers which roughly amounts to $300 and will ask a minimum buying guarantee of 350,000 francs or roughly $1,000 from American manufacturers . . . Jean Dessès will charge 100,000, Bruyère 50,000, Manguin 40,000 but other couturiers have not yet announced deposits required." Christian Dior Archives, Paris.

[19] Eugenia Sheppard, "Rented for Reproductions in US . . .," [New York Herald?] *Tribune*, 18 March 1951, B51.1, Alison Settle Archives, University of Brighton.

[20] The arrangements and regulations of these sales were intricate. In a memorandum issued by the Chambre syndicale as a subsection of "Vente de toiles," the author, D. Gorin, refers to a memo circulated in October 1948 regarding the sale of symmetrical "toiles entières." "Saison de Printemps 1949," memorandum, 12 January 1949, Christian Dior Archives, Paris. I have seen only one *demi-toile*, a 1953 Christian Dior dress given to the Brooklyn Museum of Art (55.199.1-2) by Kay Wynne Dress Company of 7th Avenue, New York. Information about the *référence* comes from Booton Herndon, *Bergdorf's on the Plaza: The Story of Bergdorf Goodman and a Half-Century of American Fashion* (New York: Alfred A. Knopf, 1956), 148–9.

[21] Christian Dior, *Christian Dior and I*, trans. Antonia Fraser (New York: E.P. Dutton and Company, 1957), 46, 50.

[22] Jarnow and Judelle, *Inside the Fashion Business*, 94.

[23] Bernard Roshco, *The Rag Race: How New York and Paris Run the Breakneck Business of Dressing American Women* (New York: Funk and Wagnalls, 1963), 162. The date 15 October for the fall season release date is given by Dora Miller in the Appendix to Bernice G. Chambers, *Fashion Fundamentals* (New York: Prentice-Hall, 1947), 475.

[24] The Royal Ontario Museum has the Balenciaga suit made up in camel wool, ROM 958.85.1ab.

[25] William Leach discusses the role of women buyers in American department stores in the late nineteenth and early twentieth centuries, calling them the "queens" of Paris couture in *Land of Desire: Merchants, Power and the Rise of a New American Culture* (New York: Vintage Books, 1993), 95–9.

[26] Ollie Smythe, interview by author, Toronto, Canada, 4 October 1990.

[27] Ibid.

[28] F.E. West to H. Kennedy, 20 March 1952, General Merchandise Office, Buyer's Meetings Files, F229-77-1, T. Eaton Records, Archives of Ontario, Toronto (hereinafter AOO).

[29] General Merchandise Office, Toronto, to F.E. West, Vancouver, 22 March 1952, F229-7-1, T. Eaton Records, AOO.

[30] General Merchandise Office to S.R. Martin, 5 April 1952, F229-77-1, T. Eaton Records, AOO. The previous fall, the Vancouver and Victoria couture rooms had sold $33,000 and $12,500 of merchandise respectively, for a combined gross gain of 43 percent. See F.E. West to H. Kennedy, 20 March 1952, General Merchandise Office, Buyer's Meetings Files, F229-77-1, T. Eaton Records, AOO.

[31] Dora Matthews, Toronto, to Jenny Lindsay, Fashion Bureau, Montreal, 25 August 1960, F229-162-42, T. Eaton Records, AOO.

[32] *Success Story*, [1946], 15 min., 30 sec., Crawley's, Staff Training Films, F229-403-0-6, T. Eaton Records, AOO; *You Are the Star*, 195[6?], 35 mm, produced for Allied Stores Corporation by Carvel Films Inc., New York, F229-403-0-34, T. Eaton Records, AOO; Canada, Department of Labour, Women's Bureau, *Married Women Working for Pay in Eight Canadian Cities* (Ottawa: Department of Labour, Women's Bureau, 1958), 11.

[33] Ollie Smythe, interview.

[34] Ibid.

[35] Jeanne Parkin, interview by author, Toronto, Canada, 11 August 1993.

[36] Mabel Letchford was an Englishwoman who worked in theatre and film in the 1930s, and in 1940 opened a private school at 70 Bloor Street West. Might Directories, *Metropolitan Toronto City Directory*, 1940 (Toronto: McLaren Micropublishing, 1940), 65; Margery Steele, interview by author, Toronto, Canada, 7 November 1990.

[37] "Creeds," *Toronto Life Fashion* (Holiday 1987): 77.

[38] Advertisement, *Globe and Mail*, 4 October 1949, 11.

[39] Margery Steele, interview.

[40] Ollie Smythe, interview. In the 1960s, Irene Satz of Ohrbach's also went over to buy models to copy and didn't have a budget. Irene Satz, interview by author, New York, US, 16 September 1990.

[41] Elsa Jenkins, interview.

[42] Jean E. Pierce, interview.

[43] Joyce Scott and Helen Stimpson, interview.

[44] Susan Porter Benson, *Counter Cultures: Saleswomen, Managers, and Customers in American Department Stores 1890–1940* (Urbana and Chicago: University of Illinois Press, 1986), 147–53.

[45] Mrs Matthews was divorced. Her ex-husband was an officer in the military and lived in Ottawa. "Ideas for Article on History of Fashion Shows and Models," notes, F229-162-41, T. Eaton Records, AOO.

[46] Dora Matthews, "Unpublished memoirs" (Documentary Files, Textile and Costume Section, Royal Ontario Museum, manuscript), 27, 4.

[47] Marion John, interview by author, Toronto, Canada, 4 July 1993.

[48] "Fashion Picture for Fall, 1951, Seen by Staff," *Flash*, 17 September 1951, 4, F229-141-0-179, T. Eaton Records, AOO.

[49] "Staff Training Holds Spring Show," *Flash*, 5 March 1951, 4, and "Fashions and Their Selling Outlined at Early Show," *Flash*, 4 September 1951, 4, F229-141-0-179, T. Eaton Records, AOO; Eaton's, *A Capsule Course in the New Fashion Story*, fall and winter 1947 booklet, F229-162-37, T. Eaton Records, AOO; Eaton's Fashion Bureau, *Gifted New Fashions*, spring and summer 1948 booklet, F229-62-37, T. Eaton Records, AOO.

[50] "'Fashions on Trial' in the Georgian Room," *Flash*, 10 September 1945, 6, F229-141-0-173, T. Eaton Records, AOO.

[51] Minutes of Sales Promotion Committee meeting, 20 February 1945, F229-151-4, file 116, T. Eaton Records, AOO.

[52] "New York City," report, 23 October 1945, F229-151-5, file 143, T. Eaton Records, AOO; Dorothy Coleman, "Fashion Dolls/Fashionable Dolls," *Dress* 3 (1997): 1–8. Harriet Quick, in *Catwalking: A History of the Fashion Model* (London: Hamlyn, 1997), 65, shows a photograph of would-be fashion models at the Mayfair School in New York during the 1940s, who were taught how to pose with the aid of metre-high wooden dolls. Artists also used articulated wooden dolls, complete with wardrobe, for painting a portrait while a sitter was not available. In the eighteenth century, large-scale fashion dolls dressed in the latest styles were sent to England from Paris twice a year. See Edward Maeder, *An Elegant Art: Fashion and Fantasy in the Eighteenth Century* (Los Angeles and New York: H.N. Abrams in association with Los Angeles County Museum of Art, 1983), 163.

[53] "Headlines in Outline, Spring 1952," *Flash*, 18 February 1952, 6–7, F229-141-0-180, T. Eaton Records, AOO.

[54] *Fashionably Yours*, spring show staff training booklet, 1961, F229-162-37, T. Eaton Records, AOO; "Remember

When Selling . . ." *Eaton News* 6, 3 (1961): 4, F229-141-0-156, T. Eaton Records, AOO.

Chapter 4: Couture, Fashion Shows, and Marketing

1 Bettina Ballard, *In My Fashion* (New York: David McKay, 1960), 83.

2 The Syndicale Suisse des Exportateurs de l'Industrie de l'Habillement set up an arrangement whereby 400 members paid 1 percent of all export profits to a central promotion fund. Their designs were then presented anonymously and fourteen countries sent fashion critics. Alison Settle, A Woman's Viewpoint column, *Observer* (London), 12 June 1955, A55.17 and L50.27, Alison Settle Archives, University of Brighton.

3 Alison Settle, A Woman's Viewpoint column, *Observer* (London), 31 August 1952, A52.33, Alison Settle Archives, University of Brighton.

4 Some extensive research is just beginning on these centres. More often they are acknowledged only briefly, and work tends to focus on the big designer names. See Anthea Jarvis' section on fashion in Lesley Jackson's *The New Look Design in the Fifties* (London: Thames and Hudson, 1991), 117–22. Quotation from Ballard, *In My Fashion*, 250. Alison Adburgham also writes of the sensation of seeing collections at the Pitti Palace in an article, originally published in 1957, called "Warm Squash at the Palazzo Pitti," in her book *View of Fashion* (London: Allen and Unwin, 1966), 132–5.

5 "New Era for Air Travel Overseas," *Mayfair*, February 1952, 55, 58. The new tourist fares were $510 Montreal-London return, down from the old luxury fare of $733. When one considers that a 1952 dollar is worth 6.5 cents today, it is clear that air travel was still a considerable expense. Sir Miles Thomas, "Canada's Amazing Future in the Air," *Mayfair*, January 1954, 21.

6 Lotta Dempsey, "Five Countries Represented in Fashions at Simpson's," *Globe and Mail*, 11 September 1951, 10; Margaret Cragg, "Sportswear to Mink in a Fast Paced Show," *Globe and Mail*, 17 September 1958, 17. This show probably comprised high-end ready-to-wear and couture.

7 "Paris Influence Strong. Remembers New-Look Jokes." *Globe and Mail*, 18 November 1948, 14; "Fath Skirts Are So Tight, Models Seem on Wheels," *Globe and Mail*, 9 August 1949, 10.

8 Dora Matthews, notes, 3 August 1950, F229-151-3, file 100, T. Eaton Records, Archives of Ontario, Toronto (hereinafter AOO).

9 Miss D. Weston, European report, spring 1953, F229-77-1, T. Eaton Records, AOO.

10 "London Export Fashions by the Big Ten," *Mayfair*, April 1950, 69.

11 Settle, A Woman's Viewpoint column, *Observer* (London), 31 August 1952.

12 "Husband of Canadian Girl Joins London's Top Twelve," *Mayfair*, April 1954, 68; "A New Fame for Ireland," *Mayfair*, October 1953, 47; "The Shape of Spring Is Lithe and Lovely," fashion show program, spring 1955, F229-135-4, file 2, T. Eaton Records, AOO; "Irish Fashions in the News," *Mayfair*, April 1954, 68; "Dublin Designs Make Much of Native Fabrics and Handwork," *Mayfair*, October 1954, 9; *CBC Newsmagazine*, 13 March 1955, NFA 76-11-261, 13-0823, National Archives of Canada, Moving Image and Sound Archives, Ottawa; "Top Designer at Staff Show," *Flash*, April 1955, 4–5, F229-141-183, T. Eaton Records, AOO; Iona Monahan, "The Irish Spirit in Fashion," *Mayfair*, March 1957, 42–3. For more on Irish fashion see Elizabeth McCrum, *Fabric and Form: Irish Fashion since 1950* (Ulster, Ireland: Sutton Publishing in association with Ulster Museum, 1996).

13 For work on Italian fashion, see Gloria Bianchino, *Italian Fashion Designing 1945–80* (Los Angeles and Parma: Centro studi e archivio della comunicazione, Università di Parma, 1987), 63; Luigi Settembrini, "From Haute Couture to Prêt-à-Porter," in *The Italian Metamorphosis, 1945–1968*, ed. Germano Celant (New York: Guggenheim Museum, 1994), 485–7; Valerie Steele, "Italian Fashion and America," in *Italian Metamorphosis, 1945–1968*, 496–505; Ornella Morelli, "The International Success and Domestic Debut of Postwar Italian Fashion," in *Italian Fashion: The Origins of High Fashion and Knitwear*, ed. Gloria Bianchino, trans. Paul Blanchard (Milan: Electa, 1987), 58–77; Nicola White, *Reconstructing Italian Fashion: America and the Development of the Italian Fashion Industry* (Oxford and New York: Berg, 2000).

14 "Italian Fashions Come to Canada," *Mayfair*, October 1951, 63.

15 Advertisement, *Mayfair*, September 1952, 14.

16 "For the Coronation Season," *Mayfair*, April 1953, 51.

17 In many respects, Rosemary Boxer was the 1950s precursor to Jeanne Beker and Citytv's *Fashion Television*. She hosted the fashion segment of *CBC Newsmagazine*. Her beauty salon was described as follows: "Opening of Rosemary Boxer's dazzling new Fashion and Beauty Clinic . . . [in] harmonizing shades of grey, pink, red, white and black, the salon is about as feminine as a frilly negligée . . . the colour based on a Monet painting in Rosemary Boxer's office . . . She is dropping radio and television and all fashion shows except the very big ones and is keeping on as a fashion and beauty editor of *Chatelaine* . . . [Her] fashion co-ordinator is Eveleen

Dollery . . . [She offers] a six week course, . . . one week-ly 3 hour class on makeup, hairstyling and fashion that will cost $75.00. Or Rosemary will give single consul-tations . . . Almost all glamour gals . . . who attended Rosemary's celebrations had on eye-makeup . . . if you walk around downtown Toronto, you'll notice eye-makeup is being worn more and more in the daytime." Jean Armstrong, "Here's Looking at You," *Globe and Mail*, 6 October 1955, 18. See *CBC Newsmagazine*, 4 April 1954, NFA 76-11-198, 13-0835; 22 August 1954, NFA 76-11-219, 13-0780; 6 February 1955, NFA 76-11-254, 13-0786; 24 April 1955, NFA 76-11-265, 13-0828; and 18 March 1956, NFA 76-11-309, 13-0861, National Archives of Canada, Moving Image and Sound Archives, Ottawa. A Casa da Silva ensemble similar to or the same as fig. 4.7 is described in F229-0-135-4, file 2, The T. Eaton Records, Archives of Ontario.

[18] Boxer quoted from *CBC Newsmagazine*, 24 April 1955, NFA 76-11-265, 13-0828, National Archives of Canada, Moving Image and Sound Archives, Ottawa; Balmain quoted from "Dior, Dictator by Demand," *Time*, 4 March 1957, 36.

[19] Posy Chisholm Feick, interview by author, New York, US, 1 July 1991; Mona Campbell, interview by author, Toronto, Canada, 24 January 1991. Two Mingolini Guggenheim dresses worn by Mona Campbell are in the Seneca Fashion Resource Centre, 1-995-14-00930 and 1-956-14-00943, Seneca College of Applied Arts and Technology, Toronto, Canada.

[20] As in Simpson's St Regis advertisement for "Swiss creations," *Mayfair*, November 1951, 33.

[21] Miss D. Weston, European report.

[22] Best-dressed list, *Toronto Telegram*, 22 March 1960, 27–8; Betty Cassels, interview by author, Toronto, Canada, 29 October 1992; "Ellington's Way with the National Ballet," *Toronto Telegram*, 11 December 1959, 31.

[23] Cragg, "Sportswear to Mink," 17; Miss D. Weston, European report; fig. 4.10 from *Mayfair*, September 1952, 40.

[24] "Fall Fashion Wears a Gentle or Dramatic Air," *Flash*, September 1952, 3, F220-141-0-180, T. Eaton Records, AOO

[25] "Madrid: Simple Wool Dresses — Again, Long Lines; Easy Fit," *Mayfair*, October 1954, 47; Iona Monahan, "Madrid — Cosmopolitan Setting for Spanish Fashion," *Mayfair*, April 1958, 41; fig. 4.11 from *Mayfair*, April 1953, 59.

[26] For instance, the following advertised Dutch designs: Eaton's in *Globe and Mail*, 16 February 1950, 28; Simp-son's in *Globe and Mail*, 3 September 1944, 14; Eaton's in *Globe and Mail*, 7 March 1955, 40; Eaton's in *Globe and Mail*, 17 March 1955, 48; Eaton's in *Globe and Mail*, 18 January 1955, 30. Swiss designs were also advertised: "Eaton's from Zurich," in *Globe and Mail*, 6 September 1950, 28; fashion show dispersal advertised by Simpson's in *Globe and Mail*, 4 March 1950, 14; Eaton's in *Globe and Mail*, 18 January 1955, 30; Marty of Switzerland sold by Eaton's, fashion show program, fall 1955, F229-135-4, T. Eaton Records, AOO; Creeds in *Globe and Mail*, 3 November 1955, 14; Eaton's in *Globe and Mail*, 29 December 1955, 32; Morgan's in *Canadian Jewish Review* 37, 51 (1955): 162; Simpson's in *Globe and Mail*, 12 October 1955, 16. Eaton's also advertised designs from Brussels in *Globe and Mail*, 12 October 1955, 16.

[27] Holt Renfrew advertised its exclusive licence with Christian Dior regularly in *Mayfair*, beginning in August 1951, 9. Figs. 4.12 and 4.13 from *Mayfair*, May 1952, 11 and April 1953, 9.

[28] Diana de Marly, *Christian Dior* (London: B.T. Batsford, 1990), 73.

[29] Christian Dior, *Christian Dior and I*, trans. Antonia Fraser (New York: E.P. Dutton and Company, 1957), 33; Jacques Rouët, interview by author, Paris, France, 29 April 1991.

[30] Jacques Rouët, interview.

[31] Leonard Shavick, telephone interview by author, 8 April 1991; Jacques Rouët, interview; Carolyn Druion, author's questionnaire, March 1992.

[32] Leonard Shavick, interview; Barbara Shavick, inter-view by author, 2 January 1999, Montreal, Canada.

[33] Advertisement, *Mayfair*, September 1952, 14.

[34] Advertisement, *Mayfair*, May 1953, 15; Leonard Shavick, interview.

[35] Florette Chelot, interview by author, Paris, France, 3 May 1991. For discussion of Dior in Australia see *Christian Dior: The Magic of Fashion* (Sydney: Powerhouse Museum, 1994).

[36] Teresa Richey, interview by author, London, England, 5 December 1991.

[37] "Magic of Dior Name $50 Million a Year," *Financial Post*, 8 November 1958, 16. Fig. 4.17 from *Mayfair*, March 1958, 9.

[38] "Fashions Fluid and Flattering," *Eaton News* 2, 10 (1957): 10, F229-141-0-153, T. Eaton Records, AOO; Advertisement, *Globe and Mail*, 14 October 1960, 13; "Ele-gance Is Trademark of Parisian Design, Pierre Balmain," *Globe and Mail*, 18 October 1960, 12. The Florilège col-lection was not ready-to-wear but produced by Pierre Balmain himself. See Didier Grumbach, *Histoires de la mode* (Paris: Seuil, 1993), 169, 178.

[39] Palais Galliera, Musée de la mode et du costume, *Pierre Balmain, 40 années de création* (Paris: Paris-Musées,

1985), 242. This catalogue does not mention or explain his Florilège collection. "Elegance Is Trademark," 12.

[40] Ollie Smythe, interview by author, Toronto, Canada, 4 October 1990; and interview by author, with Ida Hewett and Lucille Gauthier, Toronto, Canada, 14 September 1990.

[41] See discussions of late-nineteenth- and early-twentieth-century North American department stores by William Leach. Leach, "Transformations in a Culture of Consumption: Women and Department Stores, 1890–1925," *Journal of American History* 71, 2 (1984): 319–42; William Leach, *Land of Desire: Merchants, Power and the Rise of a New American Culture* (New York: Vintage Books, 1993), 101–4; and William Leach, "Strategists of Display and the Production of Desire," in *Consuming Visions: Accumulation and Display of Goods in America, 1880–1920*, ed. Simon J. Bronner (New York: W.W. Norton and Company, 1989), 99–132.

[42] Though Eaton's College Street building still exists, the auditorium is not open to the public. It is still intact and there is a movement to preserve this important architectural site. Cynthia Jane Wright, "'The Most Prominent Rendezvous of the Feminine Toronto': Eaton's College Street and the Organization of Shopping in Toronto, 1920–1950" (PhD diss., OISE, University of Toronto, 1993), 140–3; William Dendy, *Lost Toronto: Images of City's Past* (Toronto: McClelland and Stewart, 1993), 159.

[43] Auditorium Attendance Records, F229-138-1, T. Eaton Records, AOO.

[44] Minutes of the Joint Advertising and Merchandise Display meeting, 16 January 1947, F229-151-2, file 2/4, T. Eaton Records, AOO.

[45] Marion John, interview by author, Toronto, Canada, 4 July 1993.

[46] Norma Wildgoose, interview by author, Toronto, Canada, 22 October 1991.

[47] Ibid.

[48] "Long Lean Line for Fall '55," *Flash*, October 1955, 18–19, F229-141-0-183, T. Eaton Records, AOO; "This Autumn . . . the Defined Line," fashion show program, fall 1955, F229-135-4, file 1, T. Eaton Records, AOO.

[49] "Training Department Sponsors Spring Fashion Preview," *Flash*, March 1953, 8, F229-141-0-181, T. Eaton Records, AOO. *Millinery*, spring 1953, F229-403-0-39, T. Eaton Records, AOO, was another film interlude produced as part of a fashion show. Other Eaton's fashion films include: *Fall Hats*, 1953, 9 min., Staff Training Films, F229-403-0-25; *Spring Millinery Film*, 1955, 6 min., 30 sec., Staff Training Films, F229-403-0-31; *Flattery from the Hands of Talented Milliners*, 1957, 6 min., Staff Training Films, F229-403-0-35; *Feminine Flattery*, 1952, approx. 15 min., flashcut reel 1, Eaton's History, F229-401-0-103; *The Mystery of Fashion*, fall 1952, 32 min., Staff Training Films, F229-403-0-17; *Through the Fashion Looking Glass*, 1952, 25 min., flashcut reel 2, Eaton's Photographic Studio, Eaton's History, F229-401-0-105; *New Focus in Fashion and Figure*, 1961, 10 min., Staff Training Films, F229-403-0-43, T. Eaton Records, AOO.

[50] *Paris and London*, 1952, 6 min., 30 sec., Staff Training Films, F229-403-015, T. Eaton Records, AOO.

[51] H.E.R. King, Paris Office, to J.A. Brockie, Toronto, 10 August 1950, F229-151-3, file 100, T. Eaton Records, AOO; J.A. Brockie to H.E.R. King, 29 January 1951, F229-151-3, file 97, T. Eaton Records, AOO.

[52] "Fall Fashion Wears a Gentle or Dramatic Air," 3; *Paris and London*, film, 1952.

[53] Minutes of Sales Promotion Committee meeting, 17 January 1947, F229-151-2, file 58, T. Eaton Records, AOO; Conference, Merchandise Display Division meeting, 16, 17, 18, 19 June 1947, F229-151-2, file 2/4, T. Eaton Records, AOO.

[54] Minutes of the Merchandise Display and Sales Promotion meeting, 11 May 1948, F229-151-4, file 118, T. Eaton Records, AOO.

[55] "Women's groups sponsoring Eaton's fashion presentations," notes from Merchandise Display and Sales Promotion Office, 3 April 1948, F229-151-2, file 60, T. Eaton Records, AOO.

[56] Minutes of Sales Promotion Committee meeting, 6 April 1948, F229-151-4, file 118, T. Eaton Records, AOO.

[57] Minutes of Sale Promotions Committee meeting, 25 September 1945, F229-151-4, file 116, T. Eaton Records, AOO.

[58] "Women's groups sponsoring Eaton's fashion presentations," 3 April 1948.

[59] Minutes of Sales Promotion Committee meeting, 2 January 1948, F229-151-86, file 118, T. Eaton Records, AOO; Memo re: Spring Fashion Presentations, 5 March 1948, F229-151-2, file 60, T. Eaton Records, AOO.

[60] A donor dinner for B'nai B'rith to be held February 1949 at the Royal York Hotel was turned down. Minutes of Sales Promotion Committee meeting, 21 September 1948, F229-151-4, file 118, T. Eaton Records, AOO.

[61] Minutes of Sales Promotions Committee meeting, 20 January 1948, F229-151-2, file 118, T. Eaton Records, AOO.

[62] Minutes of Sales Promotion Committee meeting, 16 March 1948, F229-151-2, file 118, T. Eaton Records, AOO.

63 *Toronto Telegram*, 8 September 1955, 33; *Globe and Mail*, 20 October 1955, 13; "M'sieu Dior was Here," *Mayfair*, February 1956, 4; *CBC Newsmagazine*, 6 November 1955, NFA 76-11-292, 13-0852, National Archives of Canada, Moving Image and Sound Archives, Ottawa. See 1955–6 in Art Gallery of Ontario, *Fortytude, A History to Celebrate 40 Years of the Volunteer Committee of the Art Gallery of Ontario, formerly the Women's Committee of the Art Gallery of Toronto, 1945–6 to 1985–6*, ed. Mrs R. Burns Lind, Mrs J.L. Goad, and Mrs John Stohn (pamphlet, May 1986).

64 Jean E. Pierce, interview by author, Toronto, Canada, 20 January 1991.

65 The Wimodausis (*wives, mothers, daughters, sisters*) Club of Toronto was founded in 1902. In 1915, it formed a partnership with the Earlscourt Children's Home, a Methodist institution founded to meet the emergency needs of families "fragmented by illness or the death of a parent or parents." See Carol Thora Baines, "From Women's Social Benevolence to Professional Social Work: The Case of the Wimodausis Club and the Earlscourt Children's Home, 1902–1971" (PhD diss., OISE, University of Toronto, 1991), 1; Morgan's advertisement, *Globe and Mail*, 20 September 1951, 11. Fig. 4.23 is an advertisement from *Globe and Mail*, 18 September 1951, 14.

66 Margaret Cragg, "Top Imported Fashions Feature of Morgan Show," *Globe and Mail*, 15 March 1951, 15.

67 Morgan's advertisement for fall fashion show under the auspices of the Women's Auxiliary of Toronto Western Hospital, held 23–4 September, *Globe and Mail*, 11 September 1958, 17; advertisement, *Globe and Mail*, 18 September 1958, 17; Kay Rex, "Hartnell Sees Gowns Modelled at Morgan's," *Globe and Mail*, 24 September 1958, 11; *Tabloid*, CBC Canada, 23 September 1958, NFA V1 8205 002-2, National Archives of Canada, Visual and Sound, Ottawa. Fig. 4.24 from *Mayfair*, September 1958, 17.

68 C. Tait, Merchandise Display and Sales Promotion Office, to J.A. Brockie, Merchandise Display and Sales Promotion Office, 8 April 1947, F229-151-1, file 41, T. Eaton Records, AOO; Merchandise Display and Sales Promotion Office to W.D. McMaster, Merchandise Office, 9 January 1948, F229-151-1, file 23/2, T. Eaton Records, AOO; Minutes of Sales Promotion Committee meeting, 17 January 1947, F229-151-2, file 58, T. Eaton Records, AOO.

69 For spring 1948, the forty purchases comprised three ensembles by Lelong, three by Balenciaga, three by Schiaparelli, three by Dessès, three by Fath, four by Piguet, four by Balmain, five by Dior, three by Rouff, four by Griffe, three by Lanvin, and two by Lafaurie. "Paris Couture Models — Spring 1948," 12 February 1948, Paris,

and 20 February 1948, Fashion Bureau, F229-151-2, file 60, T. Eaton Records, AOO. The dispersal to other branches is recorded in Minutes of the Combined Advertising and Merchandising Representatives Conference, 23–4 June 1952, F220-90-1, T. Eaton Records, AOO.

70 Minutes of the Combined Advertising and Merchandising Display Representative Conference, 14–15 January 1952, F229-90-1, T. Eaton Records, AOO.

71 Dora Matthews, Toronto, to Jenny Lindsay, Fashion Bureau, Montreal, 25 August 1960, F229-162-42, T. Eaton Records, AOO.

72 McKenzie Porter, "Bargain Is a Naughty Word at Morgan's," *Maclean's*, 15 June 1953, 65.

73 The practice is noted in Minutes of Sales Promotion Committee meeting, 5 October 1948, F229-151-2, file 118, T. Eaton Records, AOO. Simpson's advertised the dispersal of its fall fashions of French and British originals, Dessès, Givenchy, Piguet, Balenciaga, Ricci, and Michael Sherard, originally priced from $375 to $1,200 and selling for $195 to $295, in *Globe and Mail*, 26 October 1953, 18. Creeds advertised a dispersal sale in *Globe and Mail*, 5 October 1955, 17.

Chapter 5: Alternative Sources of Imported Couture

1 Yvonne Deslandres and Florence Müller, *Histoire de la mode au XXe siècle* (Paris: Somogy, 1986), 25.

2 Museums tend to collect actual garments, which have more public appeal in an exhibition, and technical samples are not commonly offered to museum collections. The Royal Ontario Museum was given figs. 5.1 to 5.4 by Dora Matthews of Eaton's, who was also a founding member of the Toronto Fashion Group. One important exception to this generalization is an initiative at the University of Rhode Island, under the leadership of Joy Emery, to document historical paper patterns on a computer database. Also an exhibition at The Fashion Institute of Technology, New York, *Dreams on Paper: Home Sewing in America*, February–April 1987, exhibited a collection of 1868–1959 paper patterns from the collection of the late Betty Williams.

3 Bonded models are rarely mentioned in current writing on the fashion industry. Sources from the period include Bernard Roshco, *The Rag Race: How New York and Paris Run the Breakneck Business of Dressing American Women* (New York: Funk and Wagnalls, 1963), 152; Booton Herndon, *Bergdorf's on the Plaza: The Story of Bergdorf Goodman and a Half-Century of American Fashion* (New York: Alfred A. Knopf, 1956), 76; Jeannette A. Jarnow and Beatrice Judelle, *Inside the Fashion Business* (New York: John Wiley and Sons, 1965), 100. The exception is a recent article

that explains the function of bonded models in an abbreviated context. Beate Ziegert, "American Clothing: Identity in Mass Culture, 1840–1990," *Human Ecology Forum* 19, 3 (1991): 9. The references are not documented but probably come from Ziegert's personal experience in the garment industry. Thanks to John Vollmer for this reference. Deslandres and Müller, *Histoire de la mode au XXᵉ siècle*, 25, deals with the start of the bonded system.

[4] Mary Brooks Picken and Dora Loues Miller, *Dressmakers of France: The Who, How and Why of French Couture* (New York: Harper and Bros., 1956), xiv.

[5] Quotation from Celia Bertin, *Paris à la mode: A Voyage of Discovery*, trans. Marjorie Deans (London: Victor Gollancz, 1956). Bernard Roshco notes that duty was 15 to 20 percent on a US$1,500 evening gown and could go up to 50 percent. Roshco, *The Rag Race*, 152. Booton Herndon noted duties of up to 75 percent. Herndon, *Bergdorf's on the Plaza*, 76. Information on the length of bonds is from Eugenia Sheppard, "Rented for Reproductions in US . . .," [New York Herald?] *Tribune*, 18 March 1951, B51.1, Alison Settle Archives, University of Brighton; Edmund Creed, author's questionnaire, 21 April 1992.

[6] Roshco, *The Rag Race*, 151–2.

[7] I am aware of bonded models only in Canada but they very probably exist in other collections though they may not be identified as such. The McCord Museum in Montreal also has examples of bonded models. Many of those donated by Barbara Shavick, for instance, were bonded.

[8] Quotation from Roshco, *The Rag Race*, 151–2; Irene Satz, interview by author, New York, US, 16 September 1990.

[9] For the history of the store, see Nathan M. Ohrbach, *Getting Ahead in Retail* (New York: McGraw-Hill, 1935). Irene Satz said that Ohrbach's total annual purchases from 1964 to 1977 ranged from US$50,000 to US$100,000. Irene Satz, interview.

[10] Andrew Goodman, interview by author, New York, US, 7 March 1991. Didier Grumbach noted that in 1930 alone Bergdorf Goodman imported around 150 originals, whereas its buyer, Ethel Frankau, selected only sixty-eight originals over the entire period from 1945 to 1955. *Histoires de la mode* (Paris: Seuil, 1993), 65.

[11] Advertisement, *Vogue* (New York), 1 November 1955, 2.

[12] Herndon, *Bergdorf's on the Plaza*, photo section. Another Curiel design, in a private collection, retains its original Simpson's sales tag, marked down from $759 to $110.

[13] Gertrude Cain, *The American Way of Designing* (New York: Fairchild Publications, 1950), 106.

[14] Estron was a synthetic fibre of cellulose acetate. KODA-Eastman Estron yarn and TECA-Eastman Estron staple were woven into a rich variety of fabrics that emulated silks, satins, and wool suitings and were used in day time, leisure, afternoon, and evening wear. Designs made of Estron are found in The Costume Institute, Metropolitan Museum of Art (CI 50.21.1-15) and Brooklyn Museum of Art (50.56.1-16). Two-thirds of the fabrics were woven in the United States using Teca, and the rest were "unusual French weaves of the more formal variety . . . [containing] French estron yarn." Couturiers Ardanse, Balmain, Bruyère, Carven, Dessès, Heim, Molyneux, Patou, Piguet, Schiaparelli, and Vramant all used the fabrics.

[15] Miss Heidelberger to Mr Robert Sugben, 2 September 1949, Costume Institute registration records, Metropolitan Museum of Art, New York.

[16] S. Stern, Henry and Co., Customs Brokers, New York, to W.E.H. Higman, Commissioner of Customs, 24 August 1949, Costume Institute registration records, CI5021.1-15, Metropolitan Museum of Art, New York; Roshco, *The Rag Race*, 152–3.

[17] Roshco, *The Rag Race*, 165; Irene Satz, interview. A rub-off was a copy.

[18] Andrew Goodman, interview; Herndon, *Bergdorf's on the Plaza*, 76.

[19] Christian Dior, "Note à l'Attention de Messieurs les Commissionnaires," undated memorandum regarding the spring 1949 collection, Christian Dior Archives, Paris.

[20] Choral C. Pepper, "Don't Discount Dior!" *Travel*, January 1963, 62, Christian Dior Designer File, Fashion Institute of Technology, New York.

[21] Clayton Burton, interview by author, Toronto, Canada, 22 August 1990.

[22] Edmund Creed, author's questionnaire.

[23] Carolyn Druion, author's questionnaire, March 1992.

[24] Irene Satz, interview. Prices quoted are approximations made at time of interview.

[25] Quotation from advertisement, *Globe and Mail*, 28 March 1957, 17. Another example is a Holt Renfrew advertisement for bonded models, *Globe and Mail*, 2 January 1957, 9.

[26] Edmund Creed, author's questionnaire.

[27] Roshco, *The Rag Race*, 152. This is probably a reference to Creeds.

[28] "Texte des Modifications apportées au contract original," memorandum, 1948, Christian Dior Archives, Paris.

[29] Judith James, interview by author, Toronto, Canada, 28 March 1991.

[30] Joan Rosefield Lepofsky, interview by author, Toronto, Canada, 18 September 1990.

31 Photograph, *L'Officiel de la Haute Couture*, September 1951, 173.

32 Naomi Bristol, "Hourglass Fashions Applauded at Simpson's Show," *Globe and Mail*, 9 September 1947, 10. Strapless gowns were a new postwar style, considered rather dangerous and risqué. It was noticed that for Eaton's spring 1946 fashion show the store "showed no strapless evening gowns but featured a 'cold shoulder' model which leaves one shoulder bare and is just as attractive and probably safer than the strapless models." Helen Beattie, "Feminine Softness Returns to Spring Show," *Globe and Mail*, 12 March 1946, 9.

33 "From Bob Bugnand, I paid $75 apiece for them. Mind you there were some dogs in them, but I sold them for $495 apiece and they cost about $113 laid down [with tax and brokerage fees] . . . And we used to send them up to a great cleaners and they'd estimate how much they cost new . . . And they would estimate what it cost to clean the clothes." Ollie Smythe, interview by author, Toronto, Canada, 4 October 1990.

34 Ibid.; Margery Steele, interview by author, Toronto, Canada, 7 November 1990; Carolyn Druion, questionnaire; and Edmund Creed, questionnaire.

35 Rose Torno, interview by author, Toronto, Canada, 26 July 1990.

36 Margery Steele, interview.

37 Joyce Carter, "Memories Recalled at Party," *Globe and Mail*, 1 November 1988, C6.

38 June McLean, interview by author, Toronto, Canada, 15 March 1991.

39 Mary Carr-Harris, interview by author, Toronto, Canada, 15 January 1991; Rosemary Rathgeb, interview by author, Toronto, Canada, 20 February 1991; and Rose Torno, interview.

40 Barbara McNabb, interview by author, Toronto, Canada, 4 February 1991. During the postwar period, she was one of the first Canadian women business editors. She worked for a paper reporting on china and glass, *Current Publications Limited*, and her job required her to go to trade shows in North America and Europe.

41 Roshco, *The Rag Race*, 158.

42 Ibid.

43 Thanks to the late Otto Thieme for informing me of this suit and noting that it was published in American *Vogue* without the cuffs.

44 Patricia Harris, telephone interview by author, 17 March 1992; Joanne Stoddart, "Gala Hunt Club Supper Climaxes Horse Show Events," *Globe and Mail*, 21 November 1953, 16; fig. 5.16 from *Toronto Telegram*, 22 March 1955, 11.

45 Caroline Rennolds Milbank, *New York Fashion: The Evolution of American Style* (New York: Harry N. Abrams, 1989), 62, 122.

46 Joan Rosefield Lepofsky, interview. Chanel suit, spring 1960 collection, "tailleur marinière en lainage grège de Burg," advertised in *Vogue* (Paris), April 1960, 125. Thanks to the Chanel archives for this reference.

47 Frances M. Weir and Mary S. Bunnett, interview by author, Toronto, Canada, 6 June 1991. Frances M. Weir confirmed that the dress was the same style and colour as the one in an advertisement, *Harper's Bazaar*, April 1954, 148.

48 The percentages are estimates. It seems practically impossible to fix this in Canadian terms as the designs were rarely advertised. My assessment is based on personal interviews with Toronto women, who all knew about the system, and on the large number of extant bonded models uncovered in this research.

49 Roshco, *The Rag Race*, 120.

50 Edmund Creed, author's questionnaire. "Line-for-line" copies were not launched in France until 1962, when Pierre Cardin initiated the practice for Printemps department store. Natalie Pernikoff, "Behind Couture's £800 Million Turnover Lies a Problem," B62.3, Alison Settle Archives, University of Brighton.

51 Carolyn Druion, author's questionnaire.

52 Roshco, *The Rag Race*, 191.

53 Jessica Daves, *Ready-Made Miracle* (New York: G.P. Putnam's Sons, 1967), 145.

54 Roshco, *The Rag Race*, 165.

55 The most celebrated essay is by Walter Benjamin, "The Work of Art in the Age of Mechanical Reproduction," in *Illuminations*, ed. Hannah Arendt, trans. Harry Zohn (New York: Harcourt, Brace and World, 1968), 219–53. See also Pierre Bourdieu's work in *The Field of Cultural Production: Essays on Art and Literature*, ed. Randal Johnson (New York: Columbia University Press, 1993), 29–141.

56 Jean Baudrillard, "The System of Objects," in *Design after Modernism: Beyond the Object*, ed. John Thackera (London: Thames and Hudson, 1988), 171–82. Anny Latour writes that Fath signed with 7th Avenue in 1948, and his spring collection was reproduced in the thousands. In the course of two years, the turnover trebled. Latour, *Kings of Fashion*, trans. Mervyn Savill (London: Weidenfeld and Nicolson, 1956), 27.

57 Peter Dormer, *The Meanings of Modern Design: Towards the Twenty-First Century* (London: Thames and Hudson, 1990), 120–33, 116–17.

58 Irene Satz, interview.

59 Umberto Eco, "Travels in Hyperreality," in *Travels in*

Hyperreality, trans. William Weaver (New York: Harcourt Brace Jovanovich, 1986), 36, 39, 44. Emphasis added.

60 Roshco, *The Rag Race*, 153. Emphasis added.

61 Irene Satz, interview.

62 Dior would not permit his name to be used on merchandise that retailed below $100. See Olive Dickason, "Paris and London Fashions Are Quickly Copied Here," *Globe and Mail*, 8 September 1955, 17. Ohrbach's showed "Monsieur X " designs in its fashion shows. Irene Satz, personal archives.

63 Roshco, *The Rag Race*, 123–4; Marvin Klapper and Fairchild News Service, "Dior Won't Be Easy Mark, Takes Case to High Court," newspaper clipping *Women's Wear Daily*, 16 February 1962, Christian Dior Designer File, Fashion Institute of Technology, New York.

64 See reprint of an article by Samuel Hopkins Adams that appeared in the *Ladies' Home Journal* in 1913, "The Dishonest Paris Label: How American Women Are Being Fooled by a Country-Wide Swindle," *Dress* 4 (1978): 17–23; Nancy Troy, "Fashion As Art/Art As Fashion," (Teezel Lecture series "Couture and Culture: Fashion and the Marketing of Modernism, c. 1880–1918" University of Toronto, 11 March 1997).

65 Daves, *Ready-Made Miracle*, 145.

66 The sales figures are found in the Christian Dior Archives, Paris. The same situation occurred in the late eighteenth century when a Lyonnais designer for the silk industry could no longer produce his own designs as they had already been copied. This is discussed by Lesley Ellis Miller in "Innovation and Industrial Espionage in Eighteenth-Century France: An Investigation of the Selling of Silks through Samples," *Journal of Design History* 12, 3 (1999): 279–80.

67 Roshco, *The Rag Race*, 166.

68 Herndon, *Bergdorf's on the Plaza*, 225.

69 Irene Satz, interview.

70 Jarnow and Judelle, *Inside the Fashion Business*, 99.

71 Advertisements in *Globe and Mail*, 20 March 1951, 16; 4 March 1951, 14; 16 April 1951, 18; fig. 5.23 from *Globe and Mail*, 7 October 1955, 12.

72 Roshco, *The Rag Race*, 161; fig. 5.24 from *Globe and Mail*, 13 October 1960, 17.

73 "Overture to Fashion," fashion show script, fall 1948, F229-162-42, T. Eaton Records, Archives of Ontario, Toronto (hereinafter AOO); figs. 5.26, 5.27, 5.28 from *Globe and Mail*, 25 September 1950, 18, *Mayfair*, May 1958, 9, and *Globe and Mail*, 22 February 1950, 28.

74 Dickason, "Paris and London Fashions," 17.

75 Roshco, *The Rag Race*, 143.

76 Latour, *Kings of Fashion*, 256; Christian Dior–New York, Christian Dior Archives, Paris. "Barometre" in *Vogue* (New York), January 1950, 95, is reproduced in Polly Devlin, *Vogue Book of Fashion Photography* (Quill: New York, 1979), 99. For more on Christian Dior–New York, see Marie-France Pochna, *Christian Dior: The Man Who Made the World Look New*, trans. Joanna Savill (New York: Archade, 1996), 192–4.

77 Roshco, *The Rag Race*, 124; "Dictator by Demand," *Time*, 4 March 1957, 34.

78 The arrangements were very complex and deserve further detailed study. Nicola White begins to discuss this in "The Commercialization of the Paris Couture Industry" (MA thesis, Brighton Polytechnic, 1986). Also see Grumbach, *Histoires de la mode*, 167–201.

79 Applications for Couture-Création, 1955, F12/10505, Archives nationales, Paris.

80 Alison Settle, "New Trends in the Paris Collections," A Woman's Viewpoint column, *Observer* (London), 7 February 1949, A49.7, Alison Settle Archives, University of Brighton.

81 Règlement intérieur de la Commission de Contrôle et de Classement "Couture-Création," article 3, 12 January 1955, F12/10505, Archives nationales, Paris.

82 Classification Couture-Création, Monsieur Dupouy, Rapport de contrôle, 1952, F12/10504, Archives nationales, Paris.

83 Ibid., reporting on Nina Ricci boutique, Dior boutique, and Lanvin boutique, March 1952.

84 Jurors' decisions, 1955, F12/10505, Archives nationales, Paris. At the house of Dessès in 1951, the boutique models were not shown as part of the main collection. "Observations regarding Jean Dessès," report, 20 December 1951, F12/10504, Archives nationales, Paris.

85 Advertisement, *Mayfair*, November 1950, 71; "Fashions Fluid and Flattering," *Eaton News* 2, 10 (1957), 10, F229-141-0-153, T. Eaton Records, AOO.

86 Advertisement, *Mayfair*, July 1951, 6; quotation from Elizabeth James in caption to fig. 5.33 in "Irish Fashions in the News," *Mayfair*, March 1954, 68.

87 Alison Settle, A Woman's Viewpoint column, *Observer* (London), 14 December 1952, A52.48 and 22 February 1953, A53.8, Alison Settle Archives, University of Brighton.

88 Latour, *Kings of Fashion*, 27. For more information, see Valérie Guillaume, *Jacques Fath* (Paris: Adam Biro, 1993), 39–42; Grumbach, *Histoires de la mode*, 92.

89 Fig. 5.34 from *Mayfair*, March 1952, 27; Simpson's advertisement for Jean Dessès knock-offs, *Globe and Mail*, 11 April 1951, 14; Palais Galliera, Musée de la

mode et du costume, *Pierre Balmain, 40 années de création* (Paris: Paris-Musées, 1985), 235; Vivian Wilcox, "The Empire and the Princess," *Mayfair*, February 1954, 34–5.

[90] This has been discussed by Grumbach, *Histoires de la mode*, 170–3; and Guillaume, *Jacques Fath*, 43–7.

[91] "Accords à intervenir entre la haute couture et la couture en grosse," notes, 1 June 1944, F12.10503, Archives nationales, Paris.

[92] Olive Dickason, "Paris Couture Group Plan to Do Their Own Copying," *Globe and Mail*, 27 October 1950, 17. See Grumbach, *Histoires de la mode*, 170–3.

[93] Palais Galliera, Musée de la mode et du costume, *Pierre Balmain, 40 années de création*, 235.

[94] Olive Dickason, "Paris Couture Group," 17. See also Guillaume, *Jacques Fath*, 46, who says that London department store John Lewis purchased the models.

[95] Grumbach, *Histoires de la mode*, 172–3.

[96] Grumbach gives a very useful account of the development of *prêt-à-porter* in section 2 of *Histoires de la mode*.

[97] Alison Settle, "Couture Enters Ready-to-Wear," A Woman's Viewpoint column, *Observer* (London), 17 November 1957, A57.42, Alison Settle Archives, University of Brighton.

[98] Grumbach, *Histoires de la mode*, 178–90; Jarnow and Judelle, *Inside the Fashion Business*, 98.

[99] Iona Monahan, "Paris News: Prêt-à-Porter Collections," *Mayfair*, November 1957, 45.

[100] "Exclusive in Toronto with Creeds," *Globe and Mail*, 21 January 1959, 10; Iona Monahan and Jennifer Stowell, "Mayfair Fashion Show Report," *Mayfair*, April 1959, 42; Richard Morais, *Pierre Cardin: The Man Who Became a Label* (London: Bantam Press, 1991), 91.

[101] Roshco, *The Rag Race*, 192.

[102] One of the only studies of the second-hand trade to encompass the late twentieth century is by Madeleine Ginsburg, "Rags to Riches: The Second-Hand Clothes Trade 1700–1978," *Costume* 14 (1980): 121–35. Other studies of the history of the second-hand clothes trade include the important work by Beverly Lemire, *Dress, Culture and Commerce: The English Clothing Trade before the Factory, 1660–1800* (London: Macmillan Press, 1997); and Angela McRobbie, ed., *Zoot Suits and Second-Hand Dresses: An Anthology of Fashion and Music* (Boston: Unwin Hyman, 1988). A volume of essays is in progress on the history of second-hand clothes, tentatively entitled "Re-used and Reinterpreted: Second-Hand Dress" and edited by Alexandra Palmer and Hazel Clark.

[103] Sheila Kieran, "In Toronto Cast-Off Shop Items of Haute Couture Sell at Bargain Prices," *Style*, 11 March 1956, 29.

[104] According to Kieran, ibid., the most important was the 139 Shoppe. Today it is known as Shoppe D'Or and run by Norma King-Wilson, granddaughter of the original owner. The Toronto Symphony Women's Committee also ran a shop, called Symphony Band Box, at 4 Roxborough Street West, which opened in February 1960. Photo caption, *Globe and Mail*, 17 February 1960, 15.

[105] "Junior League Success: The Story of a Store," *Mayfair*, May 1957, 72. It was originally located at 2 Walton Street behind a barber shop and in 1930 moved to Cumberland Street. In 1933, the shop moved to larger premises near Maple Leaf Gardens, and in approximately 1936 the League hired a paid worker to organize it. The store moved again before the war, to an ex-butcher shop at 1116 Yonge Street, and Eaton's undertook and paid for the renovations. At this time, a quota of $10 worth of goods per member per year was introduced. In 1946, the store moved to smaller premises at 75 Gerrard Street, paying $23 a month in rent. In spring 1948, it moved to 1095 Yonge Street, paying $175 a month, and it was here that the Next-to-New section was opened. Marjorie Finlayson, "Junior League Opportunity Shop — 1928–1948," *The Key*, November 1948, 12–13.

[106] Anne Fromer, "Mayfair Merit Award: They Pay for the Privilege," *Mayfair*, April 1959, 32; "Your Key to the Opportunity Shop," *The Key*, October 1957, 22. The shop sold over $64,000 worth of second-hand goods over the 1943–8 period and realized a profit of over $53,000. Finlayson, "Junior League Opportunity Shop," 13. The New Look was given as the reason for raising the quota in 1948, as the profits were not up to par. Sales gross for 1947–8 was $15,114.08, with a net profit of $12,554.27. "Spotlight on Reports," *The Key*, May 1948, 4. See also June Gibson, "Shop News," *The Key*, April 1960, 32, 8.

[107] "Your Key to the Opportunity Shop," 22–3.

[108] "Junior League Shop Aids Budget, Next-to-New Department," *Toronto Telegram*, 14 February 1951, 13; Junior League Scrapbook, newspaper clippings 1950–1, Junior League Toronto; "Your Key to the Opportunity Shop," 23; "Shop News," *The Key*, October 1948, 12.

[109] Gibson, "Shop News," 7.

[110] A handwritten label marked "Eaton" identifies the dress as made for Signy Eaton.

[111] Signy Eaton, interview by author, Toronto, Canada, 11 July 1991.

[112] Mrs Morrison, née Hare, was married three times, to James Creek, David Sykes, and Pearce Morrison. Norma King-Wilson, interview by author, Toronto, Canada, 11 June 1991. The Clothes Horse was at 534A St Clair Avenue West. Might Directories, *Metropolitan*

Toronto City Directory, 1950 (Toronto: McLaren Micropublishing, 1950), 160.

[113] In 1960, the City of Toronto expropriated the building for the subway. Vera Morrison moved it to 119 Yorkville and called it the 119 Shoppe. Norma King-Wilson, interview.

[114] Kieran, "In Toronto Cast-Off Shop," 29.

[115] Norma King-Wilson, interview. At the time of this interview, 11 June 1991, 15,284 people had consigned goods to the store since its opening. All the records and ledgers are held by the store.

[116] Kieran, "In Toronto Cast-Off Shop," 29.

[117] Martha S. Crase, interview, Toronto, Canada, 5 June 1991; Norma King-Wilson, interview.

[118] Virginia Denton, "On and Off the Avenue," *The Key*, May 1958, 40.

[119] Toronto Symphony Women's Committee, *The Toronto Symphony Women's Committee, 1923–1985* (Toronto: Toronto Symphony Women's Committee, 1984), 10.

[120] "Customers No Problem for TSO Rummage Sale," *Globe and Mail*, 20 February 1957, 12.

[121] Toronto Symphony Women's Committee, *The Toronto Symphony Women's Committee*, 9.

[122] Alan Suddon, interview by author, Toronto, Canada, 22 January 1993. The Alan and Mary Suddon Collection of fashionable dress and accessories from the nineteenth century to the present has been acquired largely locally. Alan Suddon would try to find out who had donated the dress and sometimes the information was forthcoming.

[123] "Hadassah Soars from Humble Start," *Toronto Telegram*, 23 October 1959, 33; Helen Allen, "Imagine a Party Raising $40,000 — It's Next Week," *Toronto Telegram*, 18 January 1955, 23. Fig. 5.37 from *Globe and Mail*, 20 October 1960, 13.

[124] John B. Swinney, *Merchandising of Fashions: Policies and Methods of Successful Specialty Stores* (New York: The Ronald Press, 1945), 262.

[125] "Shop News," October 1948.

[126] Denton, "On and Off the Avenue."

[127] Quotation from Fromer, "Mayfair Merit Award," 31; "Junior League Success," 72.

[128] Kieran, "In Toronto Cast-Off Shop," 29.

[129] Photo caption, *Globe and Mail*, 14 February 1951, 11.

[130] Barbara McNabb to author, 28 November 1990; Barbara McNabb, interview.

[131] Harriet "Sis" Bunting Weld, interview by author, Toronto, Canada, 30 January 1992.

[132] "If you don't need it — If you don't wear it — Pass it on," *Harper's Bazaar*, September 1947, 181; Velga Jan-sons, interview by author, Toronto, Canada, 23 March 1993. For more on this history, see Alexandra Palmer, "Virtual Home Dressmaking: Dressmakers and Seamstresses in Post-War Toronto," in *The Culture of Sewing: Gender, Consumption and Home Dressmaking*, ed. Barbara Burman (Oxford and New York: Berg, 1999), 207–19.

[133] Norma King-Wilson, interview.

[134] Kieran, "In Toronto Cast-Off Shop," 29.

Chapter 6: The Value of Couture

[1] "Fashions Wear an Elegant Air," *Flash*, October 1953, 8, F229-141-0-181, T. Eaton Records, Archives of Ontario, Toronto (hereinafter AOO); Marion John, interview by author, Toronto, Canada, 4 July 1993.

[2] Canada, Dominion Bureau of Statistics, Census Division, *Census of Canada, 1961* (Ottawa: Queen's Printer, 1962), Table 1E.

[3] Canada, Dominion Bureau of Statistics, *Census of Canada, 1951* (Ottawa: Queen's Printer, 1953–5), Table 2; Canada, *Census of Canada, 1961*, Table 1.4, Table 3.

[4] These estimates are conservatively taken from Appendix C.

[5] This figure for income is taken from Canada, *Census of Canada, 1961*, and verified by Elizabeth Bryce, interview by author, Toronto, Canada, 5 November 1991. Most of Mrs Bryce's wardrobe was made by local designer Mrs Rasing. See Alexandra Palmer, "Virtual Dressmaking: Dressmakers and Seamstresses in Post-War Toronto" in *The Culture of Sewing: Gender, Consumption and Home Dressmaking*, ed. Barbara Burman (Oxford and New York: Berg, 1999), 207–19.

[6] Lachasse Records, Archive of Art and Design, National Art Library, London. See notes on Lachasse in Amy de la Haye, ed., *The Cutting Edge: 50 Years of British Fashion, 1947–1997* (London: V&A Publications, 1997), 205. Figures for Mrs Plow's purchases come from the Lachasse Records, AAD 6/10-1989 P.195, Archive of Art and Design, National Art Library, London, and are based on the average annual exchange rate of $2.69 to £1.0.0.

[7] Olive Dickason, "Paris and London Fashions Are Quickly Copied Here," *Globe and Mail*, 8 September 1955, 17.

[8] For more on these social events, see Alexandra Palmer, "The Myth and Reality of Haute Couture: Consumption, Social Function and Taste in Toronto, 1945–1963" (PhD diss., University of Brighton, 1994), ch. 2.

[9] Creeds advertisement, *Globe and Mail*, 19 October 1953, 23; Simpson's advertisement, *Globe and Mail*, 26 October 1955, 18; Holt's advertisement, *Globe and Mail*, 6 November 1956, 21; Creeds advertisement, *Globe and Mail*, 7 November 1950, 13.

10 Dickason, "Paris and London Fashions," 17.

11 Fig. 6.2 from *Globe and Mail*, 30 September 1955, 18; fig. 6.3 from *Globe and Mail*, 21 September 1955, 15.

12 Olive Dickason, "City's Increasing Gaiety Sets Fashion Show Theme," *Globe and Mail*, 27 September 1955, 12.

13 Rodolphe and his fellow Canadian couturiers are outlined in Palmer, "The Myth and Reality of Haute Couture." The Association of Canadian Couturiers is also the subject of a chapter in a work in progress tentatively entitled "Moose, Mountains, Mounties, and Canadian Fashion," edited by Alexandra Palmer.

14 Rodolphe Liska, interview by author, Toronto, Canada, 16 August 1991.

15 Ginette Spanier, *It Isn't All Mink* (New York: Random House, 1959), 209. Similarly, British milliner John Reed Crawford said that buyers were willing to pay more for a hat if it was large, thus ignoring the hours of workmanship and quality. John Reed Crawford, interview by author, London, England, 26 November 1991.

16 Grant McCracken, *Culture and Consumption: New Approaches to the Symbolic Character of Consumer Goods and Activities* (Bloomington and Indianapolis: Indiana University Press, 1988), 99; Helen Allen, "Best-Dressed List Shows Many Interests of Toronto Women," *Toronto Telegram*, 13 March 1956, 31.

17 Edna Woolman Chase and Ilka Chase, *Always in Vogue* (London: Victor Gollancz, 1954), 216. For more discussion on suits, see Anne Hollander, *Sex and Suits* (New York: Alfred A. Knopf, 1994).

18 Nancy Boxer, interview by author, Toronto, Canada, 6 December 1990. The dress was donated to the Seneca Fashion Resource Centre, Seneca College of Applied Arts and Technology, Toronto.

19 Gertrude Pringle, *Etiquette in Canada: The Blue Book of Canadian Social Usage*, 2nd ed. (Toronto: McClelland and Stewart, 1949), 92.

20 Bettina Ballard, *In My Fashion* (New York: David McKay, 1960), 115.

21 Christian Dior, *Christian Dior and I*, trans. Antonia Fraser. (New York: E.P. Dutton and Company, 1957), 76–7.

22 Flavia Redelmeier, interview by author, Toronto, Canada, 12 December 1990. Her mother, Catherine Elliott, was on the Toronto best-dressed lists. Mrs Elliott's concern for correct purchasing is recorded in great detail in her seasonal wardrobe lists, which date from 1937 to 1971. I am indebted to Flavia Redelmeier for permitting me access to her mother's records and also for her meticulousness in keeping them as well as several pieces from her mother's wardrobe.

23 Rose Torno, interview by author, Toronto, Canada, 26 July 1990; Rosemary Rathgeb, interview by author, Toronto, Canada, 20 February 1991; Nancy Boxer, interview.

24 Olive Dickason, "For Loyal Fans of the Designer, Old Diors Never Die," *Globe Magazine*, 13 February 1958, cover, 16–17.

25 Mary Carr-Harris, interview by author, Toronto, Canada, 15 January 1991.

26 Ballard, *In My Fashion*, 114.

27 Judith R. Wilder, interview by author, Toronto, Canada, 18 March 1991; Katherine Mackay Stewart, interview by author, Toronto, Canada, 14 March 1991. Continued wearing of "good" couture designs was an idea reiterated by Mrs Osler-Martin, who said, "Evening gowns didn't go out of fashion too much. They survived well." Cecily Martin, interview by author, Toronto, Canada, 7 June 1991.

28 Amy Vanderbilt, *Amy Vanderbilt's Complete Book of Etiquette: A Guide to Gracious Living* (New York: Doubleday and Company, 1954), 196; Emily Post, *Emily Post's Etiquette: The Blue Book of Social Usage* (New York: Funk and Wagnalls, 1945), 457–8.

29 Signy Eaton, interview by author, Toronto, Canada, 11 July 1991; Sonja Bata, interview by author, Toronto, Canada, 22 August 1990.

30 Margaret Cragg, "900 Attend State Dinner, Dignity Keynotes Evening," *Globe and Mail*, 15 October 1951, 18; "Toronto and North York Hunt Club Entertains Winter Fair Exhibitors," *Mayfair*, January 1950, 21; "Hunt Club Supper Dance Winter Fair Social Event," *Globe and Mail*, 17 November 1951, 12. Lady Eaton was mother-in-law to Signy Eaton.

31 Former fashion costume curator Mary Holford told me where the dress was bought. It was received into the Royal Ontario Museum with the hem and back panel taken up several inches and has since been let down to the original length.

32 Rose Torno, interview. Mrs Elliott's records indicate that she had leather accessories repaired; hats retrimmed and altered; clothes dyed, cleaned, shortened, lengthened, and changed in the revers, shoulders, and sleeve lengths; coats and jackets retrimmed; and sizes in general altered.

33 Belle Greenberg, "Jim Boylen: Prospector with the Midas Touch," *Mayfair*, November 1956, 51. Among the books and articles on the subject of clothing care are Betsy Wade, *Encyclopedia of Clothes Care* (New York: Royal Books, 1961); and "Maid Yourself," *Harper's Bazaar*, February 1950, 102, 185–7.

34 Zena Cherry, "'Compact Luxury' Describes Apartment Living at Its Best," *Mayfair*, August 1954, 47. Rose

Torno's current dressing room is also beautifully designed specifically for her wardrobe requirements. The information about Nora Vaughan was obtained in conversation with Dr Adrienne Hood, who visited her house in 1992 for donations to the Royal Ontario Museum. Gifts given at this time were primarily from her "white" collection.

35 Pringle, *Etiquette in Canada*, 94.

36 Liudja Stulginskas, telephone interview by author, 18 April 1993.

37 "Maid Yourself," 102.

Chapter 7: The Couture Society Wardrobe As a Model of Taste

1 Rose Torno, interview by author, Toronto, Canada, 26 July 1990.

2 Flavia Redelmeier, "Catherine Canfield Elliott Wilson" (Redelmeier Document Files, Textiles and Costume Section, Royal Ontario Museum, unpublished notes), unpaginated.

3 Best-dressed list, *Toronto Telegram*, 11 March 1952, 9; Joyce Kofman, interview by author, Toronto, Canada, 4 June 1991. Quotation from Ruth H. Frankel, *Three Cheers for Volunteers* (Toronto: Clarke, Irwin and Company, 1965), viii.

4 Frances Benton, *Etiquette: The Complete Modern Guide for Day-to-Day Living the Correct Way* (New York: Random House, 1956); Christian Dior, *Christian Dior's Little Dictionary of Fashion* (London: Cassel and Company, 1954); Millicent Fenwick, *Vogue's Book of Etiquette* (New York: Simon and Schuster, 1948); Emily Post, *Emily Post's Etiquette: The Blue Book of Social Usage* (New York: Funk and Wagnalls, 1945); Gertrude Pringle, *Etiquette in Canada: The Blue Book of Canadian Social Usage*, 2nd ed. (Toronto: McClelland and Stewart, 1949); Amy Vanderbilt, *Amy Vanderbilt's Complete Book of Etiquette: A Guide to Gracious Living* (New York: Doubleday and Company, 1954); Amy Vanderbilt, *Amy Vanderbilt's Everyday Etiquette* (New York: Hanover House, 1956); Claire Wallace, *Canadian Etiquette Dictionary* (Winnipeg: Harlequin Books, 1960); Margery Wilson, *The Pocket Book of Etiquette: The Modern Social Guide* (New York: Pocket Books, 1940).

5 Pringle, "Preface to the First Edition," *Etiquette in Canada*, 2nd ed., vii–viii.

6 "Authority on Etiquette Brings out New Edition," *Globe and Mail*, 2 November 1949, 13.

7 Pringle, *Etiquette in Canada*, v.

8 Georgie Henschel, *Georgie Henschel's Book of the Well-Dressed Woman* (London: Phoenix House, 1951), 14.

9 Julia Ruby Lean, interview by author, Toronto, Canada, 31 May 1991; June McLean, interview by author, Toronto, Canada, 15 March 1991.

10 "If . . . [the guest] doesn't know the customs of the household and neighbourhood he's visiting, he should find out in advance what wardrobe is expected of him." Vanderbilt, *Amy Vanderbilt's Complete Book of Etiquette*, 315.

11 Post, *Emily Post's Etiquette*, 459.

12 Ibid., 454.

13 "Favour Fur Coats for Coronation Stakes," *Globe and Mail*, 25 September 1950, 18.

14 Holly Brubach, "The Annals of Glory," *The Atlantic* 259, 5 (1987): 81.

15 "Canada's Ten Best-Dressed Women," *New Liberty*, 24 January 1948, 5–16.

16 "10 Best-Dressed Women All Married in Canada," *Globe and Mail*, 23 January 1950, 13.

17 "From the Younger Business and Professional Women *Liberty* Chooses Canada's Ten Best-Dressed," *Liberty*, January 1955, 40.

18 Best-dressed list, *Toronto Telegram*, 17 March 1953, 11.

19 Editorial, *Mayfair*, February 1956, 3; portraits, *Mayfair*, March 1956, 44.

20 "Friends of Mrs Exeter," *Vogue* (New York), 15 February 1950, 107; "At My Age . . ." *Harper's Bazaar*, February 1949, 148.

21 Pringle, *Etiquette in Canada*, 93.

22 There is little work on twentieth-century women's wardrobes. Most historical work is drawn from wills or probate records. See Janet Arnold, ed., *Queen Elizabeth's Wardrobe Unlock'd: The Inventories of the Wardrobe of Robes Prepared in July 1600* (Leeds: Maney, 1988); and Daniel Roche, *The Culture of Clothing: Dress and Fashion in the Ancien Regime*, trans. Jean Birrell (Cambridge: Cambridge University Press, 1994). An interesting article on a woman's nineteenth-century wardrobe is by Erika Rappaport, "'A Husband and His Wife's Dresses': Consumer Credit and the Debtor Family in England, 1864–1914," in *The Sex of Things: Gender and Consumption in Historical Perspective*, ed. Victoria de Grazia with Ellen Furlough (Berkeley and Los Angeles: University of California Press, 1996), 163–87. She discusses an 1878 court case in which the wife had run up debts that the husband would not pay. She claimed that "her dress allowance of five hundred pounds was far too low for her requirements and that her purchases were necessary for her social position. To test this the court sought to establish what 'ladies of fashion' usually spent on their 'feminine fripperies.'" The court upheld the husband's case, though the judge admonished him for previously pandering to his wife's indulgences. Rappaport, "A Husband," 171. More recently, an exhibition of parts of

23 Elizabeth Bryce, interview by author, Toronto, Canada, 5 November 1991; Wallace, *Canadian Etiquette Dictionary*, 50.

24 The New Look was synthesized in Christian Dior's spring 1947 collection. Its main features were rounded shoulders, a cinched-in waist, and long, full skirts. This was in direct contrast to the square-shouldered, male-inspired, knee-length wartime fashions. Quotation from "Large Trousseau Replaced by Few Planned Outfits," *Globe and Mail*, 24 May 1949, 16. See Benton, *Etiquette*, 222.

25 Benton, *Etiquette*, 127–8.

26 Helen Allen, "Best-Dressed in Toronto," *Toronto Telegram*, 11 March 1952, 9. The co-ordinated look adopted by Mrs Frankel was first introduced in the 1920s and was popular with Chanel.

27 Best-dressed list, *Toronto Telegram*, 22 March 1955, 14.

28 Pringle, *Etiquette in Canada*, 98; Post, *Emily Post's Etiquette*, 458.

29 Mary Cragg, "Low Curtsy, Chic Clothes Must for Meeting Royalty," *Globe and Mail*, 6 October 1951, 12. Photographs appeared in the *Globe and Mail*, 11 October 1951, 14.

30 Mona Campbell, interview by author, Toronto, Canada, 24 January 1991; Joyce Kofman, interview.

31 Joan Rosefield Lepofsky, interview by author, Toronto, Canada, 18 September 1990; Mary Carr-Harris, interview by author, Toronto, Canada, 15 January 1991; Rosemary Rathgeb, interview by author, Toronto, Canada, 20 February 1991.

32 Signy Eaton, interview by author, Toronto, Canada, 11 July 1991.

33 Pringle, *Etiquette in Canada*, 96; Mary Carr-Harris, interview; June McLean, interviews. June McLean also commented that late November and early December tended to be dressier than spring.

34 Stephen de Pietri and Melissa Leventon, *New Look to Now: French Haute Couture 1947–1987* (New York: Rizzoli; San Francisco: Fine Arts Museums of San Francisco, 1989), 30.

35 Joan Rosefield Lepofsky, interview.

36 Signy Eaton, interview; "Visitors to Eaton Hall Enjoy Christmas Charm," *Globe and Mail*, 18 December 1951, 14.

37 Joan Rosefield Lepofsky, interview.

38 Maggie Grant, "Ballet Opening Sparkling Affair," *Globe and Mail*, 7 January 1950, 9; Mona Campbell, interview.

39 Betty Cassels, interview by author, Toronto, Canada, 29 October 1992; best-dressed list, *Toronto Telegram*, 22 March 1960, 27–8.

40 Cragg, "Low Curtsy, Chic Clothes," 12.

41 Figs. 7.14 and 7.15 from *Globe and Mail*, 12 October 1951, 14 and 13 October 1951, 142; Margaret Cragg, "900 Attend State Dinner, Dignity Keynotes Evening," *Globe and Mail*, 15 October 1951, 18.

42 The dress was also shown by Simpson's at the Canadian National Exhibition and advertised in the *Globe and Mail*, 11 September 1951, 12. Quotation from Lillian Foster, "Norman Hartnell Is Designer of Most Famous Glamor Gowns in World, but When He Started His Career He Was a Clerk at $10 a Week," *Toronto Telegram*, 11 September 1954, 11.

43 Jeanne Stoddart, "Gala Hunt Supper Dance Climaxes Horse Show Events," *Globe and Mail*, 21 November 1953, 16. This notice also confirms that Mrs Harris never wore this dress with mink bands as it was designed and shown in Paris.

44 Lillian Foster, "Fashion Facts," *Toronto Telegram*, 7 January 1955, 19.

45 Signy Eaton, interview; Mona Campbell, interview; "Start of a Season," *Mayfair*, January 1957, 30.

46 Edna Woolman Chase and Ilka Chase, *Always in Vogue* (London: Victor Gollancz, 1954), 216.

47 Signy Eaton, interview; Post, *Emily Post's Etiquette*, 469; Wilson, *Pocket Book of Etiquette*, 49.

48 Anne C. Smith, interview by author, Toronto, Canada, 6 June 1991; Judith James, interview by author, Toronto, Canada, 28 March 1991; Anne C. Smith, née Burton, photographed in *Globe and Mail*, 25 October 1947, 12.

49 Flavia Redelmeier, interview by author, Toronto, Canada, 12 December 1990.

50 Pringle, *Etiquette in Canada*, 50; Wallace, *Canadian Etiquette Dictionary*, 188; Sally Brenzel, interview by author, Toronto, Canada, 22 March 1991; Joan Rosefield Lepofsky, interview; conversation with Claire Becker, who spoke with donor.

51 Wallace, *Canadian Etiquette Dictionary*, 78.

52 Fenwick, *Vogue's Book of Etiquette*, 632–3.

53 Rose Torno, interview.

54 Fenwick, *Vogue's Book of Etiquette*, 633; Wilson, *Pocket Book of Etiquette*, 61, 60; Pringle, *Etiquette in Canada*, 252.

55 Vivian Wilcox, "What to Wear Getting There," *Mayfair*, May 1953, 38–43.

56 The Canadian Monarch non-stop flights Montreal to London were advertised in *Mayfair*, April 1952, 66 (fig. 7.24), and January 1953, 6. Flying time from New York to Paris took about fourteen and a half hours. Airlines permitted sixty-six pounds of luggage per person. "Why Not Paris — By Air?" *Mayfair*, June 1949, 65.

57 "Fashions in Travel," *Mayfair*, May 1952, 49; Vivian Wilcox, "Flight Fashions for '54," *Mayfair*, January 1954, 35.

58 Quotation from Fenwick, *Vogue's Book of Etiquette*, 633; Rose Torno, interview.

59 Muriel Penn, "Horseless Carriage Left Behind: New London Fashion Designed for the Atom Age," *Globe and Mail*, 23 January 1957, 11.

60 Pringle, *Etiquette in Canada*, 93.

61 Olive Dickason, "Paris and London Fashions Are Quickly Copied Here," *Globe and Mail*, 8 September 1955, 17.

62 Post, *Emily Post's Etiquette*, 455; Fenwick, *Vogue's Book of Etiquette*, 11.

63 *Tabloid*, CBC Canada, 27 February 1953, NFA VI 8204 043-2, National Archives of Canada, Visual and Sound, Ottawa.

64 During the 1930s, Catherine Elliott had a dressmaker, Mrs Jarvis, went to Vassallo and Maria, Ruth McDougal, Meme Dystée, Creeds, Holt Renfrew, Eaton's, and Simpson's, and favoured Joan Rigby. Flavia Redelmeier, interview. The Royal Ontario Museum has several pieces from the family, dating from 1890s onward.

65 A turn-of-the-century Paris custom-designed dress for Mrs Sheldon Stephens of Montreal was never worn; the basting stitches are still in the garment at the McCord Museum of Canadian History. Perhaps this was another instance of a design being "too French," or flamboyant.

66 Signy Eaton was on the 1952 best-dressed in Toronto list, published by *Liberty* magazine, and the first *Toronto Telegram* best-dressed in Toronto list, published in 1952. She was also voted onto the Hall of Fame list published by the *Toronto Telegram* in 1962. Signy Eaton, interview. The Royal Ontario Museum has a Henry à la Pensée from her with a bond tag inside (fig. 5.12, pp. 158–9).

67 Daniel Miller, "Consumption as the Vanguard of History: A Polemic by Way of an Introduction," in *Acknowledging Consumption: A Review of New Studies*, ed. Daniel Miller (New York: Routledge, 1995), 9.

68 Margaret Maynard, *Fashioned from Penury: Dress As Cultural Practice in Colonial Australia* (Hong Kong: Cambridge University Press, 1994), 100.

69 Prudence Glynn, "The Life and Hard Times of British Couture," *Times* (London), 18 January 1972, clipping from Peter Hope Lumley.

70 Denis William Brogan, "Is Canada Ready for Greatness?" *Mayfair*, March 1954, 23.

71 Canada, *Report of the Royal Commission on National Development in the Arts, Letters and Sciences, 1949–51* (Massey Report) (Ottawa: King's Printer, 1951), 254.

72 Alison Settle, typescript, *Radio Times*, January 1952, L50.6, Alison Settle Archives, University of Brighton.

73 Daniel Miller, *Material Culture and Mass Consumption* (Oxford: Basil Blackwell, 1987), 157.

SELECTED BIBLIOGRAPHY

Newspapers, Magazines, and Periodicals

The Ambassador: The British Export Journal for Textiles and Fabrics, 1946–9.

Chatelaine, Toronto, 1945–65

Flash, Eaton's, Toronto, 1945–55. Succeeded by *Eaton News*, 1956

Globe and Mail, Toronto, 1945–65

Gossip! Toronto, 1945–65

Harper's Bazaar, New York, 1945–65

The Key, Toronto, 1945–65

Liberty. Toronto, 1950–65. Name varies, also *New Liberty*, 1945–9

Mayfair, Toronto, 1945–65

New Mount Sinai Hospital Highlights, Toronto, 1945–65

Style, Toronto, 1945–65

Toronto Star, 1945–65

Toronto Telegram, 1945–65

Vogue, New York, 1945–65

Archives

Alison Settle Archives, University of Brighton, Brighton.

Archive of Art and Design, National Art Library, London.

Archives Balenciaga, Paris.

Archives nationales, Paris.

Art and Design Archives, Victoria and Albert Museum, London.

Christian Dior Archives, Paris.

City of Toronto Archives, Toronto.

National Archives of Canada, Visual and Sound, Ottawa.

Pierre Balmain Archives, Paris.

Seeberger Frères collection, Bibliothèque nationale de France, Paris.

Archives of Ontario, Toronto.

Toronto Reference Library, Toronto.

Union Française des Arts du Costume, Paris.

Museums and Private Collections

Alan and Mary Suddon Collection, Toronto.

Brooklyn Museum of Art, Brooklyn, New York.

Canadian Museum of Civilization, Hull, Quebec.

Costume Institute, Metropolitan Museum of Art, New York.

Royal Ontario Museum, Toronto.

Seneca Fashion Resource Centre, Seneca College of Applied Arts and Technology, Toronto.

Victoria and Albert Museum, London.

Film and Video

CBC Newsmagazine. Various dates. National Archives of Canada, Moving Image and Sound Archives, Ottawa.

Fall Hats. 1953. 9 min. Staff Training Films. F229-403-0-25. T. Eaton Records, Archives of Ontario, Toronto.

Feminine Flattery. 1952. Approx. 15 min. Flashcut reel 1. Eaton's History. F229-401-0-103. T. Eaton Records, Archives of Ontario, Toronto.

Flattery from the Hands of Talented Milliners. 1957. 6 min. Staff Training Films. F229-403-0-35. T. Eaton Records, Archives of Ontario, Toronto.

The Mystery of Fashion. 1952. 32 min. Staff Training Films. F229-403-0-17. T. Eaton Records, Archives of Ontario, Toronto.

New Focus in Fashion and Figure. 1961. 10 min. Staff Training Films. F229-403-0-43. T. Eaton Records, Archives of Ontario, Toronto.

Paris and London. 1952. 6 min., 30 sec. Staff Training Films. F229-403-015. T. Eaton Records, Archives of Ontario, Toronto.

Spring Millinery Film. 1955. 6 min., 30 sec. Staff Training Films. F229-403-0-31. T. Eaton Records, Archives of Ontario, Toronto.

Success Story. [1946]. 15 min., 30 sec. Crawley's. Staff Training Films. F229-403-0-6. T. Eaton Records, Archives of Ontario, Toronto.

Tabloid. 23 September 1958. CBC Canada. NFA V1 8205 002-2. NFT&SA, National Archives of Canada, Moving Image and Sound Archives, Ottawa.

Through the Fashion Looking Glass. 1952. 25 min. Flashcut reel 2. Eaton's Photographic Studio. Eaton's History. F229-401-0-105. T. Eaton Records, Archives of Ontario, Toronto.

You Are the Star. 195[6?]. 35 mm. Produced for Allied Stores Corporation by Carvel Films Inc., New York. F229-403-0-34, T. Eaton Records, AOO.

Books, Articles, Pamphlets, Theses

Abelson, Elaine S. *When Ladies Go A-Thieving: Middle-class Shoplifters in the Victorian Department Store.* New York and Oxford: Oxford University Press, 1989.

Adams, Ruth. *A Woman's Place, 1910–75.* London: Chatto and Windus, 1975.

Adburgham, Alison. *Shopping in Style: London from the Restoration to Edwardian Elegance.* London: Thames and Hudson, 1979.

____. *Shops and Shopping, 1800–1914.* London: Allen and Unwin, 1964.

____. *View of Fashion.* London: Allen and Unwin, 1966.

Amies, Hardy. *Just So Far.* London: Collins, 1954.

Appadurai, Arjun, ed. *The Social Life of Things: Commodities in Cultural Perspective.* Cambridge: Cambridge University Press, 1986.

Aragno, Bonizza Giordani. *40 Years of Italian Fashion, 1940–1980.* Rome: The Made in Ltd., 1983.

Arch, Nigel, and Joanna Marschner. *Splendour at Court: Dressing for Royal Occasions since 1700.* London and Sydney: Unwin Hyman, 1987.

Arnold, Janet, ed. *Queen Elizabeth's Wardrobe Unlock'd: The Inventories of the Wardrobe of Robes Prepared in July 1600.* Leeds: Maney, 1988.

Art Gallery of Ontario. *Fortytude, A History to Celebrate 40 Years of the Volunteer Committee of the Art Gallery of Ontario, formerly the Women's Committee of the Art Gallery of Toronto, 1945–6 to 1985–6.* Edited by Mrs R. Burns Lind, Mrs J.L. Goad, and Mrs John Stohn. Pamphlet. May 1986.

Arthur, Eric. *Toronto: No Mean City,* 3rd ed. Revised by Stephen Otto. Toronto: University of Toronto, 1986.

Ash, Juliet, and Elizabeth Wilson, eds. *Chic Thrills: A Fashion Reader.* London: Pandora Press, 1992.

Baines, Carol Thora. "From Women's Social Benevolence to Professional Social Work: The Case of the Wimodausis Club and the Earlscourt Children's Home, 1902–1971." PhD diss., OISE, University of Toronto, 1991.

Ballard, Bettina. *In My Fashion.* New York: David McKay, 1960.

Balmain, Pierre. *My Years and Seasons.* London: Cassell, 1964.

Baltzell, E. Digby. "'Who's Who in America' and 'The Social Register': Elite and Upper Class Indexes in Metropolitan America." In *Class, Status and Power,* edited by Bernard Barber and Lyle Lobel, 172–85. New York: The Free Press, 1953.

Bara, Jana. "Cradled in Furs: Winter Fashions in Montreal in the 1860s." *Dress* 16 (1990): 38–47.

Barber, Bernard, and Lyle Lobel, eds. *Class, Status and Power.* New York: The Free Press, 1953.

Barthes, Roland. *The Fashion System.* Translated by Matthew Ward and Richard Howard. Toronto: McGraw-Hill Ryerson, 1983.

Bayley, Stephen, ed. *Commerce and Culture: From Pre-Industrial Art to Post-Industrial Value.* London: Fourth Estate, 1989.

Beard, Madeleine. *English Landed Society in the Twentieth Century.* London: Routledge, 1989.

Beaudoin-Ross, Jacqueline. *Form and Fashion: Nineteenth-Century Montreal Dress.* Montreal: McCord Museum of Canadian History, 1992.

Beaudoin-Ross, Jacqueline, and Pamela Blackstock. "Costume in Canada: An Annotated Bibliography." *Material History Bulletin* 19 (Spring 1984): 59–92.

____. "Costume in Canada: The Sequel." *Material History Review* 34 (Fall 1991): 42–67.

Benson, Susan Porter. *Counter Cultures: Saleswomen, Managers, and Customers in American Department Stores 1890–1940.* Urbana and Chicago: University of Illinois Press, 1986.

Benton, Frances. *Etiquette: The Complete Modern Guide for Day-to-Day Living the Correct Way.* New York: Random House, 1956.

Bertin, Celia. *Paris à la mode: A Voyage of Discovery.* Translated by Marjorie Deans. London: Victor Gollancz, 1956.

Bianchino, Gloria. *Italian Fashion Designing 1945–1980.* Los Angeles and Parma: Centro studi e archivio della comunicazione, Università di Parma, 1987.

____, ed. *Italian Fashion: The Origins of High Fashion and Knitwear.* Translated by Paul Blanchard. Milan: Electa, 1987.

Blaszczyk, Regina Lee. *Imagining Consumers: Design and Innovation from Wedgwood to Corning.* Baltimore, MD: Johns Hopkins University Press, 2000.

Blishen, Bernard R., Frank E. Jones, Kasper D. Naegele, and John Porter, eds. *Canadian Society: Sociological Perspectives,* rev. ed. Toronto: Macmillan of Canada, 1964.

Bliss, Michael. *Northern Enterprise: Five Centuries of Canadian Business.* Toronto: McClelland and Stewart, 1987.

Bluestone, Barry, Patricia Hanna, Sarah Kuhn, and Lauren Moore, eds. *The Retail Revolution: Market Transformations, Investment and Labor in the Modern Department Store.* Boston: Auburn House, 1981.

Blumer, H. "Fashion: From Class Differences to Collective Selection." *Sociological Quarterly* 10, 3 (1969): 275–91.

Boas, William S. *Canada, Post-War Possibilities* (Montreal: William S. Boas and Company, 1948)

Bottomore, T.B. *Classes in Modern Society*. London: Allen and Unwin, 1965.

____. *Elites and Society*. New York: Basic Books, 1964.

Bourdieu, Pierre. *Distinction: A Social Critique of the Judgement of Taste*. Translated by Richard Nice. Cambridge, MA: Harvard University Press, 1984.

____. *The Field of Cultural Production: Essays on Art and Literature*. Edited by Randal Johnson. New York: Columbia University Press, 1993.

Brandt, Gail Cuthbert. "Organizations in Canada: The English Protestant Tradition." In *Women's Paid and Unpaid Work: Historical and Contemporary Perspectives*, edited by Paula Bourne, 79–95. Toronto: New Hogtown Press, 1985.

Bratlinger, Patrick. *Bread and Circuses: Theories of Mass Culture As Social Decay*. Ithaca, NY: Cornell University Press, 1983.

Brett, Katherine B. *From Modesty to Mod: Dress and Underdress in Canada, 1780–1967*. Toronto: Royal Ontario Museum/University of Toronto, 1967.

Brodie, Janine. *Women and Politics in Canada*. Toronto: McGraw-Hill Ryerson, 1985.

Bronner, Simon J., ed. *Consuming Visions: Accumulation and Display of Goods in America, 1880–1920*. New York: W.W. Norton and Company, 1989.

Brubach, Holly. "The Annals of Glory." *The Atlantic* 259, 5 (1987): 81–3.

Bryant, James. *Department Store Disease*. Toronto: McClelland and Stewart, 1977.

Burton, Allan G. *A Store of Memories*. Toronto: McClelland and Stewart, 1986.

Burton, C.L. *A Sense of Urgency: Memoirs of a Canadian Merchant*. Toronto: Clarke, Irwin and Company, 1952.

Byrnes, Garrett. *Fashion in Newspapers*. New York: Columbia University Press, 1951.

Cain, Gertrude. *The American Way of Designing*. New York: Fairchild Publications, 1950.

Campbell, Colin. "Consumption and the Rhetoric of Need and Want." *Journal of Design History* 11, 3 (1998): 235–46.

Canada. *Royal Commission on National Development in the Arts, Letters and Sciences, 1949–51* (Massey Report). Ottawa: King's Printer, 1951.

Canada, Department of Labour, Women's Bureau. *Married Women Working for Pay in Eight Canadian Cities*. Ottawa: Department of Labour, Women's Bureau, 1958.

Canada, Dominion Bureau of Statistics. *Census of Canada, 1941*. Ottawa: E. Cloutier, Printer to the King, 1944–50.

____. *Census of Canada, 1951*. Ottawa: Queen's Printer, 1953–5.

____. *Department Store Sales and Stocks, 1941 to 1948*. DBS Reference Papers no. 4. Ottawa: Dominion Bureau of Statistics, 1949.

____, Census Division. *Census of Canada, 1961*. Ottawa: Queen's Printer, 1962.

The Canadian Who's Who. Toronto: Trans-Canada Press, 1910–75.

Cannadine, David. *The Decline and Fall of the British Aristocracy*. New Haven, CT: Yale University Press, 1990.

Carter, Ernestine. *With Tongue in Chic*. London: Michael Joseph, 1974.

Caton, S.G. Turnbull. "Fashion Marches On: A Canadian Snapshot of the Second World War." *Canadian Home Economics Journal* 44 (Fall 1994): 167–9.

____. "Government Control and Canadian Civilian Clothing during World War II." *Ars Textrina* 22 (1994): 175–92.

Celant, Germano, ed. *The Italian Metamorphosis, 1943–1968*. New York: Guggenheim Museum, 1994.

Centro de Promoción de Diseno y Moda. *España, 50 Años de Moda*. Barcelona: Aduntemante de Barcelona Area de Cultura, 1988.

Chambers, Bernice G. *Fashion Fundamentals*. New York: Prentice-Hall, 1947.

Chambre syndicale de la couture parisienne. *L'exposition le théâtre de la mode . . .* Paris: N.p., 1945.

Charles-Roux, Edmonde. *Chanel and Her World*. London: Vendôme Press, 1979.

____. *Théâtre de la mode*. New York: Rizzoli, 1991.

Chase, Edna Woolman, and Ilka Chase. *Always in Vogue*. London: Victor Gollancz, 1954.

Clark, S.D. *The Suburban Society*. Toronto: University of Toronto Press, 1968.

Coleman, Elizabeth Ann. *The Opulent Era: Fashions of Worth, Doucet and Pingat*. London: The Brooklyn Museum in association with Thames and Hudson, 1989.

Corina, Maurice. *Fine Silks and Oak Counters: Debenhams 1778–1978*. London: Hutchinson Benham, 1978.

Covington, William J., ed. *The Torontonian Society Blue Book and Club Membership Register*. Toronto: William J. Covington, 1946.

Crawford, M.D.C. *The Ways of Fashion*. New York: Fairchild Publications, 1948.

Dariaux, Geneviève Antoine. *Elegance: A Complete Guide for Every Woman Who Wants to Be Well and Properly Dressed on All Occasions*. New York: Doubleday and Company, 1964.

Daves, Jessica. *Ready-Made Miracle*. New York: G.P. Putnam's Sons, 1967.

Davidoff, Leonore. *The Best Circles*. Totowa, NJ: Rowman and Littlefield, 1973.

Davidoff, Leonore, and Catherine Hall. *Family Fortunes: Men and Women of the English Middle Class, 1780–1850*. Chicago: University of Chicago Press, 1987.

Davis, Dorothy. *A History of Shopping*. Toronto: University of Toronto Press, 1966.

Dawnay, Jean. *Model Girl*. London: Weidenfeld and Nicolson, 1956.

de Grazia, Victoria, ed., with Ellen Furlough. *The Sex of Things: Gender and Consumption in Historical Perspective*. Berkeley and Los Angeles: University of California Press, 1996.

de la Haye, Amy, ed. *The Cutting Edge: 50 Years of British Fashion, 1947–1997*. London: V&A Publications, 1997.

de Marly, Diana. *Christian Dior*. London: B.T. Batsford, 1990.

——. *The History of Haute Couture, 1850–1950*. London: B.T. Batsford, 1980.

——. *Worth: Father of Haute Couture*. London: Elm Tree Books, 1980.

de Pietri, Stephen, and Melissa Leventon. *New Look to Now: French Haute Couture 1947–1987*. New York: Rizzoli; San Francisco: Fine Arts Museums of San Francisco, 1989.

Deslandres, Yvonne, and Florence Müller. *Histoire de la mode au XXᵉ siècle*. Paris. Somogy, 1986.

Devlin, Polly. *Vogue Book of Fashion Photography*. Quill: New York, 1979.

Dior, Christian. *Christian Dior and I*. Translated by Antonia Fraser. New York: E.P. Dutton and Company, 1957.

——. *Christian Dior's Little Dictionary of Fashion*. London: Cassel and Company, 1954.

——. *Talking about Fashion: Christian Dior As Told to Élie Rabourdin and Alice Chavane*. Translated by Eugenia Sheppard. New York: G.P. Putnam's Sons, 1954.

Dormer, Peter. *The Meanings of Modern Design: Towards the Twenty-First Century*. London: Thames and Hudson, 1990.

Douglas, Mary, and Baron Isherwood. *The World of Goods: Towards an Anthropology of Consumption*. London: Allan Lane, 1979.

Drummond, Ian, Robert Bothwell, and John English. *Canada since 1945: Power, Politics and Provincialism*, rev. ed. Toronto: University of Toronto Press, 1989.

Eco, Umberto. *Travels in Hyperreality*. Translated by William Weaver. New York: Harcourt Brace Jovanovich, 1986.

English, John. *The Years of Growth, 1948–1967*. Toronto: Grolier, 1986.

Evans, Caroline, and Minna Thornton. *Women and Fashion: A New Look*. London: Quartet Books, 1989.

Fairley, Roma. *A Bomb in the Collection: Fashion with the Lid Off*. Brighton, UK: Clifton Books, 1969.

The Fashion Group. *Your Future in Fashion Design*. New York: Richards Rosen Press, 1966.

Fenwick, Millicent. *Vogue's Book of Etiquette*. New York: Simon and Schuster, 1948.

Fernandez, Nancy Page. "'If a Woman Had Taste' . . . Home Sewing and the Making of Fashion 1850–1910." PhD diss., University of California, Irvine, 1987.

Ferry, John William. *A History of the Department Store*. New York: Macmillan, 1960.

Finkel, Alvin, and Margaret Conrad, with Veronica Strong-Boag. *History of the Canadian Peoples*. Vol. 2, *1867 to the Present*. Toronto: Copp Clark Pitman, 1993.

Finlayson, Marjorie. "Junior League Opportunity Shop, 1928–1948." *The Key* (November 1948): 12–13.

Fivel, Sharon. *From Carriage Trade to Ready-Made: St. Louis Clothing Designers, 1880–1920*. St Louis: Missouri Historical Society Press, 1992.

Fox, Richard Wrightman, and T.J. Jackson Lears, eds. *The Culture of Consumption: Critical Essays in American History, 1880–1980*. New York: Pantheon Books, 1983.

——. *The Power of Culture: Critical Essays in American History*. Chicago: University of Chicago Press, 1993.

Frankel, Ruth H. *Three Cheers for Volunteers*. Toronto: Clarke Irwin and Company, 1965.

Fraser, Blair. *The Search for Identity: Canada 1945–1967*. Toronto: Doubleday Canada, 1967.

Freedman, Adele. "Out of Fashion." *Saturday Night* 6, 10 (1991): 12–16, 93–6.

Gamber, Wendy E. *The Female Economy: The Millinery and Dressmaking Trades, 1860–1930*. Urbana and Chicago: University of Illinois Press, 1997.

——. "A Precarious Independence: Milliners and Dressmakers in Boston, 1860–1890." *Journal of Women's History* 4 (Spring 1992): 60–80.

Ginsburg, Madeleine. "Rags to Riches: The Second-Hand Clothes Trade 1700–1978." *Costume* 14 (1980): 121–35.

Giroud, Françoise. *Dior: Christian Dior, 1905–1957*. Translated by Stewart Spencer. New York: Rizzoli, 1987.

Gold, Anna Lee. *How to Sell Fashion*. New York: Fairchild Publications, 1968.

Gottesman, Eli. *Who's Who in Canadian Jewry*. Compiled and prepared by the Canadian Jewish Literary Foundation. Montreal: Jewish Institute of Higher Research, Central Rabbinical Seminary of Canada, 1965.

Granatstein, J.L. *Canada 1957–67: The Years of Uncertainty and Innovation*. Toronto: McClelland and Stewart, 1986.

Grumbach, Didier. *Histoires de la mode*. Paris: Seuil, 1993.

Guenther, Irene. "Nazi 'Chic'? German Politics and Women's Fashions, 1915–1945." *Fashion Theory: The Journal of Dress, Body and Culture* 1, 1 (1997): 29–58.

Guernsey, Betty. *Gaby: The Life and Times of Gaby Bernier, Couturière Extraordinaire*. Toronto: Martincourt Press, 1982.

Guillaume, Valérie. *Jacques Fath*. Paris: Adam Biro, 1993.

Hamburger, Estelle. *Fashion Business: It's All Yours*. San Francisco: Canfield Press, 1967.

Hartnell, Norman. *Silver and Gold*. London: Evans Bros., 1955.

Henschel, Georgie. *Georgie Henschel's Book of the Well-Dressed Woman*. London: Phoenix House, 1951.

Herndon, Booton. *Bergdorf's on the Plaza: The Story of Bergdorf Goodman and a Half-Century of American Fashion*. New York: Alfred A. Knopf, 1956.

Hollander, Anne. *Sex and Suits*. New York: Alfred A. Knopf, 1994.

Ironside, Janey. *Janey*. London: Michael Joseph, 1973.

Jackson, Lesley. *The New Look Design in the Fifties*. London: Thames and Hudson, 1991.

Jarnow, Jeannette A., and Beatrice Judelle. *Inside the Fashion Business*. New York: John Wiley and Sons, 1965.

Jouve, Marie-Andrée, and Jacqueline Demornex. *Balenciaga*. New York: Rizzoli, 1989.

Kennett, Frances. *The Collector's Book of Fashion*. New York: Crown Publishers, 1983.

Kirkham, Pat. *The Gendered Object*. Manchester and New York: Manchester University Press, 1996.

Kopytoff, Igor. "The Cultural Biography of Things: Commoditization As Process." In *The Social Life of Things: Commodities in Cultural Perspective*, edited by Arjun Appadurai, 64–91. Cambridge: Cambridge University Press, 1986.

Lafitte, Pierre, ed. *La collection d'hiver de Jacques Fath, 1949–1950*. Paris: Libraire Hachette, 1949.

Lambert, Richard B. *The Universal Provider: A Study of William Whiteley and the Rise of the London Department Store*. London: G.G. Harrap, 1938.

LaPick, Gaeton J. *Scientific Designing of Women's Clothes*. New York: Fairchild Publications, 1949.

Latour, Anny. *Kings of Fashion*. Translated by Mervyn Savill. London: Weidenfeld and Nicolson, 1956.

Leach, William. *Land of Desire: Merchants, Power and the Rise of a New American Culture*. New York: Vintage Books, 1993.

——. "Transformations in a Culture of Consumption: Women and Department Stores, 1890–1925." *Journal of American History* 71, 2 (1984): 319–42.

Lee, Sarah Tomerlin, ed. *American Fashion*. New York: The Fashion Institute of Technology, 1975.

Lemire, Beverly. *Dress, Culture and Commerce: The English Clothing Trade before the Factory, 1660–1800*. London: Macmillan Press, 1997.

Light, Beth, and Ruth Roach Pierson. *No Easy Road: Women in Canada 1920s–1960s*. Toronto: New Hogtown Press, 1990.

Lipovetsky, Gilles. *The Empire of Fashion: Dressing Modern Democracy*. Translated by Catherine Porter. Princeton, NJ: Princeton University Press, 1994.

Litt, Paul. *The Muses, the Masses and the Massey Commission*. Toronto: University of Toronto Press, 1992.

Locke, Jeanine. "Canadian Society." *Chatelaine*, April 1958, 18–20, 78–80.

Lynam, Ruth, ed. *Couture: An Illustrated History of the Great Paris Designers and Their Creations*. New York: Doubleday and Company, 1972.

McCarthy, Kathleen D. *Women's Culture: American Philanthropy and Art, 1830–1930*. Chicago: University of Chicago Press, 1991.

——, ed. *Lady Bountiful Revisited: Women, Philanthropy and Power*. New Brunswick, NJ: Rutgers University Press, 1990.

McCracken, Grant. *Culture and Consumption: New Approaches to the Symbolic Character of Consumer Goods and Activities*. Bloomington and Indianapolis: Indiana University Press, 1988.

McCrum, Elizabeth. *Fabric and Form: Irish Fashion since 1950*. Ulster, Ireland: Sutton Publishing in association with the Ulster Museum, 1996.

McDowell, Colin. *Forties Fashion and the New Look*. London: Bloomsbury, 1997.

McRobbie, Angela, ed. *Zoot Suits and Second-Hand Dresses: An Anthology of Fashion and Music*. Boston: Unwin Hyman, 1988.

Maeder, Edward. *An Elegant Art: Fashion and Fantasy in the Eighteenth Century*. Los Angeles and New York: H.N. Abrams in association with the Los Angeles Country Museum of Art, 1983.

Marwick, Arthur. *British Society since 1945*. London: Allen Lane, 1982.

____, ed. *Class in the Twentieth Century*. Brighton, UK: Harvester, 1986.

Massey, Vincent. *On Being Canadian*. Toronto: J.M. Dent and Sons, 1948.

Matheson, Gwen, ed. *Women in the Canadian Mosaic*. Toronto: Peter Martin Associates, 1976.

May, Elaine Tyler. *Homeward Bound: American Families in the Cold War Era*. New York: Basic Books, 1988.

Mayfield, Franklin. *The Department Store Story*. New York: Fairchild Publications, 1949.

Maynard, Margaret. *Fashioned from Penury: Dress As Cultural Practice in Colonial Australia*. Hong Kong: Cambridge University Press, 1994.

Might Directories. *Metropolitan Toronto City Directory*. Toronto: McLaren Micropublishing, 1940, 1950, 1952, 1960.

Milbank, Caroline Rennolds. *Couture: The Great Designers*. New York: Stewart, Tabori and Chang, 1985.

____. *New York Fashion: The Evolution of American Style*. New York: Harry N. Abrams, 1989.

Miller, Daniel. *Material Culture and Mass Consumption*. Oxford: Basil Blackwell, 1987.

____, ed. *Acknowledging Consumption: A Review of New Studies*. New York: Routledge, 1995.

Miller, Lesley Ellis. *Cristóbal Balenciaga*. London: B.T. Batsford, 1993.

Miller, Michael B. *The Bon Marché: Bourgeois Culture and the Department Store, 1869-1920*. Princeton, NJ: Princeton University Press, 1981.

Morais, Richard. *Pierre Cardin: The Man Who Became a Label*. London: Bantam Press, 1991

Morelli, Ornella. "The International Success and Domestic Debut of Postwar Italian Fashion." In *Italian Fashion: The Origins of High Fashion and Knitwear*, edited by Gloria Bianchino, 58-71. Milan: Electa, 1987.

Morgan, David. *The Morgans of Montreal*. Montreal: D. Morgan, 1992.

Musée de la mode et du costume. *Robes du soir, 1850-1990*. Paris: Paris-Musées, 1990.

Musée de la mode et du textile. *Garde-robes: Intimités dévoilées, de Cléo de Mérode à . . .* Paris: Musée de la mode et du textile, 1999.

Musée des arts de la mode. *Hommage à Christian Dior, 1947-1957*. Paris: Union des arts décoratifs, 1986.

National Ballet Guild, Women's Committee. *Presiding Genius*. Pamphlet. N.d.

Newman, Peter C. *The Canadian Establishment*. Toronto: McClelland and Stewart, 1975.

____, ed. *Debrett's Illustrated Guide to the Canadian Establishment*. Agincourt, ON: Methuen Publishers, 1983.

O'Hara, Georgina. *The Encyclopedia of Fashion*. New York: Harry N. Abrams, 1986.

Ohrbach, Nathan M. *Getting Ahead in Retail*. New York: McGraw-Hill, 1935.

Packard, Vance. *The Status Seekers*. New York: David McKay, 1959.

Palais Galliera, Musée de la mode et du costume. *Pierre Balmain, 40 années de création*. Paris: Paris-Musées, 1985.

Palmer, Alexandra. "The Myth and Reality of Haute Couture: Consumption, Social Function and Taste in Toronto, 1945-1963." PhD diss., University of Brighton, 1994.

____. "Virtual Dressmaking: Dressmakers and Seamstresses in Post-War Toronto." In *The Culture of Sewing: Gender, Consumption and Home Dressmaking*, edited by Barbara Burman, 207-19. Oxford and New York: Berg, 1999.

Park, Julian, ed. *The Culture of Contemporary Canada*. New York: Cornell University Press, 1957.

Parker, Rozsika. *The Subversive Stitch: Embroidery and Making of the Feminine*. London: Routledge, 1989.

Parr, Joy. *Domestic Goods: The Material, the Moral, and the Economic in the Postwar Years*. Toronto: University of Toronto Press, 1999.

Pepper, Gordon. "Millionaire in Mink." *New Liberty* 28, 12 (1952): 18-19, 68ff.

Perkins, Alice K. *Paris Couturiers and Milliners*. New York: Fairchild Publications, 1949.

Perreau, Geneviève. *Portrait of Christian Dior*. Paris: Helpé, 1953.

Picken, Mary Brooks, and Dora Loues Miller. *Dressmakers of France: The Who, How and Why of French Couture*. New York: Harper and Brothers, 1956.

Pierson, Ruth Roach. *"They're Still Women After All": The Second World War and Canadian Womanhood*. Toronto: McClelland and Stewart, 1986.

Pochna, Marie-France. *Christian Dior: The Man Who Made the World Look New*. Translated by Joanna Savill. New York: Archade, 1996.

Porter, John A. *Canadian Social Structure: A Statistical Profile*. Toronto: McClelland and Stewart, 1967.

____. *The Vertical Mosaic: An Analysis of Social Class and Power in Canada*. Toronto: University of Toronto Press, 1965.

Porter, John Chester. *The Men Who Put the Show on the Road: Simpson's 100*. Toronto: N.p., 1972.

Porter, McKenzie. "'Bargain' Is a Naughty Word at Morgan's." *Maclean's*, 15 June 1953, 24–5, 64–7, 71.

Post, Emily. *Emily Post's Etiquette: The Blue Book of Social Usage*. New York: Funk and Wagnalls, 1945.

Pound, Reginald. *Selfridges*. London: Heinemann, 1960.

Prentice, Alison. *Canadian Women: A History*. Toronto: Harcourt Brace Jovanovich, 1988.

Pringle, Gertrude. *Etiquette in Canada: The Blue Book of Canadian Social Usage*. 2nd ed. Toronto: McClelland and Stewart, 1949.

Prown, Jules David. "Mind in Matter: An Introduction to Material Culture Theory and Method." *Winterthur Portfolio* 17, 1 (1982): 1–19.

Pullar, Philippa. *Gilded Butterflies: The Rise and Fall of the London Season*. London: Hamish Hamilton, 1978.

Quick, Harriet. *Catwalking: A History of the Fashion Model*. London: Hamlyn, 1997.

Rappaport, Erika. "'A Husband and His Wife's Dresses': Consumer Credit and the Debtor Family in England, 1864–1914." In *The Sex of Things: Gender and Consumption in Historical Perspective*, edited by Victoria de Grazia with Ellen Furlough, 163–87. Berkeley: University of California Press, 1996.

Reekie, Gail. *Temptations: Sex, Selling and the Department Store*. Sydney: Allen and Unwin, 1993.

Riley, Robert. *The Fashion Makers: A Photographic Record*. New York: Crown Publishers, 1968.

Roche, Daniel. *The Culture of Clothing: Dress and Fashion in the Ancien Regime*. Translated by Jean Birrell. Cambridge: Cambridge University Press, 1994.

Roshco, Bernard. *The Rag Race: How New York and Paris Run the Breakneck Business of Dressing American Women*. New York: Funk and Wagnalls, 1963.

Ross, Alexander. *The Booming Fifties, 1950/1960*. Toronto: Natural Sciences of Canada, 1977.

Routh, Caroline. *In Style: 100 Years of Canadian Fashion*. Toronto: Stoddart Publishing, 1993.

Royal Ontario Museum. *Haute Couture: Notes on Designers and Their Clothes in the Collections of the Royal Ontario Museum*. Notes on clothes by Katharine B. Brett. Toronto: Royal Ontario Museum, 1969.

Royal Pavilion, Art Gallery and Museums. *Norman Hartnell*. Brighton, UK: Art Galleries and Museums; Bath: Bath City Council, 1985.

Runciman, W.G. *A Treatise on Social Theory*. Cambridge and New York: Cambridge University Press, 1983.

Santink, Joy. *Timothy Eaton and the Rise of His Department Store*. Toronto: University of Toronto Press, 1990.

Schumpeter, Joseph Alois. *Imperialism and Social Classes*. Translated by Heinz Norden. New York: Meridian Books, 1955 [c. 1951].

Sifton, Elizabeth. "Retailing Fashion in Montreal: A Study of Stores, Merchants and Assortments, 1845–1915." MA thesis, Concordia University, 1994.

Smith, Kathleen M. "Study the Family Tree and You'll Find Haute-to-Hip History of Fashion in Toronto." *Toronto Life Fashion* (Holiday 1987): 77–8.

Snow, Carmel, with Mary Louise Aswell. *The World of Carmel Snow*. New York: McGraw-Hill, 1962.

Social Register of Canada. *The Social Register of Canada*. Montreal: Social Register of Canada, 1958.

Spanier, Ginette. *It Isn't All Mink*. New York: Random House, 1959.

Stanley, Louis T. *The London Season*. London: Hutchinson, 1955.

Statistics Canada. *Department Stores in Canada, 1927–76*. Ottawa: Merchandising and Service Division, Statistics Canada, 1976.

Steedman, Carolyn. *Landscape for a Good Woman: A Story of Two Lives*. London: Virago Press, 1986.

Steele, Valerie. *Fifty Years of Fashion*. New Haven and London: Yale University Press, 1997.

––––. *Paris Fashion: A Cultural History*. New York and Oxford: Oxford University Press, 1988.

––––. *Women of Fashion: Twentieth-Century Designers*. New York: Rizzoli, 1991.

Stephenson, William. *The Store That Timothy Built*. Toronto: McClelland and Stewart, 1969.

Stern, Suzanne Pierette. "Memories of a Parisian Seamstress." *Threads* (April–May 1992): 45–9.

Strasser, Susan. *Satisfaction Guaranteed: The Making of the American Mass Market*. New York: Pantheon Books, 1989.

Strong-Boag, Veronica. "Home Dreams: Women and the Suburban Experiment in Canada, 1945–60." *Canadian Historical Review* 72, 4 (1991): 471–504.

Strong-Boag, Veronica, and Anita Clair Fellman, eds. *Rethinking Canada: The Promise of Women's History*. Toronto: Copp Clark Pitman, 1986.

Stuart, Ewen. *All Consuming Images*. New York: Basic Books, 1988.

Swinney, John B. *Merchandising of Fashions: Policies and Methods of Successful Specialty Stores*. New York: The Ronald Press, 1945.

Taylor, Lou. "Paris Couture, 1940–44." In *Chic Thrills: A Fashion Reader*, ed. Juliet Ash and Elizabeth Wilson, 127–44. London: Pandora Press, 1992.

Thackera, John, ed. *Design after Modernism: Beyond the Object*. London: Thames and Hudson, 1988.

Thornton, Peter. *Baroque and Rococo Silks*. London: Faber and Faber, 1965.

Tippett, Maria. *Making Culture: English-Canadian Institutions and the Arts before the Massey Commission*. Toronto: University of Toronto Press, 1990.

Toronto Symphony Women's Committee. *The Toronto Symphony Women's Committee, 1923–1983*. Toronto: Toronto Symphony Women's Committee, 1984.

Vancouver Museum. *Panache: 200 Years of the Fashionable Woman*. Vancouver: Vancouver Museum, 1991.

Vanderbilt, Amy. *Amy Vanderbilt's Complete Book of Etiquette: A Guide to Gracious Living*. New York: Doubleday and Company, 1954.

_____. *Amy Vanderbilt's Everyday Etiquette*. New York: Hanover House, 1956.

Vaudoyer, Mary. *Le livre de la haute couture*. Paris: V & O Editions, 1990.

Veblen, Thorstein. *The Theory of the Leisure Class*. 1899. Reprint, New York: Penguin Books, 1979.

Veillon, Dominique. *La mode sous l'Occupation: Débrouillardise et coquetterie dans la France en guerre (1939–1945)*. Paris: Documents Payot, 1990.

Vergani, Guido. *The Sala Bianca: The Birth of Italian Fashion*. Milan: Electa, 1992.

Vineberg, Ethel. *The History of the National Council of Jewish Women of Canada*. Montreal: N.p., 1967.

Vollmer, John. *Dressed to Celebrate: Evening Wear in the Twentieth Century*. Houston: Museum of Fine Art, 1988.

Wade, Betsy. *Encyclopedia of Clothes Care*. New York: Royal Books, 1961.

Walker, John A. *Design History and the History of Design*. London: Pluto Press, 1990.

Wallace, Claire. *Canadian Etiquette Dictionary*. Winnipeg: Harlequin Books, 1960.

Warburton, Gertrude, and Jane Maxwell. *Fashion for a Living*. New York: McGraw-Hill, 1939.

White, Nicola. "The Commercialization of the Paris Couture Industry." MA thesis, Brighton Polytechnic, 1986.

_____. *Reconstructing Italian Fashion: America and the Development of the Italian Fashion Industry*. Oxford and New York: Berg, 2000.

White, Palmer. *Elsa Schiaparelli, Empress of Fashion*. New York: Rizzoli, 1986.

Who's Who in Canada. Toronto: International Press, 1958–68.

Williams, Beryl. *Fashion Is Our Business*. New York: J.B. Lippincott, 1945.

Williams, Rosalind H. *Dream Worlds: Mass Consumption in Late-Nineteenth-Century France*. Berkeley: University of California Press, 1982.

Wilson, Elizabeth. *Adorned in Dreams: Fashion and Modernity*. London: Virago Press 1985.

Wilson, Margery. *The Pocket Book of Etiquette: The Modern Social Guide*. New York: Pocket Books, 1940.

Winnipeg Art Gallery. *Achieving the Modern: Canadian Abstract Painting and Design in the 1950s*. Winnipeg: Winnipeg Art Gallery, 1993.

Woodcock, George. *A Social History of Canada*. Markham, ON: Viking, 1988.

Wright, Cynthia Jane. "'Feminine Trifles of Vast Importance': Writing Gender into the History of Consumption." In *Gender Conflicts: New Essays in Women's History*, edited by Franca Iacovetta and Mariana Valverde, 229–60. Toronto: University of Toronto Press, 1992.

_____. "'The Most Prominent Rendezvous of the Feminine Toronto': Eaton's College Street and the Organization of Shopping in Toronto, 1920–1950." PhD diss., OISE, University of Toronto, 1993.

Yoxall, H.W. *A Fashion of Life*. London: Heinemann, 1966.

Ziegert, Beate. "American Clothing: Identity in Mass Culture, 1840–1990." *Human Ecology Forum* 19, 3 (1991): 9.

CREDITS

A reasonable attempt has been made to secure permission to reproduce all material used. If there are errors or omissions they are wholly unintentional and the publisher would be grateful to learn of them.

The following people kindly gave permission for parts of their interviews or information from their interviews with the author to be reproduced: Agnes "Nan" Allen, Sonja Bata, Russel Berg, Nancy Boxer, Marian Bradshaw, Sally Brenzel, Elizabeth Bryce, Mary S. Bunnett, Mrs E.G. (Clayton) Burton, Mona Campbell, Mary Carr-Harris, Betty Cassels, Martha Crase, Eveleen Dollery, Thor Eaton (for Signy Eaton), Madeleine Epstein, Rosemary "Posy" Chisholm Feick (Boxer), Diana L. Goad, Diana Gooderham (for Grace Gooderham), Patricia Harris, Jeanie Hersenhoren, Judith James, Velga Jansons, Elsa Jenkins, Norma King-Wilson, Joyce Kofman, Julia Ruby Lean, Joan Rosefield Lepofsky, Joy McGillawee, June McLean, Barbara McNabb, Cecily Martin (Osler), Margaret R. Morison, Ollie O'Connor (Smythe), Jeanne Parkin, Marian Postlethwaite, Rosemary Rathgeb, Flavia Redelmeier, Elizabeth Rhind, Beverley Rockett, Jacques Rouët, Irene Satz, Joyce Scott, Barbara Shavick, Anne C. Smith, Margery Steele, Katherine Mackay Stewart, Helen Stimpson, Suzanne Stohn, Rose Torno, Frances M.Weir, Harriet "Sis" Bunting Weld, Vivian Wilcox, Judith Wilder, Norma Wildgoose.

Photographs

All photographs of artifacts from the ROM collection are copyrighted images of the Royal Ontario Museum, Toronto, Canada.

0.1 Courtesy Pierre Balmain, Paris / 2

0.2 ROM 959.8.1ab, gift of Mrs Dora Matthews, photography by Brian Boyle / 4

0.3 ROM 969.241.4, gift of Mrs Graham Morrow, photography by Brian Boyle / 5

0.4 ROM 964.164, gift of Mrs Anne Gardiner, photography by Brian Boyle / 5

0.5 *Globe and Mail*, 25 August 1955, 14, photograph from Toronto Reference Library, credit unknown / 9

0.6 ROM 961.83.1, gift of Mrs John David Eaton, photography by Irving Solero / 10–11

0.7 *Harper's Bazaar*, April 1955, 157, photography by Louise Dahl-Wolfe, © 1989 Center for Creative Photography, Arizona Board of Regents / 12

1.1 ROM 969.223, photography by Brian Boyle / 14

1.2 Courtesy Archives Balenciaga, Paris / 15

1.3 *Mayfair*, April 1945, 27, photograph from the Toronto Reference Library / 21

1.4 *Mayfair*, April 1945, 28, photography by I. Bandy, photograph from the Toronto Reference Library / 22

1.5 ROM 959.8.2, gift of Mrs Dora Matthews, photography by Irving Solero / 24

1.6 Courtesy Pierre Balmain, Paris / 27

1.7 Photograph courtesy Suzanne D. Stohn, reprinted with permission from Ashley and Crippen / 28

1.8 *Mayfair*, April 1947, 53, photograph from the Toronto Reference Library, reprinted with permission from Sears Canada Inc. / 29

1.9 F229-306-0-1670-4, T. Eaton Records, Archives of Ontario, reprinted with permission from Sears Canada Inc. / 30

1.10 F229-306-0-1679-6, T. Eaton Records, Archives of Ontario, reprinted with permission from Sears Canada Inc. / 31

1.11 Courtesy Christian Dior Archives, Paris / 32

1.12 Courtesy Christian Dior Archives, Paris / 33

1.13 Courtesy Christian Dior Archives, Paris / 34

1.14 Courtesy Christian Dior Archives, Paris / 35

1.15 ROM 975.297.2ab, gift of Mrs Kenneth Laidlaw Campbell, photography by Irving Solero / 36–7

1.16 F229-308-0-1060, T. Eaton Records, Archives of Ontario, reprinted with permission from Sears Canada Inc. / 38

1.17 ROM 957.50, gift of Mrs Dora Matthews, photography by Irving Solero / 39

2.1 *Mayfair*, October 1956, 51, photography by Hans Wild, photograph from the Toronto Reference Library / 48

2.2 ROM 969.51.1, gift of Mrs Laurie Norstad, photography by Irving Solero / 50

2.3 Courtesy Pierre Balmain, Paris / 51

2.4 ROM 974.318abc, gift of Mrs Noah Torno, photography by Irving Solero / 52

2.5 Courtesy Archives Balenciaga, Paris / 53

2.6 ROM 981.206.3, gift of Mrs George Gooderham, photography by Irving Solero / 56–7

2.7 Author's collection / 59

2.8 Courtesy Pierre Balmain, Paris / 63

2.9 ROM 970.358.8a-b, gift of Mrs James Boylen, photography by Irving Solero / 64–5

2.10 ROM 964.258.1ab, gift of Mrs W.C. Harris, photography of mannequin by Irving Solero and of details by Brian Boyle / 66–7

3.1 *Toronto Telegram*, 4 December 1954, 27, photography courtesy the Junior League of Toronto, reprinted with permission from The Toronto Telegram Photograph collection, York University Archives and Special Collections / 68

3.2 *Globe and Mail*, 2 November 1956, 16, photograph from the Toronto Reference Library, reprinted with permission from the Hudson's Bay Company / 70

3.3 F229-308-0-1657, T. Eaton Records, Archives of Ontario, reprinted with permission from Sears Canada Inc. / 71

3.4 *Mayfair*, September 1953, 8, photograph from the Toronto Reference Library / 73

3.5 ROM 961.136.3, gift of Mrs David Meltzer, photography by Irving Solero / 74–5

3.6 Courtesy Archives Balenciaga, Paris / 80

3.7 ROM 971.162.2ab, gift of Mrs Graham Morrow, photography by Irving Solero / 80–1

3.8 ROM 975.232.3, gift of Mrs Ian Crookston, photography by Irving Solero / 82–3

3.9 Courtesy Christian Dior Archives, Paris, photography by Sartony / 84–5

3.10 Courtesy Archives Balenciaga, Paris / 86

3.11 Courtesy Archives Balenciaga, Paris / 87

3.12 *Toronto Star*, 30 July 1998, E2, photography by Cheryl Hnatiuk/Toronto Star, reprinted with permission of the Toronto Star, photograph from the Toronto Reference Library / 90

3.13 Courtesy Mr Christopher Matthews, photography by Ballard and Jarrett / 92

3.14 *Flash*, 10 September 1945, 6–7, F229-141-0-173, T. Eaton Records, Archives of Ontario, reprinted with permission from Sears Canada Inc. / 93

3.15 *Flash*, 18 February 1952, 7, F229-141-0-180, T. Eaton Records, Archives of Ontario, reprinted with permission from Sears Canada Inc. / 94

4.1 ROM 970.358.7a-d, gift of Mrs M. James Boylen, photography by Irving Solero / 98–9

4.2 ROM 981.109.8, gift of Mrs John D. Eaton, photography by Irving Solero / 100–1

4.3 ROM 959.8.1ab, gift of Mrs Dora Matthews, photography by Irving Solero / 102–3

4.4 ROM 957.119, gift of The Fashion Group Inc. of Toronto, photography by Irving Solero / 104–5

4.5 *Mayfair*, September 1952, 14, photograph from the Toronto Reference Library, courtesy Holt Renfrew / 107

4.6 ROM 979.15.2ab, gift of Mrs Peter Cragg, photography by Irving Solero / 108–9

4.7 ROM 962.21.3ab, gift of Mrs Dora Matthews, photography by Irving Solero / 110–11

4.8 ROM 2000.85.1.1-2, gift of Mrs Patrick Cassels, photography by Irving Solero / 112–13

4.9 *Gossip!* 16 April 1960, cover, courtesy Betty Cassels, photography by Gerald Campbell with permission from Ashley and Crippen / 114

4.10 *Mayfair*, September 1952, 40, photograph from the Toronto Reference Library, reprinted with permission from Sears Canada Inc. / 115

4.11 *Mayfair*, April 1953, 59, photography by Forlano, photograph from the Toronto Reference Library / 116

4.12 *Mayfair*, May 1952, 11, photograph from the Toronto Reference Library, courtesy Holt Renfrew with permission from Christian Dior / 117

4.13 *Mayfair*, April 1953, 9, photograph from the Toronto Reference Library, courtesy Holt Renfrew with permission from Christian Dior / 117

4.14 ROM 964.152.1a-d, gift of Mrs David Meltzer, photography by Irving Solero / 118

4.15 ROM 962.216.1b, gift of Mrs Saul A. Silverman, photography by Brian Boyle / 119

4.16 Courtesy Ann Levitt, photography by Studio C Marcil, Ottawa / 120

4.17 *Mayfair*, March 1958, 9, photograph from the Toronto Reference Library, courtesy Holt Renfrew with permission from Christian Dior / 121

4.18 F229-308-0-1170 AO 5106, T. Eaton Records, Archives of Ontario, reprinted with permission from Sears Canada Inc. / 123

4.19 *Flash*, October 1955, 18–19, F229-141-0-183, T. Eaton Records, Archives of Ontario, reprinted with permission from Sears Canada Inc. / 126

4.20 *Flash*, March 1953, cover, F229-141-0-181, T. Eaton Records, Archives of Ontario, reprinted with permission from Sears Canada Inc. / 127

4.21 *Globe and Mail*, 20 October 1955, 13, Metropolitan Photos, photograph from the Toronto Reference Library, text by Pearl McCarthy reprinted with permission from The Globe and Mail / 130

4.22 ROM Textile Section Document Files, gift of Geitel Winakor / 131

4.23 *Globe and Mail*, 18 September, 1951, 14, photography by Ballard and Jarrett, photograph from the Toronto Reference Library / 132

4.24 *Mayfair*, September 1958, 17, photograph from the Toronto Reference Library / 133

5.1 ROM 964.38.1, gift of Eaton's of Canada, photography by Brian Boyle / 136

5.2 ROM 964.38.1, gift of Eaton's of Canada, photography by Brian Boyle / 136

5.3 ROM 964.38.2, gift of Eaton's of Canada, photography by Irving Solero, photography of detail by Brian Boyle / 137

5.4 ROM 964.38.5, gift of Eaton's of Canada, photography by Brian Boyle / 138

5.5 ROM 970.286.6ab, gift of Mrs M. James Boylen, photography by Irving Solero / 140–1

5.6 ROM 957.100ab, gift of The Robert Simpson Co. Ltd., photography by Irving Solero / 144–5

5.7 Courtesy Brooklyn Museum of Art, Gift — A.M. Tenney Assoc. Textile Sales & Serv. 50.56.9A-C / 146

5.8 Courtesy Christian Dior Archives, Paris / 150

5.9 M210748, Seeberger Frères collection, Cliché Bibliothèque nationale de France, Paris / 151

5.10 ROM 969.241.4, gift of Mrs Graham Morrow, photography by Irving Solero, photography of inside details by Brian Boyle / 152–3

5.11 Courtesy Archives Balenciaga, Paris / 156

5.12 ROM 956.153.16ab, gift of Mrs John David Eaton, photography by Irving Solero / 158–9

5.13 Two-piece suit, 1948, Paris, France, 1986.765 and 1986.766, courtesy Cincinnati Art Museum, gift of Mary Louise Robertson, photography Ron Forth, 6/86 / 160

5.14 Courtesy Archives Balenciaga, Paris / 161

5.15 Courtesy Pierre Balmain, Paris / 162

5.16 *Toronto Telegram*, 22 March 1955, 11, reprinted with permission from The Toronto Telegram Photograph collection, York University Archives and Special Collections, photography with permission of Ashley and Crippen / 163

5.17 ROM 973.299.1abcd, gift of Mrs Alex Levinsky, photography by Irving Solero, photography of inside detail by Brian Boyle / 164–5

5.18 Photography by Willy Maywald, Près de la Madeleine, Paris, 1959 © DACS/SODART 2001 / 166

5.19 Courtesy of and reprinted with permission of Mrs Joan Rosefield Lepofsky / 167

5.20 *Mayfair*, June 1956, 17, photograph from the Toronto Reference Library, courtesy Holt Renfrew and with permission from Christian Dior / 169

5.21 *Mayfair*, May 1953, 15, photograph from the Toronto Reference Library, courtesy Holt Renfrew / 170

5.22 ROM 979.15.1, gift of Mrs Peter Cragg, photography by Irving Solero / 172–3

5.23 *Globe and Mail*, 7 October 1955, 12, photograph from the Toronto Reference Library, reprinted with permission of the Hudson's Bay Company / 177

5.24 *Globe and Mail*, 13 October 1960, 17, photograph from the Toronto Reference Library, courtesy Holt Renfrew / 178

5.25 ROM 973.299.2ab, gift of Mrs Alex Levinsky, photography by Irving Solero / 179

5.26 *Globe and Mail*, 25 September 1950, 18, photograph from the Toronto Reference Library, courtesy Holt Renfrew / 180

5.27 *Mayfair*, May 1958, 9, photograph from the Toronto Reference Library / 180

5.28 *Globe and Mail*, 22 February 1950, 28, photograph from the Toronto Reference Library, reprinted with permission from Sears Canada Inc. / 181

5.29 F12/10505, document conservé au Centre historique des Archives nationales à Paris / 186

5.30 ROM 964.37.3ab, gift of Mrs Dora Matthews, photography by Brian Boyle / 187

5.31 ROM 969.126.2ab, gift of Mrs Harry Parker, photography by Brian Boyle / 187

5.32 ROM 964.37.3ab, gift of Mrs Dora Matthews, photography by Irving Solero; ROM 969.126.2ab, gift of Mrs Harry Parker, photography by Irving Solero / 188–9

5.33 *Mayfair*, March 1954, 15, photograph from the Toronto Reference Library, courtesy Holt Renfrew / 191

5.34 *Mayfair*, March 1952, 27, photograph from the Toronto Reference Library / 192

5.35 *The Key*, October 1948, 10–11, courtesy the Junior League of Toronto / 197

5.36 The Toronto Telegram Photograph collection, York University Archives and Special Collections, YU1650 / 200

5.37 *Globe and Mail*, 20 October 1960, 13, photography by John Boyd, photograph from the Toronto Reference Library, reprinted with permission from The Globe and Mail / 202

5.38 *Globe and Mail*, 14 February 1951, 11, photograph from Junior League Scrapbook 1950–1, reprinted with permission from The Globe and Mail / 204

6.1 ROM 970.286.4ab, gift of Mrs M. James Boylen, photography by Irving Solero / 210–11

6.2 *Globe and Mail*, 30 September 1955, 18, photograph from the Toronto Reference Library, reprinted with permission from E.M. Creed / 215

6.3 *Globe and Mail*, 21 September 1955, 15, photograph from the Toronto Reference Library, reprinted with permission from E.M. Creed / 215

6.4 ROM 991.147.4.1-2, gift of Mrs O.D. Vaughan, photography by Irving Solero / 222–3

6.5 ROM 999.102.6.1-3, gift of Mrs Flavia Redelmeier, photography by Irving Solero / 224–5

6.6 ROM 987.233, gift of Mrs Ernest Redelmeier, photography by Irving Solero / 226

6.7 *Mayfair*, October 1954, 51, photography by Hans Wild, photograph from the Toronto Reference Library / 227

6.8 ROM 909.33.1, photography by Brian Boyle / 229

6.9 Schiaparelli Archives, D-73-21-3992, Ensemble du soir, Printemps 1949, © Musée de la mode et du textile, coll. UFAC, Paris / 230

6.10 ROM 987.153.1, gift of Miss Nancy Thompson, photography by Irving Solero / 232–3

6.11 Zena Cherry, "Compact Luxury Describes Apartment Living at Its Best," in *Mayfair*, August 1954, 47, photography by Panda, photograph from the Toronto Reference Library / 235

7.1 ROM 969.241.3a-e, gift of Mrs Graham Morrow, photography by Irving Solero / 238–9

7.2 ROM 964.164, gift of Mrs Anne Gardiner, photography by Irving Solero / 240–1

7.3 *Toronto Telegram*, 17 March 1953, 11, reprinted with permission from The Toronto Telegram Photograph collection, York University Archives and Special Collections / 247

7.4 ROM 970.286.3, gift of Mrs M. James Boylen, photography by Irving Solero / 248–9

7.5 *Highlights* 4, 2 (November 1956), cover, courtesy the Mount Sinai Hospital Auxiliary / 252

7.6 *Globe and Mail*, 14 October 1953, 13, photography by Canada Pictures, photograph from the Toronto Reference Library / 253

7.7 *Globe and Mail*, 11 October 1951, 14, photograph from the Toronto Reference Library, reprinted with permission from The Globe and Mail / 254

7.8 Courtesy Christian Dior Archives, Paris / 255

7.9 Photograph courtesy of Mrs Joan Rosefield Lepofsky, reprinted with permission from Ashley and Crippen / 256

7.10 ROM 956.153.6abc, gift of Mrs John David Eaton, photography by Irving Solero / 258–9

7.11 Courtesy Archives Balenciaga, Paris / 260–1

7.12 ROM 956.153.4abc, gift of Mrs John David Eaton, photography by Irving Solero / 262–3

7.13 Courtesy Mrs Elizabeth Cassels, reprinted with permission from Ashley and Crippen / 264

7.14 *Globe and Mail*, 12 October 1951, 14, photographs from the Globe and Mail Collection, items 144862 and 144857, City of Toronto Archives, reprinted with permission from the City of Toronto Archives / 265

7.15 *Globe and Mail*, 13 October 1951, 142, photograph from the Globe and Mail Collection, item 144884, City of Toronto Archives, reprinted with permission from the City of Toronto Archives / 266

7.16 *Globe and Mail*, 11 September 1951, 12, photograph from the Toronto Reference Library, reprinted with permission from the Hudson's Bay Company / 267

7.17 ROM 956.56ab, gift of Mrs Charles S. Band, photography by Irving Solero / 268–9

7.18 ROM 963.207.2, gift of Mrs Edgar G. Burton, photography by Irving Solero / 270–1

7.19 ROM 981.109.6, gift of Mrs John David Eaton, photography by Irving Solero / 272

7.20 Courtesy Pierre Balmain, Paris / 273

7.21 ROM 956.153.8ab, gift of Mrs John David Eaton, photography by Irving Solero / 274–5

7.22 *Globe and Mail*, 25 October 1947, 12, photograph from the Toronto Reference Library, reprinted with permission from The Globe and Mail / 276

7.23 Photographs courtesy Mrs Flavia Redelmeier / 277

7.24 *Mayfair*, April 1952, 66, photograph from the Toronto Reference Library / 279

7.25 Courtesy Archives Balenciaga, Paris / 280

7.26 ROM 969.245ab, gift of Mrs Noah Torno, photography by Irving Solero / 281

7.27 Courtesy Archives Balenciaga, Paris / 281

7.28 ROM 999.102.4; 999.102.5.1-2, gift of Mrs Flavia Redelmeier, photography by Irving Solero / 284–5

7.29 M210345, dos. 127, Seeberger Frères collection, Cliché Bibliothèque nationale de France, Paris / 287

7.30 ROM 962.216.1abcd, gift of Mrs Saul A. Silverman, photography by Irving Solero / 290–1

INDEX